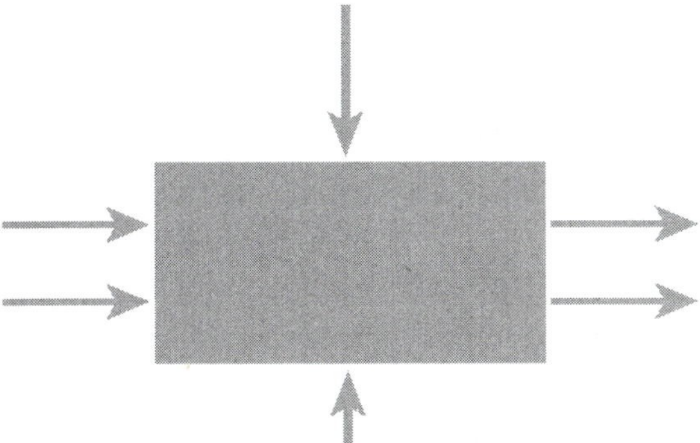

Creating Lean Corporations

Reengineering from the Bottom Up to Eliminate Waste

Jeffrey Morgan

PRODUCTIVITY
productivity press

Productivity Press • New York

Most Productivity Press books are available at quantity discounts when purchased in bulk. For more information contact our Customer Service Department (888-319-5852). Address all other inquires to:

Productivity Press
444 South Avenue South, 7th floor
New York, NY 10016
United States of America
Telephone 212-686-5900
Fax: 212-686-5411
E-mail: info@productivitypress.com

Library of Congress Cataloging-in-Publication Data

Morgan, Jeffrey (Jeffrey A.)
Creating lean corporations : reengineering from the bottom up to eliminate waste / by Jeffrey Morgan.
p. cm.
Includes bibliographical references and index.
ISBN 1-56327-324-1
1. Reengineering (Management) I. Title.
HD58.87.M67 2005
658.4'063--dc22

2005005987

08 07 06 05 6 5 4 3 2 1

Table of Contents

Dedication

To Mom, Dad, Debbie, and Sue

Introduction

Creating Lean Corporations applies lean manufacturing principles to the management of corporate business processes. These principles, called the lean philosophy, are built around one governing principle: Eliminate all forms of waste. While eliminating waste should be an obvious goal, don't be misled by the relative simplicity of this statement. Identifying and eliminating waste in large, complex processes is not trivial. It requires an understanding of the interactions between work tasks, so that they can be sequenced correctly, and an understanding of how their resulting outputs relate back to the satisfaction of one or more customers' needs or wants, so that their value can be assessed.

In addition to the lean philosophy, two seemingly unrelated disciplines, computer programming and engineering structural analysis, contribute to the new approach's methodology. The field of computer programming provides a model for creating and managing large, complex systems using a bottom-up approach. This approach is called object-oriented programming (OOP). Objects are created that are self-contained modules with clearly defined interfaces. These objects are then combined together into programs. Business processes are then created in a similar manner, with work tasks being the objects that are combined into processes. The result is that large, complex business processes can be discovered, created, and modified efficiently.

The field of engineering structural analysis provides a methodology for dividing large systems into smaller subsystems and components. The approach used is called substructuring. Substructuring allows the system's performance to be determined from subsystem and component characteristics. Thus, the effects of any subsystem and/or component characteristics on system performance can be determined. This is needed to make sure that all design decisions are based on the effect they have at the system level. Additionally, there is a condensation of the level of detail as you proceed from component to subsystems and to systems. This natural condensation of detail is critical for managing large systems. Otherwise, the amount of information needed to be comprehended at the system level would be exorbitantly large.

Three important concepts are presented in this book. The first concept is the use of hierarchies for managing large, complex systems and processes. A template for all lean organizations is presented that allows functional (horizontal) and process-oriented (vertical) groups to be integrated into a single organizational hierarchy where command-and-control is clear and direct. This is the same type of organization structure that is used by virtually all college and professional football teams but it is extended to multiple levels of management.

The second concept is the use of process models to define the organization's business processes. A standard method of process modeling, Integration Definition for Function Modeling, (IDEF0), is used along with newly defined controlling tasks that allow business processes to be represented and managed as hierarchies. The benefit of this approach is that process management is implemented in a hierarchical fashion where the level of detail increases as you move down the levels in the hierarchy. This allows management to focus on issues at the appropriate level of detail corresponding to their level of responsibility within the organization. Additionally, the hierarchical approach allows large, complex business processes to be divided into a collection of smaller, simpler subprocesses, where the coupling between subprocesses is minimized and the roll-down of business objectives is effectively implemented. Corporate financial statements are generated directly from the financial data corresponding to the hierarchical process models.

The third concept is the use of a bottom-up approach to business process reengineering. A new, lean, bottom-up approach is presented that works better on larger, more complex business processes than do traditional top-down approaches. This lean approach was successfully applied at a major automotive manufacturing company and was awarded the Charles F. "Boss" Kettering Award as one of the most important technological innovations of the year 2000.

The process for creating a lean corporation is presented in 12 chapters organized into four parts.

- **Part I: Getting an Overview of Lean Corporations** gives an overview of the lean philosophy and how these concepts are applied to business processes.
- **Part II: Understanding the Nuts and Bolts of Lean Corporations** presents the theoretical basis for the approach that includes the presentation of process models, hierarchies, decoupling of systems and processes, and requirement roll-down.
- **Part III: Making Your Business Processes Lean** presents the procedures for discovering, reengineering, and implementing business processes, along with an overview on how they can be applied to all areas of a corporation.
- **Part IV: Looking at Examples of Lean Business Processes** offers a detailed example that demonstrates the business process discovery, reengineering, and implementation procedures, using an example in the automotive field.

Acknowledgments

I would like to thank the teachers, mentors, and peers who have taught me the basics from which I have developed my own management theories. My biggest influences have come from W. Edwards Deming, Michael Hammer, James Champy, Eliyahu Goldratt, Shigeo Shingo, and Taiichi Ohno. My appreciation goes out to Dale Gerard and John Givens of the General Motors (GM) Corporation for allowing me to take a one-year leave of absence to work on this book. I would also like to thank the co-recipients of the "Boss" Kettering Award for the Virtual Powertrain project—Shawn Burns, Rohit Paranjpe, and Lonnie Ward—and everyone else who contributed to the success of that project, including Sudheer Gaddam, Anil Goli, Srinivasa Mangipudi, Glenn Griner, Uday Korde, Xu Han, and the other members of the GM Powertrain Synthesis and Analysis organization. Additionally, I would like to thank Mike Sinocchi and all the other people at Productivity Press, Inc., for making the publishing process easy. Sincere appreciation goes out to my editor, Tere Stouffer Drenth, who did a great job of transforming my manuscript into this book. Finally, my deepest appreciation goes out to my family and friends, who encouraged and supported me while writing this book.

PART I

Getting an Overview of Lean Corporations

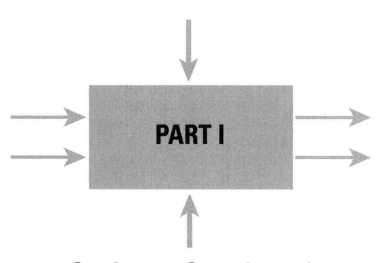

Chapter 1

Understanding the Lean Philosophy

There is always a lot of hype about new management methods and, every few months, a new one gains favor. You are well justified in having reservations about the lean philosophy presented in this book. However, the lean philosophy really is different because it utilizes a bottom-up approach, which means that workers are empowered to create and manage their own portions of business processes. This approach is essential for creating and improving business processes that are large and complex but still efficient.

The lean philosophy deserves your attention because applying its concepts results in the most efficient and profitable business processes, such as those used with great success at Toyota Motor Corporation, which is considered the world's most efficient automotive manufacturer. Drawing on Toyota's success in manufacturing, the lean philosophy can also be applied to different types of businesses with similar, dramatic results. This chapter describes the lean philosophy, explains how Toyota applies it, and relates how it can be extended to the management of any corporation, thus creating a lean corporation.

Introduction to the Lean Philosophy

The lean philosophy is based on a single principle: All forms of waste should be identified and eliminated. This seems simplistic, but it is not, because recognizing true areas of waste is difficult.

Reducing Inventory

A prime example is how inventory is treated. Traditional managers are either indifferent to inventory or consider it necessary in conducting day-to-day business. In the lean philosophy, on the other hand, inventory is considered waste because of the time value of money. The time a product sits in inventory costs the corporation money in at least three ways:

- The expenses incurred when purchasing the raw materials that could have been delayed. This costs the corporation money.
- Transporting and storing the inventory costs money.
- Products in inventory depreciate rapidly. Within a short amount of time they become obsolete and must be heavily discounted, costing the corporation money.

So why do corporations keep large inventories? Because production systems are inefficient at producing small lot sizes. As a result, corporations efficiently produce large lot sizes, but those efficiencies are offset by inventory costs. So, one objective of the lean philosophy is to reduce or eliminate inventories.

Producing Zero Defects

Another example of waste is in quality control systems. Traditional quality control is done through inspections conducted after all operations have been completed. When a defect occurs early in the process, the corporation needlessly wastes resources by processing defective parts during later operations. A potential improvement on this process is to inspect before each succeeding operation to ensure that defective parts are not further processed. However, the lean philosophy strives to do even better: Inspections are not used to find defective parts; they are used to prevent defects from occurring in the first place! When a defect is found, the cause of the defect is identified and corrected such that the same defect cannot occur in the future. This is essentially error-proofing a process. So, one objective of the lean philosophy is to create a system that inherently produces zero defects.

Designing Subsystems and Components Based on System Performance

A third example of waste is in the product design process. Products must be designed based on performance requirements that are determined by assessing potential failure modes and effects. These requirements are established at the system, subsystem, and component levels to allow the organizations responsible for design to engineer their items separately. Waste occurs when the subsystem- and component-level requirements are not determined based on their effects at the system level; this happens primarily because determining these effects can be difficult and time-consuming. The result is that the subsystems and components are optimized at their own levels instead of at the system level, causing waste when the subsystem and component designs have to be reworked several times to achieve the system performance desired. Lean corporations focus instead on the system and use specialized methods to relate system performance to subsystem- and component-level requirements. These specialized methods are presented in Chapter 5.

Identifying the Ideal Process and Optimizing the System

The governing principle of the lean philosophy is the identification and elimination of waste. Thus, the first step is to identify waste. To identify waste you first must define the ideal process, and then compare the ideal to the actual processes to determine their efficiency. For example, consider gas home-heating furnaces, which are rated based on their efficiency. The rating is ascertained by determining the heat produced by the ideal process, and then comparing this ideal value to the heat produced by the actual process. The efficiency is determined as the ratio of the actual heat produced to that of the ideal process.

Calculating efficiency in this manner has two benefits:

- **First, it forces you to know how to calculate or measure the ideal process, making you intimately familiar with the physical process.** This knowledge then leads to the identification of the factors causing the waste and tells you how to modify the system to reduce or eliminate the waste.

- **Second, the efficiency tells you how close you are to the ideal process. This is important because of the law of diminishing returns.** This law states that the closer you are to the ideal, the harder it is to make improvements. (Conversely, the farther away you are from the ideal case, the easier it is to make improvements.) In the same way, for processes that are not very efficient, you can modify and improve the system using small, incremental changes. Highly efficient systems, however, have little room for improvement, which means that radical changes are needed to invent new processes that are not governed by the same physical phenomena.

The definition of the ideal process is always subjective and depends on several factors.

- **One factor is the constraints that are applied to the process.** For the heating example, it was assumed that the gas was burned, which assumes that chemical energy is used to create heat. However, different forms of energy could have been used to create heat: electrical, solar, geothermal, and so on.
- **Another factor is the definition of the boundary of the process.** This is called the control volume. The control volume defines what is internal to the process and what is external. For the heating example, the control volume was assumed to be just the furnace. Heating costs, however, depend not only on the furnace efficiency but also on other factors, such as insulation, location and area of windows, and so on. So the furnace is really just a subsystem of a larger system. Selecting an efficient furnace is important, but balancing this selection with the other factors that affect heating costs is more important. This idea is referred to

as optimizing the system. Optimizing the system is how the most efficient business processes are created and is an important feature of the lean philosophy. This idea is further developed throughout this book.

The Ideal Manufacturing Process

As an example, consider the manufacturing process, in which a company buys raw materials (purchasing), processes them into final goods (manufacturing), and sells them (sales). If you do not consider purchasing and sales as part of the manufacturing process, you are optimizing only a part of the system, not the whole, a problem that is widespread throughout industry and is detrimental to business performance.

When considering the entire manufacturing process, the main characteristics of an ideal manufacturing process emerge:

- All products made are immediately sold.
- Raw materials are purchased and used exactly when needed.
- No defects are made.
- Minimum processing costs are used to produce the products.

These characteristics are discussed in the following sections.

All Products Made Are Immediately Sold

The first characteristic, that all products made are immediately sold, requires that production be tied to orders. To achieve this, you must be capable of producing products quickly, because customers are willing to wait a limited amount of time between when they order a product and when they receive it. Businesses are tempted to establish large inventories to anticipate these demands, but this is not the best approach. In a lean system, the manufacturing process is optimized to produce the products exactly when needed and in the exact quantities through flexible production processes that have the ability to change quickly from one product to another. This allows each product to be produced in single or small lot sizes. In addition, production process must be optimized to take the minimum amount of time. This requires that the operations be run in parallel, where possible. Sequential operations are located next to each other to eliminate transportation delays. The idea is to break a twelve-hour sequential process into, say, two parallel six-hour processes (or three parallel four-hour processes, and so on). This approach is called optimizing process threads and is presented in Chapter 7.

Raw Materials Are Purchased and Used Exactly when Needed

The second characteristic, that raw materials are purchased and used exactly when needed, requires that suppliers must be integrated into the production system. Raw materials are defect-free and are delivered directly to where they are used and in the right quantities. Methods to ensure zero defects are needed, and optimum delivery quantities and schedules need to be determined, based on statistical analysis of the production processes.

Having suppliers responsible for delivering their items is important in producing efficient processes. When suppliers take the responsibility, each operation is responsible for producing its outputs; not for getting its inputs. This separation of responsibility is extremely effective. It allows the entire manufacturing process to be managed by placing controls on the inputs of the initial operations of the process. Work then flows naturally through the process until the end. Synchronizing the supplier to the production system allows the production manager to concentrate on the controls instead of the acquisition of raw materials.

No Defects Are Made

The third characteristic, that no defects are made, requires that processes should be error-proofed. This requires that production processes consist of standardized operations that produce consistent outputs. Standardized work is created by documenting the procedures to be used and ensuring that procedures are specific enough that any qualified person can conduct the work with a small amount of training. Error-proofing the process is done by modifying the setups, procedures, and/or machinery used, and assemblies are designed so that they fit together in only one way. Product designs, therefore, become insensitive to manufacturing variation.

Minimum Processing Costs Are Used to Produce the Products

The fourth characteristic, that minimum processing costs are used, requires that the processes be optimized with respect to the resources needed to conduct them. Resources are the items that act on the materials and include people, equipment, facilities, and so on. Processes must be optimized such that the resources are used efficiently, and that means all effort conducted by the resources goes into adding value to the customer. Generally, the most expensive resource is employees (because people require retirement and healthcare benefits), so every effort to minimize labor costs is important. The best way to minimize work hours is by automating as much work as possible through the use of computers and machines.

The Toyota Lean Manufacturing System

The Toyota Motor Corporation is credited as being the first company that applied the concepts of an ideal manufacturing process to its automotive production system. The result is referred to as the Toyota Lean Manufacturing System. Toyota implemented the four characteristics of an ideal manufacturing process (described in the preceding section) over a 25-year period starting in the 1950s. The company adopted an order-based production system in which products were made only to firm orders. Inventory (stock) at all stages of production was minimized. The result was the creation of a non-stock production system. In this system, stock refers to raw materials, work-in-progress, and final goods, so a non-stock system minimizes the inventory of these items. To achieve a non-stock system, a single-part-flow production system was adopted. This means that a production lot size as low as one item of a type can be produced efficiently. To make the process efficient, a method of quick die changes was implemented, called Single Minute

Exchange of Die (SMED). Instead of taking hours to change setups, the process was improved until it took only minutes. This then made changing between products during the day quite feasible.

Suppliers were managed using a just-in-time system with a pull system. In other words, parts are used up as products are produced, and suppliers are responsible for replacing the parts that are used. Therefore, the inventory of parts is automatically synchronized to production. This type of inventory control is called the Kanban system and is the same system that supermarkets use all over the world. You may notice that many supermarkets have their suppliers stock their products themselves. Products are delivered fresh from the supplier, some having been packaged that same day. Transportation boxes are reused, which reduces expenses. Suppliers get immediate feedback on what products are selling best. All of this benefits the customer.

At Toyota, quality is designed into the process. Defects are eliminated by error-proofing processes. This was done using what are called Andon and Poka-yoke systems.

- **Andon systems** are visual displays that show work instructions, identify the correct tools and parts to use, and record information on their usage. An example is the recording of the torque applied to a bolt. If the recorded value is not within the specified range, a visual indication of the problem is given to the worker and the problem is immediately corrected.

- **Poka-yoke systems** are devices that prevent errors from being made or that detect these errors immediately. Poka-yoke systems are simpler than Andon systems. An example is a machining jig that is designed so that the workpiece fits only when it is installed correctly. Additionally, products were designed to be insensitive to manufacturing variation. Processes are made simple so that nonexperts can conduct them with minimal training, thus allowing for flexible production and optimized process flows.

The Toyota production processes were also optimized. Machines are located in a way that facilitates process flow, instead of being arranged according to function. People do tasks based on process requirements, not on organizational reporting structures. This breakdown of barriers is known as the Nagara system and requires that processes be designed so that they can be performed by nonexperts and documented in terms of standardized work tasks. Every operation is reviewed and continuously improved (a process called Kaizen) by the workers who perform the tasks.

Toyota's implementation of the characteristics of an ideal manufacturing process is summarized as follows:

- All products made are immediately sold = **Non-stock** and **SMED** systems
- Raw goods are purchased and used exactly when needed = **Just-in-time** and **Kanban** systems
- No defects are made = **Andon** and **Poka-yoke** systems
- Minimum processing costs are used to produce the products = **Nagara** and **Kaizen** systems

Toyota developed the lean manufacturing system because the company was operating under severe financial constraints and needed radical change. The Toyota lean philosophy is credited to Taiichi Ohno and Shigeo Shingo, who were influenced by the work of Henry Ford and Frederick Taylor. For a more comprehensive discussion of the Toyota lean manufacturing system, see the works cited in the bibliography.

Definition of the Lean Philosophy

The fundamental concept of the lean philosophy is the identification and elimination of waste, a concept that has been applied to manufacturing processes with great success. To apply the same concept to general business processes, consider the eight key features of the lean philosophy:

- Process orientation
- Clearly defined roles and responsibilities
- Optimized processes and systems
- Focus on the customer
- Transparency
- Standardization
- Continuous improvement
- Flexibility

These features are not an exhaustive list, but they are the main ones needed to implement lean business processes and systems. Each feature is discussed in the following sections.

Process Orientation

The lean philosophy is process oriented. This means that process requirements take precedence over all other items and a significant amount of effort is expended to define the processes that are used, using a bottom-up approach. Defining the processes in detail allows waste to be identified and eliminated.

Probably the biggest difference between lean and not-so-lean systems is in the definition of the processes. Lean systems define their processes in detail, thus leading to exceptional performance in relatively simple tasks.

Defining processes requires the definition of process models. See Chapter 2 for a generalized model that can be used to represent corporate business processes.

Clearly Defined Roles and Responsibilities

The lean philosophy uses clearly defined roles and responsibilities to establish effective command-and-control over processes and systems. This control is implemented through the organizational structure, a hierarchy that defines the positions of responsibility within the corporation, and each position has clearly defined roles and responsibilities. Individuals are then assigned to these positions.

Lean corporations utilize a hybrid organization that consists of vertical, horizontal, and support groups.

- **Vertical groups are the process and system owners.** They control the budget.
- **Horizontal groups are the task and subsystem owners.** They perform the majority of the tasks that constitute the business processes.
- **Support groups are specialized groups that perform tasks for either the vertical or horizontal groups.** They may be internal or external to the organization.

This type of organizational structure is used by virtually all lean corporations—and, incidentally, nearly all professional football teams.

Hierarchies are used to manage all corporate entities. The key feature of hierarchies is that they present general information at the top level and progressively more detailed information as you traverse down the hierarchical levels. This allows corporate information to be controlled in different levels of details corresponding to different levels of responsibility. Examples include corporate financial statements and product performance reviews. Creating and using hierarchies for managing corporations is presented in Chapter 3.

Optimized Processes and Systems

The optimization of the processes and systems, not the individual tasks and components, produces great results. Efficient tasks that are poorly linked produce inefficient processes. Likewise, quality components that are poorly integrated result in inferior systems. Therefore, all tasks, subsystems, and components must be designed based on their effect on the overall process and system performance. This design requires specialized methods of analysis that present two challenges:

- **The first is how to divide complex entities into manageable subsystems.** This is done using substructuring methods. Substructuring is a class of specialized methods developed for the analysis of large, complex systems such as airplanes and automobiles. The key feature of these methods is that they allow subsystems to be designed independently while still taking into account their effect on system level performance. An overview of substructuring is presented in Chapter 4.
- **The second area is the decoupling of systems and processes.** Coupling occurs when changes in one item result in changes in other items. Reducing or eliminating these interactions makes achieving the design requirements much easier and is especially important when large, complex systems and processes are involved. Decoupling of processes and systems is presented in Chapter 4.

Focus on the Customer

All effort conducted in the lean processes focuses on adding value to the customer; all other effort is waste. Therefore, you must understand the customer's wants and needs. This is done using design requirements, requirement roll-down, and performance reviews.

- **Design requirements quantify customers' needs and wants in terms of measurable attributes, like vehicle 0–60 mph time and overall fuel economy.** This provides an objective measure that can be used to assess the quality of the system's overall design and that of other competitors.
- **Requirement roll-down is used to relate the system level design requirements to subsystem- and component-level design requirements.** For example, vehicle 0–60 mph time and overall fuel economy can be related to engine design parameters, like

engine brake horsepower and specific fuel consumption. Then, the optimal values of these parameters based on system performance requirements are determined and specified as subsystem (engine) design requirements.

- **Performance reviews are used to present the results at achieving the design requirements.** This is where design trade-offs are made. Predicted and actual values of performance attributes are shown along with their assessments in terms of rating values. Then, each area's performance is balanced with respect to the other competing areas to achieve the best overall design. Using the automotive example again, a vehicle's 0–60 mph time would need to be balanced with respect to overall fuel economy based on the vehicle type and corresponding customer's wants and needs.

Another area of lean corporations that focuses on the customer is the pricing of products and services. In the lean philosophy, the customer dictates the sales price of products and services based solely on market conditions. All products and services are treated as commodities. Price differences between competitor products and services are assumed to be negligible. This is called the non-cost principle for the pricing of products and services, because the cost of producing an item is not taken into account in setting its price. Therefore, profitability cannot be increased by raising prices. It can be achieved only by reducing expenses, which is why the lean philosophy focuses of the identification and elimination of waste. This topic is further discussed in Chapter 2. The use of requirement roll-down to evaluate systems, subsystems, and components is presented in Chapter 5.

Transparency

Transparency is another important feature of the lean philosophy. This means information and processes must be made visible. This is important for two reasons:

- Making information and processes transparent allows management to make the most informed decisions.
- Hidden information and processes are subject to intentional and unintentional abuse. Events in the news concerning abuses in corporate governance highlight this principle.

Transparency means that information and processes are viewable at any level of detail. High-level summary views are used by upper management to set overall corporate direction. Low-level detailed views are used by the workers and their managers to accomplish their day-to-day activities. Transparency makes the activities that are going right and going wrong readily apparent. Immediate action can then be taken. Web-enabled technologies are used to make corporate information and processes transparent. These are the technologies that the Internet uses as well as most current information technology systems.

Standardization

Standardization is arguably the most important feature of the lean philosophy and applies to all aspects of lean corporations. Standardization ensures efficiency and quality. Efficiency is ensured by documenting the current, best practices. This institutionalizes these practices across the entire organization. Quality is ensured by following the procedures. By using the same procedures, the same quality of outputs is produced. Variation in product quality is thereby minimized. I suggest that the single most important aspect of successful organizations is the documentation of their processes in terms of standardized work. This is clearly demonstrated by professional football teams, military organizations, and companies that utilize lean manufacturing; all having clearly defined standardized work tasks that are performed according to specific procedures.

Standardization also applies to materials. Materials are items that are processed by the tasks and include raw materials, parts, components, and assemblies for manufacturing operations. In some businesses, the "material" needed to complete a task is actually information or documentation, but the result is the same—the material needed to complete a task must be standardized. Standardization of materials allows the work tasks to be optimized, along with the overall process. Competition among suppliers is increased by allowing standardized materials to be interchanged. This is done using standard interfaces between components. System integration and upgrading is then easier, because the new components share the same interfaces as the old ones. The computer hardware industry is a prime example.

Using standardized work to discover your business processes is presented in Chapter 6. An example of this discovery is presented in Chapter 10.

Continuous Improvement

The lean philosophy identifies the ideal processes and strives to implement them using continuous improvement. The type of changes needed depend on the efficiency of the current processes. Low efficiency processes can be significantly improved using modest changes. However, high efficiency processes require radical changes for significant improvements.

The lean philosophy takes the time to understand the current processes. This is important for two reasons:

- Understanding your processes often leads directly to new ideas for improved processes.
- Current processes are usually well entrenched in the corporate culture. Throwing them out without a fair and objective evaluation disenfranchises many people. This is usually what happens when a small team tries to reengineer a process and quite often leads to failure.

The lean philosophy reengineers processes from the bottom-up, which means that the people who perform the processes (not a small team of engineers or other professionals) are responsible for reengineering them. The workers take control of their portions of the business process and the entire process is always optimized prior to optimizing tasks. By optimizing the entire process first, the critical tasks are identified and optimized. Noncritical tasks are not modified. Proceeding in this manner focuses the company's limited capital on areas where it has the greatest benefit.

Reengineering of business processes is presented in Chapter 7. An example of a reengineered process is presented in Chapter 11.

Flexibility

Lean corporations have business processes that are designed to be flexible; in other words, easily adapted and modified. Flexible business processes are created from standardized work tasks. These tasks are related (mapped) to design requirements that are themselves related to customer needs and wants. This allows each business process to be tailored to specific business objectives. The tasks to be performed depends on the design and customer requirements. Task sequencing is determined primarily by each tasks' input and output relationships, and then is optimized for efficiency. Several different tasks may map to the same design requirement, resulting in multiple ways of addressing the requirement. The selection of the task is done by considering the cost, resource requirements, and risk associated with each one. This redundancy gives the corporation maximum flexibility.

Flexibility also applies to resource management. Lean corporations intentionally acquire resources with excess capacity in order to prevent bottlenecks from occurring. In other words, you don't purchase the machine that creates just enough products in just enough time; you purchase a machine that has more capacity than you need so that throughput can be increased (temporarily) to adjust to variations in upstream production flow without affecting downstream processes. Also, the resources that are acquired have multiple usages; these can perform several tasks, not just one. This is referred to as polymorphism. Chapter 8 shows how flexibility is demonstrated in the implementation of new business processes. An example is presented in Chapter 12.

The Ultimate Goal: The Lean Corporation

The ultimate goal is to apply the lean philosophy to an entire corporation, resulting in the creation of a lean corporation. What makes this possible is the ability to start small and grow large. Business processes are created in manageable pieces, then they are integrated as the scope of the implementation expands. This allows management to assess the benefits of the results prior to investing large amounts of effort. It also causes a transformation of the corporate culture. Workers are empowered. Managers become leaders. Dynamic organizations are created.

For simplicity, this book assumes that a corporation consists of only four departments: product engineering, manufacturing, finance, and sales and service. The activities conducted in these departments are modeled and the corporate business process is defined. The result is the creation of a lean corporation (to preview the results, see Chapter 9).

PART II

Understanding the Nuts and Bolts of Lean Corporations

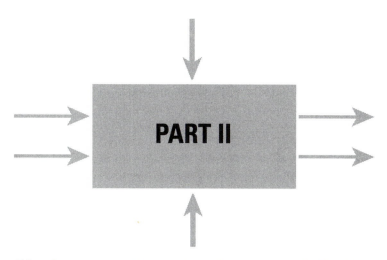

Chapter 2

Representing Corporations with a Business Process Model

The starting point for the creation of a lean corporation is the development of a corporate business process model that represents all corporate activities in a common format and facilitates the implementation of the lean philosophy. A bottom-up approach is used to create this model, such that groups and departments document their processes, and these processes are combined to form larger processes. The highest level process corresponds to the corporation's business process.

The first step in creating a corporate business process model is to determine the boundaries of the corporation. Corporations interface with external entities, so to determine the boundaries of the corporation, you must identify and manage these interfaces.

Integration Definition for Function Modeling (IDEF0) Process Model

The lean philosophy is implemented by defining business processes in terms of process models, which are defined and managed using the fundamental features of the lean philosophy. They are created using a bottom-up approach, which means that, first, the smallest elements of the processes are defined. These are referred to as tasks, and the resulting models are called task models. Tasks are sequenced together to create business processes using their input–output relationships.

But defining business processes effectively requires a model—a universal way to represent tasks and processes. Many representations exist that would work well; however, the one I prefer is the

Integration Definition for Function Modeling (IDEF0). This model was developed for the U.S. Air Force and has the advantage that it is nonproprietary and general enough to handle most situations. The general IDEF0 process model is shown in Figure 2-1.

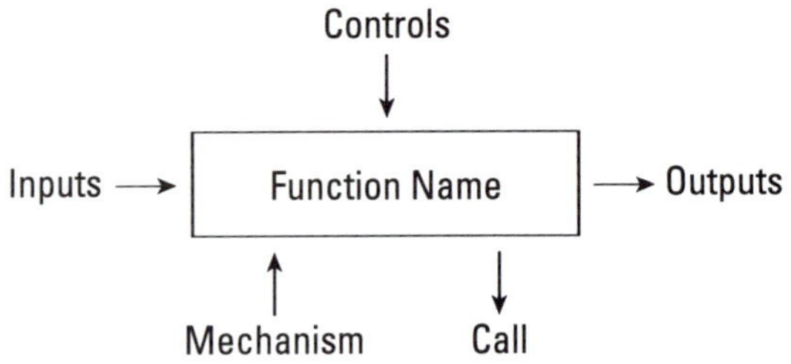

Figure 2-1. IDEF0 process model

Elements of the IDEF0 Process Model

The IDEF0 process model consists of a function name, inputs, outputs, controls, mechanism, and a call. These items are defined as follows:

- **Function name:** The verb or verb phrase placed inside an IDEF0 box to describe the modeled function.
- **Inputs:** The data or objects that are transformed by the function into output.
- **Outputs:** The data or objects produced by a function.
- **Controls:** Conditions required to produce correct output.
- **Mechanism:** The means used to perform a function; includes the special case of a call.
- **Call:** A type of mechanism that enables the sharing of detail between models (linking them together) or within a model.

Numerous rules surround the construction of IDEF0 models. Most are followed in this book, except that when process diagrams are presented, the inputs and outputs linkages are always shown, however the controls, mechanisms, and calls are sometimes not. This is done to make the process diagrams less cluttered, but as a result a process is simply a sequence of tasks: The sequence is determined by the input–output relations between tasks. A sample process consisting of several tasks is shown in Figure 2-2.

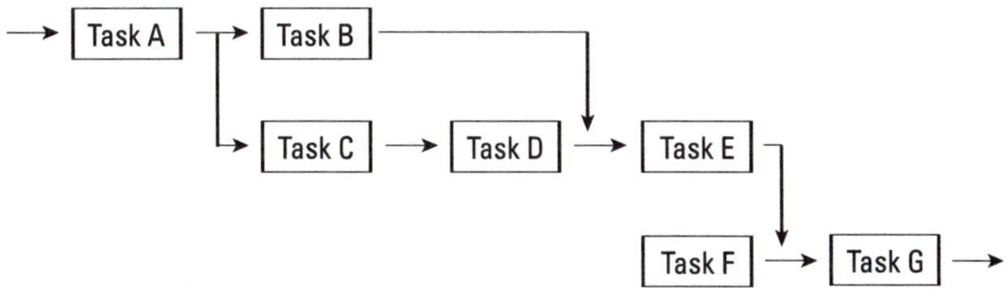

Figure 2-2. Sample process

Considering Processes and Tasks

The lean philosophy considers processes and tasks separately:

- **Processes are the sequence of tasks used to create services or products.** Processes are called vertical activities because they take low-level inputs and elevate them to higher-level outputs.
- **Tasks are the standardized units of work that are performed during a process.** Tasks are called horizontal activities because they span many processes but at the same process level.

A lean manufacturing guideline is to optimize the process first and then the tasks.

Corporate Business Process Model

The corporate business process model is defined using the IDEF0 process model. However, mechanisms are renamed resources, while calls are renamed internal controls. This change in vocabulary provides a better indication of the elements of the process model. The definition of resources is the same as the one for mechanisms. The definition of internal controls, however, is slightly different than the definition of calls.

Internal Controls

Calls allow the sharing of details between models, as do internal controls. But internal controls are also used to impose controls on other models, so as to implement command-and-control over the processes and tasks. Controls that are imposed by other process models are still called either controls or external controls. The direction of the arrows in the IDEF0 models indicates whether the controls are internal or external. Inward arrows indicated external controls, while outward arrows indicate internal controls.

The IDEF0 model explicitly defines what is internal and what is external to the process: Inputs are external to the process (because they come from outside the process), while outputs are internal (because they come from inside the process). This means that the people who perform the process are responsible for creating the outputs, but not for procuring the inputs. Instead, it is the responsibility of the process manager to supply the inputs and the external controls. The process manager also is responsible for deciding which subprocesses and activities to perform. This is consistent with the lean philosophy.

Controls and resources, however, can be internal or external. It is the responsibility of the people who perform the tasks to obtain their resources and to supply internal controls.

Analyzing the Model

The general form of a corporate business process model is shown in Figure 2-3. Representing the business process in this manner allows the entire corporation to be managed efficiently.

- Raw materials and revenues are inputs to the business process.
- Expenses and finished goods are outputs.
- Resources transform raw materials into finished goods and, in the process, consume money.
- The corporation is controlled by the CEO.

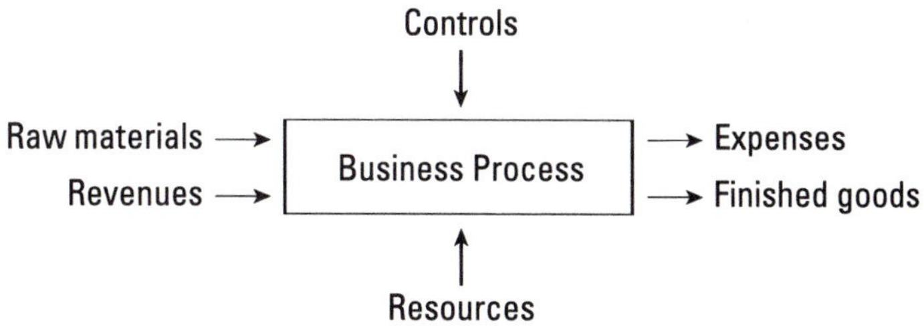

Figure 2-3. Corporate business process model

The corporate business process is just a summary of its underlying subprocesses, activities, and tasks.

- Tasks are the basic elements of work conducted by individual workers. They represent the capabilities of the corporation.
- Tasks are assembled into activities and subprocesses using their input–output linkages.
- Combining all the interacting subprocesses defines the corporate business process. This combination is represented and managed as a hierarchy. Hierarchies are important because they allow complex processes and systems to be managed using different levels of details based on different levels of management responsibility.

Materials and Resources

The model in Figure 2-3 shows that a corporation does nothing more than manage inputs, outputs, and resources.

Collectively, inputs and outputs are called materials. These are the items that get acted upon by resources. Materials usually have short-term durations, and they are either transformed into final goods or consumed in the process. The collection of all materials that are not being processed or used are called inventory.

Resources are the items that act on materials, and they usually have long-term durations. They are financed or leased and have their costs distributed over time. Unlike materials, resources are generally not considered inventory even when they are not being used; they are just extra capacity held in reserve. An exception is for service organizations, where idle workers represent an inventory of services that are available for customers to purchase. In this case, however, no accounting value is assigned.

To determine whether an item is a material or a resource, use the following simple guidelines:

- If an item gets acted upon, it is a material.
- If an item acts on things, it is a resource.

Materials and resources constitute all the property of a corporation. To facilitate their management, a property hierarchy is defined. This hierarchy is shown in Figure 2-4.

Materials

Materials are organized into three groups:

- **Cash reserves:** Cash reserves include coins, currency, and bank deposits that are used to fund daily operations. Bank deposits are checking and savings accounts from which expenses are paid.
- **Raw materials:** Raw materials include direct and indirect raw materials. Direct raw materials are materials that are transformed or assembled into final goods. Indirect raw materials are materials that are consumed by resources.
- **Final goods:** Final goods are the products and services that are produced and sold to consumers. When a raw material is removed for processing, it is removed

from the property hierarchy. When processing is completed, the resulting final good is put into the property hierarchy. This assigns zero value to any works-in-progress. Value is assigned only when processing is complete. When final goods are sold, they are replaced as cash or accounts receivable. This method of accounting was developed by Eliyahu Goldratt and is described in detail in his book, *The Goal*.

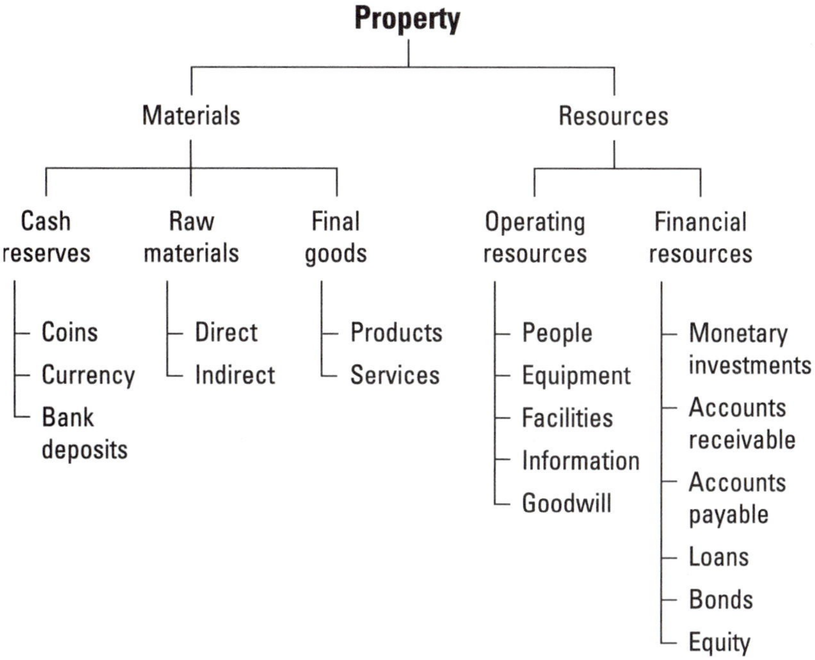

Figure 2-4. Property hierarchy

All materials are considered to be types of inventory. Services are also considered inventory, but the inventory of services is somewhat of an abstraction: It is the service that could be done by idle workers. These services are waiting for customers to purchase them, so they are a type of inventory.

Inventory should be minimized, as dictated by the lean philosophy. The value of minimizing the inventory of raw materials and final goods is probably clear (see Chapter 1 for details). The value of minimizing cash reserves, however, needs further explanation. Obviously, the goal of a corporation is to make money. But money that is not needed to sustain daily activities should be converted into resources, because resources produce higher rates of return than money held in cash reserves. So, cash reserves should be minimized. However, a cash reserve should also be kept large enough to ensure that the corporation can sustain operations in economic downturns until conditions improve. This is the same approach some people use to manage their own finances. They deposit their net income into an interest-bearing savings account (a cash reserve) and size this account to some minimum level, say two months of net income. Every month, funds are transferred to a checking account (another cash reserve) to pay daily expenses. When funds in the savings account significantly exceed the minimum value desired, a portion is invested in higher rate of return investments, such as certificates of deposit (CDs), bonds, stocks, and mutual funds (called monetary investments). Lean corporations function in a similar manner.

The actual quantities of inventory are dictated by the estimated need and restocking time. Just-in-time deliveries (deliveries that arrive exactly when they are needed) are used for materials, where applicable. All other materials are managed based on the risk associated with not having the material available when needed. Modeling the business process allows the materials and resources to be managed efficiently. This is demonstrated in the last section of this chapter.

Resources

Resources are organized into two primary groups: operating resources and financial resources. Operating resources include people, equipment, facilities, information, and goodwill.

- People, equipment, and facilities are self-explanatory.
- Information includes all corporate intellectual property, such as operating procedures, design guidelines, patents, and so on. Information is treated as a resource and not a material, because it is a valuable asset that

shouldn't be minimized.

- Goodwill is an intangible asset that represents the price paid for assets that exceed their actual value. Corporations occasionally purchase the assets of other companies at prices that exceed their actual value. This premium is accounted for as goodwill, and it represents some intangible value (such as name recognition, potential earnings, and so on) of the purchased assets. Goodwill is treated as a separate resource because it generally cannot be assigned directly to individual resources. Goodwill is depreciated just like other operating resources.

Financial resources include monetary investments, accounts receivable, accounts payable, loans, bonds, and equity.

- Monetary investments are used to make money. They include items such as CDs, stocks, bonds, and mutual funds. These investments have varying durations, which allows them to be converted into cash reserves at different intervals.
- Accounts receivable are funds owed to the corporation. They include unpaid bills for final goods the company has sold.
- Accounts payable are funds the corporation owes to others. They include unpaid bills for raw materials.
- Loans, bonds, and equity are debt instruments used to generate funds for the purchase of materials and resources.

Corporate Financial Statements

A side benefit of representing the corporate business process using an IDEF0 model is that the corporation's financial statements can be directly generated from the bottom up. This requires that all tasks that consume materials or resources be documented. However, even if only a few tasks or subprocesses are documented, their contributions to the corporate financial statements can be determined. This allows management to evaluate and quantify the effects of their area of responsibility on the corporation's financial performance.

In this section, the traditional corporate financial statements are reviewed and then it is shown how they are generated from the IDEF0 task models. The traditional corporate financial statements are the balance sheet, the income statement, and the cash flow statement. The general format of these statements is presented in the three following sections so that the relationships between the tasks that constitute the business process and the corporate financial statements can be established. The information in this section can be skipped if you are already familiar with corporate financial statements.

Balance Sheet

A balance sheet estimates the total value of a corporation from the value of the property it contains. This is expressed using the fundamental accounting equation:

Assets = Liabilities + Stockholders' Equity

Assets include materials, operating resources, monetary investments, and accounts receivable. They are sorted with respect to current and long-term durations and whether they are tangible or intangible.

- Cash-type assets have values that are known precisely. However, some are expressed in terms of promissory notes, which means there is no guarantee that the corporation will actually receive these items.
- Non-cash assets (such as final goods, operating resources, and so on) have values that are only estimates. Many corporations maintain two balance sheets: one for tax purposes, which minimizes tax expenses, and the other for stockholder purposes, attempting to quantify the actual value of the corporation. The main difference between the two is how assets are depreciated. Different depreciation schedules are used for the different valuations.

Liabilities include loans, bonds, accounts payable, and other items. The repayment schedules for some of these items are clearly defined. Others, such as pension liabilities, are only estimated. Liabilities are sorted with respect to current and long-term durations and whether they are tangible or intangible. This is the same sorting that is done for assets.

Stockholders' equity includes the funds raised through the issuing of stock and the value of retained earnings.

- The funds raised through the issuing of stock are referred to as the company's basis value. This includes the money obtained through direct stock offerings and the value of the stock issued for the purchase of assets from other companies.
- The value of retained earnings is calculated using the fundamental accounting equation: the value of the assets minus liabilities and stock basis value. All items on the balance sheet are independent (their values can change independently of one another) except for retained earnings. The value of retained earnings is an estimate because it is calculated from other items that themselves are estimates. It represents additional stockholders' equity that the company has created through its operations. This equity is created from profits that are retained as cash reserves or invested in new resources.

An example balance sheet is shown in Table 2-1, which (like all corporate reports) is displayed as a hierarchy so that it can be managed effectively. The reason hierarchies are needed is because they allow large amounts of information to be summarized at different levels of detail. This allows each level of management to view the information at the appropriate level of detail corresponding to its level of management responsibility. Creating and using hierarchies is so important in managing large organizations that an entire chapter is dedicated to this topic in this book—see Chapter 3.

Table 2-1. Example of a Balance Sheet

Period Ending:	December 31, 2002	December 31, 2001	December 31, 2000
Total Assets	**$370,782,000,000**	**$323,969,000,000**	**$303,100,000,000**
Current Assets	**$240,252,000,000**	**$47,186,000,000**	**$47,671,000,000**
Cash and Equivalents	$21,449,000,000	$18,555,000,000	$10,284,000,000
Short-Term Investments	$16,825,000,000	$790,000,000	$1,161,000,000
Net Receivables	$192,011,000,000	$13,283,000,000	$19,582,000,000
Inventory	$9,967,000,000	$14,558,000,000	$16,644,000,000
Other Current Assets	$0	$0	$0
Long-Term Assets	**$130,530,000,000**	**$276,783,000,000**	**$255,429,000,000**
Long-Term Investments	$5,044,000,000	$183,661,000,000	$162,975,000,000
Resources	$72,784,000,000	$39,724,000,000	$39,037,000,000
Goodwill	$10,265,000,000	$10,006,000,000	$10,810,000,000
Intangible Assets	$7,689,000,000	$6,921,000,000	$0
Other Assets	$34,748,000,000	$14,177,000,000	$27,737,000,000
Deferred Long-Term Asset Charges	$0	$22,294,000,000	$14,870,000,000
Total Liabilities	**$363,968,000,000**	**$304,262,000,000**	**$272,786,000,000**
Current Liabilities	**$91,281,000,000**	**$64,246,000,000**	**$63,156,000,000**
Accounts Payable	$91,281,000,000	$53,513,000,000	$63,156,000,000
Short-Term and Current Long-Term Debt	$0	$2,402,000,000	$0
Other Current Liabilities	$0	$8,331,000,000	$0
Long-Term Liabilities	**$272,687,000,000**	**$240,016,000,000**	**$209,630,000,000**
Long-Term Debt	$201,940,000,000	$163,912,000,000	$142,447,000,000
Other Liabilities	$60,949,000,000	$71,053,000,000	$66,476,000,000
Deferred Long-Term Liability Charges	$8,964,000,000	$4,305,000,000	$0
Minority Interest	$834,000,000	$746,000,000	$707,000,000
Stockholders' Equity	**$6,814,000,000**	**$19,707,000,000**	**$30,314,000,000**
Basis Value	**($3,217,000,000)**	**$10,244,000,000**	**$19,614,000,000**
Common Stock	$1,032,000,000	$1,020,000,000	$1,002,000,000
Other	($4,249,000,000)	$9,224,000,000	$18,612,000,000
Retained Earnings	**$10,031,000,000**	**$9,463,000,000**	**$10,700,000,000**

Income Statement

The income statement indicates the profits generated by the corporation over a given period of time. Profits are equal to revenues minus expenses. This can be represented using a reservoir analogy, as illustrated in Figure 2-5. Revenues are pumped into the reservoir, and expenses flow out. This analogy is reasonable. First, revenues do require a pump; you have to expend effort to generate sales (the sales and marketing department). Expenses, on the other hand, do not require a pump. They flow out rapidly if not checked. As money accumulates, the pressure for it to flow out (spend money) increases. In the end, you have only two ways to increase profits: Increase revenues or reduce expenses.

Figure 2-5. Reservoir analogy

As described in Chapter 1, the lean philosophy uses the non-cost principle for pricing goods. Thus, the selling price and, consequently, the revenues are set by the market. Therefore, the only way to increase profits is to reduce expenses. This requires that management find and control the money valve. For poorly defined business processes, the money valve is hard to find. For processes defined using the IDEF0 approach, the money valve is easy to find, because it is implemented through the controls. This transparency of the money valve is one of the reasons that processes are defined using the IDEF0 approach.

The income statement consists of three main items: total revenues, total expenses, and net income.

- Total revenues are divided into two categories: sold final goods and investment income.
- Total expenses are divided into four categories: material costs, resource costs, interest, and income taxes.
- Subtracting the total expenses from the total revenues

gives the net income (profits) for the period. The net income can then be added to the assets of the company or distributed to the stockholders in terms of dividends.

An example of an income statement is shown in Table 2-2.

Table 2-2. Example of an Income Statement

Period Ending:	December 31, 2002	December 31, 2001	December 31, 2000
Total Revenue	**$186,763,000,000**	**$177,260,000,000**	**$184,632,000,000**
Sold Final Goods	$186,763,000,000	$177,260,000,000	$184,632,000,000
Investment Income	$0	$0	$0
Other Revenues	$0	$0	$0
Total Expenses	**$185,027,000,000**	**$176,659,000,000**	**$180,180,000,000**
Material Costs	$153,344,000,000	$143,850,000,000	$145,664,000,000
Resource Costs	$23,624,000,000	$23,302,000,000	$22,252,000,000
Interest Expense	$7,715,000,000	$8,590,000,000	$9,552,000,000
Income Tax Expense	$533,000,000	$768,000,000	$2,393,000,000
Other Expenses	($189,000,000)	$149,000,000	$319,000,000
Net Income	**$1,736,000,000**	**$601,000,000**	**$4,452,000,000**

Cash Flow Statement

The cash flow statement expresses changes in the balance sheet over a given time period. The normal convention is to organize by three activity types: operating, investing, and financing activities.

- **Operating activities** include all cash flows resulting from the change in value of assets involved in the production of final goods; for example, net income. Depreciation of operating resources is included as an expense on the income statement and as a cash flow on the cash flow statement. This depreciation is equal to the reduced value of the operating resources shown on the balance sheet.

- **Investing activities** include all cash flows used to purchase resources. They are listed as negative quantities, indicating that the cash flow is going out of the corporation. Any cash flow out for investment is equal to the increase in asset value of the resources that were purchased. Thus, investment activities do not affect retained earnings.

- **Financing activities** include all cash flows received by taking on debt or by issuing equity. They are listed as positive quantities, indicating that the cash flows are going into the corporation. Any cash flow from financing activities is equal to the increase in liability or equity basis value. Thus, financing activities also do not affect retained earnings. An example of a cash flow statement is shown in Table 2-3.

Corporate Performance Reviews

The balance sheet, income statement, and cash flow statement report the results that were achieved. What is also needed is an assessment document that compares the results achieved to their target values. This allows the performance of the corporation to be assessed using specific criteria. A corporate performance review will be used for this purpose. Several important areas of performance are identified, and target values for their results are established. Examples of these areas include profits generated for a period, rate of return on net assets, stock price, and so on. The target values are based on the business objectives. Often, executive compensation and worker bonuses are directly related to achieving these targets. An example of a corporate performance review is shown in Table 2-4.

Building the Corporate Business Process from the Bottom Up

Corporate business processes are large and complex, so trying to define them from the top down is difficult or impossible. A more effective approach is to generate them from the bottom up. This is done by starting small and growing large. No attempt is made to

Table 2-3. Example of a Cash Flow Statement

Period Ending:	December 31, 2002	December 31, 2001	December 31, 2000
Cash Flow from Operating Activities	**$17,109,000,000**	**$9,166,000,000**	**$19,750,000,000**
Net Income	**$1,736,000,000**	**$601,000,000**	**$4,452,000,000**
Cash Flow Operating Activities	**$3,497,000,000**	**$9,920,000,000**	**$14,003,000,000**
Depreciation	$12,938,000,000	$12,908,000,000	$13,411,000,000
Adjustments to Net Income	($9,441,000,000)	($2,988,000,000)	$592,000,000
Changes in Operating Activities	**$11,876,000,000**	**($1,355,000,000)**	**$1,295,000,000**
Changes in Accounts Receivables	($3,059,000,000)	($2,511,000,000)	($1,351,000,000)
Changes in Liabilities Excluding Debt	$14,868,000,000	$988,000,000	$4,840,000,000
Changes in Inventories	$67,000,000	$522,000,000	($297,000,000)
Changes in Other Operating Activities	$0	($354,000,000)	($1,897,000,000)
Cash Flow from Investing Activities	**($41,377,000,000)**	**($23,171,000,000)**	**($33,773,000,000)**
Capital Expenditures	($7,443,000,000)	($8,631,000,000)	($9,722,000,000)
Investments	($33,929,000,000)	($12,473,000,000)	($14,087,000,000)
Other Cash Flows from Investing Activities	($5,000,000)	($2,067,000,000)	($9,964,000,000)
Cash Flow from Financing Activities	**$26,667,000,000**	**$22,372,000,000**	**$14,120,000,000**
Dividends Paid	($1,168,000,000)	($1,201,000,000)	($1,294,000,000)
Sale of Stock	($16,000,000)	$253,000,000	$1,179,000,000
Net Borrowings	$27,851,000,000	$22,820,000,000	$13,166,000,000
Other Cash Flows from Financing Activities	$0	$500,000,000	$1,069,000,000
Effect of Exchange Rate	**$495,000,000**	**($96,000,000)**	**($255,000,000)**
Change in Cash and Cash Equivalents	**$2,894,000,000**	**$8,271,000,000**	**($158,000,000)**

Table 2-4. Example of a Performance Review

Period Ending: 12/31/2002	Target	Actual Data	Rating
Overall Performance			**80**
Market Capitalization	$28,250,000,000	$20,740,627,000	85
Revenues	$205,000,000,000	$186,763,000,000	95
Earnings	$5,400,000,000	$1,736,000,000	70
Assets	$350,000,000,000	$370,782,000,000	95
Stockholders' Equity	$20,000,000,000	$6,814,000,000	70
Stock Price	$50.00	$36.86	75
Earnings/Share	$5.00	$3.35	90
Dividends/Share	$2.00	$2.00	100
Price/Earnings	20.00	11.00	70
Return on Net Assets	12.50%	3.27%	70
Total Return to Investors	10.00%	–20.04%	65

generate the entire corporation's financial statements at the beginning; instead, small groups and departments define their activities using IDEF0 models. The linkages to the corporate financial statements are defined by the materials and resources that are used. By adding additional groups and departments, more and more of the corporate business process is defined. When all groups and departments are included, the corporate business process is completely defined. Then, the entire corporation's financial statements can be created automatically.

A specific procedure for defining tasks and processes is presented in Chapter 6. A simple preview of the results is given here to show how defining the tasks and processes allow the corporate financial statements to be automatically generated. This example is simple and is used only to demonstrate the basic concepts. Extending these concepts to actual business activities is straightforward.

Consider a single manufacturing task that processes raw materials into finished goods. This task is represented in the IDEF0 format as shown in Figure 2-6.

1.0 Example Manufacturing Task

Inputs
0.1-1 Raw materials
Outputs
1.0-1 Final Good
Resources
R.1-1 Worker
R.1-2 Equipment
R.1-3 Facility
Controls
C.1-1 Requirements

Figure 2-6. Example of a manufacturing task

Assume that the task processes $250 worth of raw materials into a single final good worth $1,000. This activity takes one day and requires $50,000 in equipment with a useful life of 10 years. One worker is required at $36,000 per year. Assume that $5,000 worth of raw goods (X = 20) is processed each month, and all final goods are sold immediately. Facility rental is $500 a month. These cash flows are shown in Table 2-5.

At start-up, $10,000 worth of equity is issued, and the resulting funds are put into cash reserves. A $50,000 loan at 9 percent interest is obtained and used to purchase the equipment needed for the activity. This equipment is depreciated over a 5-year period using the straight-line method. Facility rental and raw materials are purchased using a debit account and are settled within one month. All other cash flows are assumed to be settled immediately. Income taxes are calculated at 24 percent of net income minus interest expense. The resulting balance sheet, income statement, and cash flow statement are calculated from the task definition as shown in Tables 2-6 through 2-8.

The preceding example was constructed using generalized inputs, outputs, resources, and controls. Actual activity definitions list the specific items—see Chapters 6 through 8 for detailed instructions on how to do this. For example, the worker resource is defined by the skills necessary to conduct the activity, so when

Table 2-5. Example of a Manufacturing Cash Flow

Date	Loan	Equipment	Worker	Facility	Raw Materials	Final Goods
12/31/2001	$50,000	$0	$0	($500)	($5,000)	$0
01/31/2002	($633)	($1,667)	($3,000)	($500)	($5,000)	$20,000
02/28/2002	($633)	($1,667)	($3,000)	($500)	($5,000)	$20,000
03/31/2002	($633)	($1,667)	($3,000)	($500)	($5,000)	$20,000
04/30/2002	($633)	($1,667)	($3,000)	($500)	($5,000)	$20,000
05/31/2002	($633)	($1,667)	($3,000)	($500)	($5,000)	$20,000
06/30/2002	($633)	($1,667)	($3,000)	($500)	($5,000)	$20,000
07/31/2002	($633)	($1,667)	($3,000)	($500)	($5,000)	$20,000
08/31/2002	($633)	($1,667)	($3,000)	($500)	($5,000)	$20,000
09/30/2002	($633)	($1,667)	($3,000)	($500)	($5,000)	$20,000
10/31/2002	($633)	($1,667)	($3,000)	($500)	($5,000)	$20,000
11/30/2002	($633)	($1,667)	($3,000)	($500)	($5,000)	$20,000
12/31/2002	($633)	($1,667)	($3,000)	($500)	($5,000)	$20,000

the activity is actually performed, an individual worker is assigned. Also, several items, such as the income tax calculation, are simplified here to make the example easier to understand. In an actual implementation, the proper methods of calculation would be used.

Defining the corporation's capabilities in terms of tasks allows the business process to be created from the bottom-up. Each task represents a building block from which the business processes are constructed. Linking together tasks using their input–output relations establishes their sequences. Then, relating the task's items back to the corporate financial statements allows these statements to be created automatically.

Generally, relating the task's items to the corporate financial statements is done in two stages. The first stage is to use approximate resource and material costs. The second stage is to convert the item's approximate cost to actual cost, as it becomes the responsibility of the people who perform the tasks. The second stage requires a higher level of management commitment than the first, and that commitment usually takes time to obtain. However,

Table 2-6. Balance Sheet Entries for the Manufacturing Activity Example

Period Ending:	December 31, 2002	December 31, 2001
Total Assets	**$148,515**	**$65,000**
Current Assets	**$118,519**	**$15,000**
Cash and Cash Equivalents	$113,519	$10,000
Short-Term Investments	$0	$0
Net Receivables	$0	$0
Inventory	$5,000	$5,000
Other Current Assets	$0	$0
Long-Term Assets	**$29,996**	**$50,000**
Long-Term Investments	$0	$0
Resources	$29,996	$50,000
Goodwill	$0	$0
Intangible Assets	$0	$0
Other Assets	$0	$0
Deferred Long-Term Asset Charges	$0	$0
Total Liabilities	**$52,268**	**$55,500**
Current Liabilities	**$5,500**	**$5,500**
Accounts Payable	$5,500	$5,500
Short-Term and Current Long-Term Debt	$0	$0
Other Current Liabilities	$0	$0
Long-Term Liabilities	**$46,768**	**$50,000**
Long-Term Debt	$46,768	$50,000
Other Liabilities	$0	$0
Deferred Long-Term Liability Charges	$0	$0
Minority Interest	$0	$0
Stockholders' Equity	**$96,247**	**$9,500**
Basis Value	**$10,000**	**$10,000**
Common Stock	$10,000	$10,000
Other	$0	$0
Retained Earnings	**$86,247**	**($500)**

Table 2-7. Income Statement Entries for the Manufacturing Activity Example

Period Ending:	December 31, 2002	December 31, 2001
Total Revenue	**$240,000**	**$0**
Sold Final Goods	$240,000	$0
Investment Income	$0	$0
Other Revenues	$0	$0
Total Expenses	**$153,253**	**$5,500**
Material Costs	$60,000	$5,000
Resource Costs	$62,000	$500
Interest Expense	$4,369	$0
Income Tax Expense	$26,884	$0
Other Expenses	$0	$0
Net Income	**$86,747**	**($5,500)**

using approximate costs allows the process managers to estimate the effect of their processes on the corporate financial statements. This begins the transformation from the current corporate state to the new lean state.

Table 2-8. Cash Flow Statement Entries for the Manufacturing Activity Example

Period Ending:	December 31, 2002	December 31, 2001
Cash Flow from Operating Activities	**$106,751**	**$0**
Net Income	**$86,747**	**($5,500)**
Cash Flow Operating Activities	**$20,004**	**$0**
Depreciation	$20,004	$0
Adjustments to Net Income	$0	$0
Changes in Operating Activities	**$0**	**$5,500**
Changes in Accounts Receivables	$0	$0
Changes in Liabilities excluding Debt	$0	$500
Changes in Inventories	$0	$5,000
Changes in Other Operating Activities	$0	$0
Cash Flow from Investing Activities	**$0**	**($50,000)**
Capital Expenditures	$0	($50,000)
Investments	$0	$0
Other Cash Flows from Investing Activities	$0	$0
Cash Flows from Financing Activities	**($3,232)**	**$60,000**
Dividends Paid	$0	$0
Sale of Stock	$0	$10,000
Net Borrowings	($3,232)	$50,000
Other Cash Flows from Financing Activities	$0	$0
Effect of Exchange Rate	**$0**	**$0**
Change in Cash and Cash Equivalents	**$103,519**	**$10,000**

Chapter 3

Creating and Using Hierarchies

Managing large amounts of anything is difficult, which is why hierarchies were developed. Hierarchies are used to organize a large number of items into smaller, more manageable groups. Most people can easily comprehend lists of up to ten items. It becomes more difficult to comprehend lists of up to a hundred items. Comprehending lists larger than this requires a high degree of mental effort. So it is natural to divide large lists into smaller groups. Hierarchies are just a formalized way of doing this. They define how the items are organized into groups. The key is that hierarchies use multiple levels to divide the items. Items are organized into groups that themselves are organized into other groups. This proceeds until a single top level is obtained. By doing this, every group can be constrained to have a specified maximum number of items that are easily comprehended.

Hierarchies also allow information to be summarized, corresponding to different levels of detail. Summaries at each level describe the attributes of all the items in that level and those contained in lower levels, but in a more general manner. Thus, hierarchies present general information at the top level and progressively more detailed information as you travel down the hierarchy levels. This allows management to view information at the different levels of detail corresponding to their levels of responsibility.

A simple example of a hierarchy is the way electronic files are stored in a computer. Files are the items, and folders are the groupings. The computer user organizes his or her files into folders, and then organizes folders into a hierarchy. Summary information is available at each level of the hierarchy. For example, each file has a size, so each folder will also have a size that is equal to the sum of all the sizes of the files and folders that it contains. Each folder also indicates the number of files and folders in it. If the organization of the hierarchy is done well, the computer user can easily manage files. If the organization of the hierarchy is done poorly, the computer user has difficulty managing files. These same issues apply to the management of corporate processes and systems. The difference is that the consequences are amplified due to the size and complexity of the entities involved. This explains why hierarchies are important and justifies the careful attention given to them in this chapter.

Definition of Hierarchies

Most people consider the groupings and items together as constituting hierarchies. In this book, hierarchies are defined as the groupings only, not the items. Viewing specific items in a specific hierarchy produces a report. For example, organization charts are people (items) viewed in the organization structure (hierarchy). It is important to understand why this distinction is made:

- First, separating the groupings from the items allows different types of items to be put into the same hierarchy, and different hierarchies to be used to organize the same set of items.
- Second, items and groupings are different types of entities. Items are the objects that are organized into hierarchies. They have measurable attributes such as cost, weight, size, and so on. Groupings are how the items are organized. They inherit their attributes from the items they contain. It is common to view the groupings as a collection of buckets and the items as the objects that are placed into the buckets to sort them. This is illustrated in Figure 3-1.

The bucket analogy reinforces a fundamental feature of hierarchies: that each item should be placed in one (and only one) grouping for any specific hierarchy. The consequence of this is that all items are "owned" by only one grouping, which is responsible for managing the item. This is critical for implementing the lean philosophy in terms of clearly defined roles and responsibilities. If items are placed in two or more groupings, you lose direct control over the items. This is illustrated with matrix organization structures where the same person reports to two or more bosses. Each boss has only partial control over the shared worker, which is not consistent with the lean philosophy. Therefore, only direct-reporting organization structures are used in lean corporations. The inherent matrix-type relationships are handled as customer–supplier relationships, as described in the "Organization Structure" section later in this chapter.

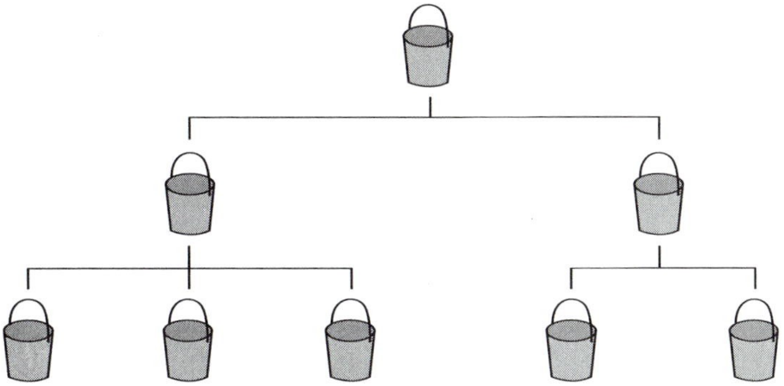

Figure 3-1. Hierarchy viewed as a collection of buckets

Each grouping in a hierarchy is called a node. Nodes are created by giving them a unique name and identification number. Hierarchies are created by establishing parent–child relationships between the nodes. This can be done in three ways:

- By defining the parent node(s) only
- By defining the child node(s) only
- By defining both the parent and child nodes

The best choice in this case is to define the child node(s) only. This causes every node to have a unique set of child nodes and also allows the same node to be used in different hierarchies. To put it another way, hierarchies are used primarily for management. Thus, they are defined using a top-down approach.

In contrast, items are placed in hierarchies by defining the parent node(s) only. This allows the same item to be placed in several different hierarchies. It also decouples the definition of the hierarchies from the definition of the items. The primary advantage of this is that it allows management to create the hierarchies based on how it wants to view the information. Then the workers define the items and place them in the appropriate nodes. This is a lean way of creating corporate reports. It utilizes a bottom-up approach. The owners of the items are responsible for supplying their information directly. Reports are generated quickly because many people are responsible for small amounts of information instead of a few people being responsible for large amounts of information.

When creating hierarchies or placing items in hierarchies, only the child nodes or parent nodes, respectively, are specified. This means that knowledge about nodes that are two or more levels away is not needed. This is an example of the concept of local knowledge, which is very powerful. If you ask someone who they work for, you will probably get the correct answer. If you ask who his or her boss works for, you may get the right answer. If you ask who the boss's boss works for, chances are you'll get no answer or the wrong answer. This illustrates the point that the farther you get away from an item, the less accurate the information becomes.

The concept of local knowledge is that the people closest to the information should be responsible for entering it. This eliminates other people from being introduced into the process and, thereby, reduces errors. How many times have you given information to somebody else and they have entered it incorrectly? Often, adding two people to a process results in the process taking twice as long instead of half as long. This can be a big problem with corporate management structures. Managers must be empowered to make decisions using local knowledge. Relying on decisions from executives far removed from the information is an indication of a poor management structure. If a manager can't make the majority of decisions that workers need and must take it up to the next level, there is at least one too many levels of management. Lean corporations implement local knowledge through the use of hierarchies. It becomes embedded in the corporate culture.

Every hierarchy has one root node (sometimes this node is not displayed). All other nodes in the hierarchy are descendants of the root node. In this book, the root node is considered the *highest* level of the hierarchy. This convention may be different to what you are used to (for example, sometimes the root node is considered the lowest level of the hierarchy; level 0). The reason I specify the root node as being the highest level of the hierarchy is because parent nodes are always shown above their child nodes. Thus, it makes sense for the parent's level to have a higher numerical value than that of its child nodes. Generally, each root node corresponds to a specific corporate report. Reports are created by displaying specific items in a specific hierarchy and specifying how a given attribute should be summarized. This summary can be done using linear or nonlinear methods, but linear methods are the most common.

Summarizing Attributes

Linear methods summarize the attributes by adding the values of subordinate items with specified weighting factors. The most common weighting is to use 1.0 for all items, because it results in a simple summation of all the attribute values corresponding to the child nodes. The computer file system example illustrates the use of a simple summation. If some items are more important than other items, then weighting values that are either higher or lower than 1.0 can be used. Often, this is done in performance reviews, where each node is the average value of the attribute values corresponding to the child nodes.

Nonlinear summations are used less often. The idea is the same, except that nonlinear equations are used for the calculation of the summarized values.

Minimizing Overlapping Groupings

To be useful, a hierarchy should define nonoverlapping groupings that span the entire population of items. Nonoverlapping groupings mean that all items to be placed in the hierarchy must belong to one and only one grouping based on some attribute or combination of attributes of the items. To span the entire population of items, every possible grouping must be defined based on the selected attribute or combination of attributes. The reason this property is needed is so that the items are summarized properly at each level and none is left out unintentionally. This is important for virtually all hierarchies that are used to manage corporations.

Minimizing Couplings

A useful hierarchy minimizes coupling between groupings. To minimize coupling between the groupings, the boundaries should be selected such that changes in one grouping has minimum effects on the others. This is a somewhat advanced topic that is explained in greater detail in Chapter 4. The key idea to understand at this point is that all management structures attempt to minimize the coupling between entities. This allows each entity to perform their activities with minimal interaction with others. It is the interactions between entities that are the major source of inefficiency and waste.

Clearly Defining a Purpose

Each hierarchy should also have a clearly defined purpose. This purpose should be included in the hierarchy's definition. When creating a hierarchy, don't try to anticipate too far into the future. Create a hierarchy that works with all the items available today and those that can be reasonably anticipated. Each node should have a maximum of ten to twenty child nodes. Separate the groupings that are likely to change from those that are not. This makes changing them in the future a little easier.

The best way to learn to create clearly defined, effective hierarchies is through demonstrations. Several examples are presented in this chapter for this purpose. The standard ways of displaying hierarchies are described in the following section.

Display of Hierarchies

Hierarchies can be displayed with or without items. However, displaying hierarchies without items is usually done only when they are being created or modified. It is more common to use hierarchies to create corporate reports (reports that are used to manage the corporation). A report is created by displaying specific items in a specific hierarchy using a specific display format.

To further clarify the report, a sorting code can be applied to one or more levels of the hierarchy. A sorting code is just an additional subgrouping of the items using a different characteristic. Sort codes can be unrelated to any hierarchy or can correspond to a specific level of a hierarchy. For example, a balance sheet sorts corporate properties based on whether they are short-term or long-term. Thus, short-term and long-term can be considered sorting codes. Filters, which are used to exclude unwanted information from a report, can also be used to clarify reports. Most people are familiar with these topics, so they are not discussed in detail.

There are three common ways to display hierarchies: node-descendant view, tree view, and tree-table view; each view is described in the following sections.

Node-Descendant View

The node-descendant view is the most common way to display hierarchical information. In this view, a node is displayed along with one or more descendant levels below it. Figure 3-1 is displayed in this format (also see Figure 2-4 in Chapter 2), as are most organization charts. This type of view is easy to understand and needs no further explanation. However, a variation of the node-descendant view can be used to display complex processes and systems. This variation is to show two node-descendant views at the same time, with one being the child view of the other. This type of view was incorporated into the IDEF0 specification and is demonstrated in Figures 3-2 through 3-4.

The process shown in Figures 3-2 through 3-4 is the same as that shown previously in Chapter 2 (Figure 2-2). Using this variation of the node-descendant view, any process or system, regardless of size and complexity, can be represented as a series of simple views. This type of view is extremely useful when implemented on a computer, so that navigation can be done by clicking on the node for which details are desired. Upward (less detailed) and downward (more detailed) navigation is then easily conducted.

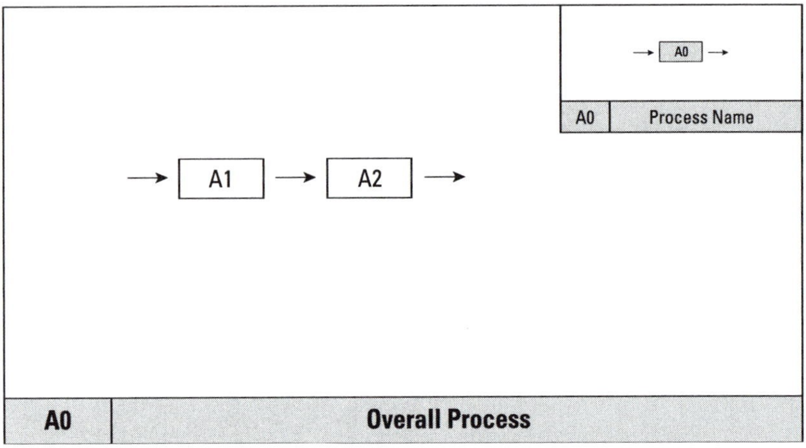

Figure 3-2. Overall process

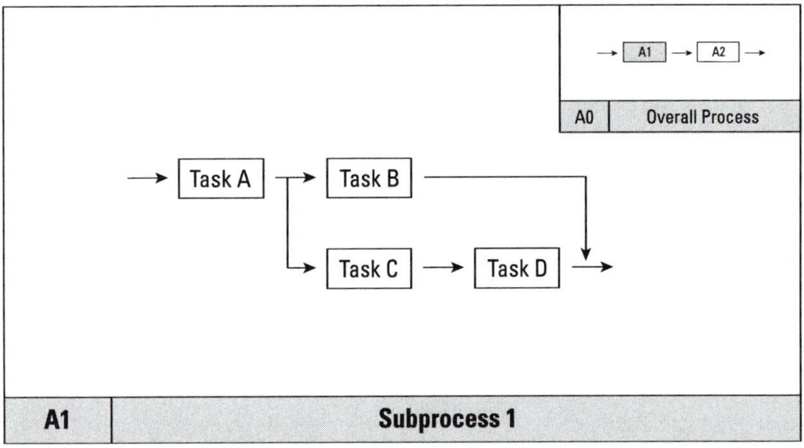

Figure 3-3. Subprocess 1

Tree View

Another common way to view hierarchical data is to use tree views. Tree views display hierarchies in the form of an outline, where each descendant node is indented below its parent node. An example of this is how folders are displayed in computer applications. Each node in a tree view can be expanded to show—or

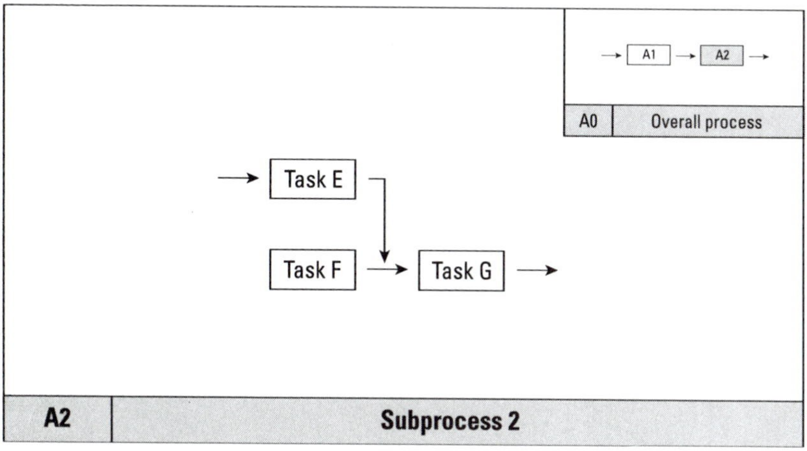

Figure 3-4. Subprocess 2

collapsed to hide—its child nodes. This allows individual branches of the tree to be navigated independently, which is useful when looking for a particular descendent node or item in the hierarchy. Tree views are popular because they offer a compact view of hierarchies. Summary data usually is not displayed in tree views. When summary data is desired, tree-table views (discussed in the following section) are used instead. The property hierarchy shown in Chapter 2 (Figure 2-4) is redisplayed using a tree view in Figure 3-5.

The groupings in corporate financial statements can also be displayed in tree views. All that is needed is to determine the parent–child relationships between the groupings in these statements. Then, by establishing the relationships between the groupings and the constitutive items, reports can be generated that allow the financial data to be viewed at any level of detail. This is incredibly powerful and would increase investor confidence in these statements. Auditors would be able to track information all the way down to the individual items, if desired. It is even conceivable that this data could be made public, and investors could review the information as they see fit. The balance sheet shown in Chapter 2 (Table 2-1) is redisplayed using a tree view in Figure 3-6.

- Property
  - Materials
    - Cash Reserves
      - Coins
      - Currency
      - Bank Deposits
    - Raw Materials
      - Direct Raw Materials
      - Indirect Raw Materials
    - Final Goods
      - Products
      - Services
  - Resources
    - Operating Resources
      - People
      - Equipment
      - Facilities
      - Information
      - Goodwill
      - Other Operating Resources
    - Financial Resources
      - Monetary Investments
      - Accounts Receivable
      - Accounts Payable
      - Loans
      - Bonds
      - Equity
      - Other Financial Resources

Figure 3-5. Tree view of the property hierarchy

- Balance Sheet
  - Total Assets
    - Current Assets
      - Cash and Cash Equivalents
      - Short-Term Investments
      - Accounts Receivable
      - Inventory
      - Other Current Assets
    - Long-Term Assets
      - Long-Term Investments
      - Resources
      - Goodwill
      - Intangible Assets
      - Other Long-Term Assets
      - Deferred Long-Term Asset Charges
  - Total Liabilities
    - Current Liabilities
      - Accounts Payable
      - Short-Term and Current Long-Term Debt
      - Other Current Liabilities
    - Long-Term Liabilities
      - Long-Term Debt
      - Other Long-Term Liabilities
      - Deferred Long-Term Liabilitiy Charges
      - Minority Interest
  - Stockholders' Equity
    - Basis Value
      - Common Stock
      - Other Basis Value
    - Retained Earnings

Figure 3-6. Tree view of the balance sheet hierarchy

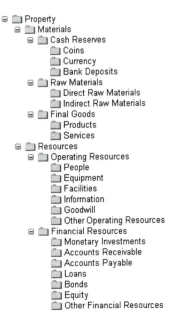

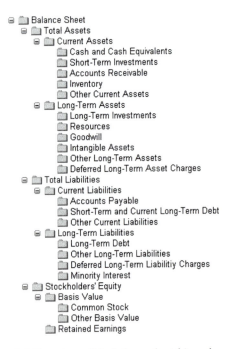

Establishing these hierarchies should be straightforward, based on the definition and examples presented in this chapter. Chapter 4 presents the decoupling of systems and processes, that is needed to create efficient business processes and management structures.

Tree-Table View

The tree-table view is a combination of a tree view and a table view. A table view is simply a display of data in rows and columns. A tree-table view displays the rows in the table next to the nodes in the tree and links them together. This allows the rows in the table to be shown or hidden by expanding or collapsing their associated nodes. Tree-table views are not very popular yet, probably because they are more difficult to program than node-descendant and tree views. However, I expect that when people start to see how useful they are, tree-table views will become the standard format for displaying corporate data.

To demonstrate the tree-table view, a set of generic property items was created and displayed in the property and balance sheet hierarchies. This is done to show how the same set of items can be displayed in different hierarchies and how nodes can be shared between hierarchies. The generic set of property items is shown in Table 3-1.

The generic property items are defined at a much higher (more general) level than would be done in an actual implementation to keep the resulting hierarchies small in size. The item's accounting value was selected as the attribute to be displayed in the tree-table view. These values are shown in Table 3-2.

The property and balance sheet hierarchies have their summary values calculated using a linear summation, with all weighting values equal to 1.0 except for those that are indicated in parentheses next to the hierarchy node names. Then, the accounting values corresponding to the generic property items can be summarized all the way up to the corporate level. This is shown in Figures 3-7 and 3-8.

Table 3-1. Generic Property Items

Generic Property Item Name	Property Hierarchy Node	Balance Sheet Hierarchy Node
Coins	Coins	Cash and cash equivalents
Currency	Currency	Cash and cash equivalents
Checking accounts	Bank deposits	Cash and cash equivalents
Savings accounts	Bank deposits	Cash and cash equivalents
Direct raw materials	Direct raw materials	Inventory
Indirect raw materials	Indirect raw materials	Inventory
Products	Products	Inventory
Services	Services	Inventory
People	People	Resources
Equipment	Equipment	Resources
Facilities	Facilities	Resources
Information	Information	Intangible assets
Goodwill	Goodwill	Goodwill
Short-term monetary investments	Monetary investments	Short-term investments
Long-term monetary investments	Monetary investments	Long-term investments
Accounts receivable	Accounts receivable	Accounts receivable
Accounts payable	Accounts payable (–1.0)	Accounts payable
Short-term loans	Loans (–1.0)	Short-term & current long-term debt
Current long-term loans	Loans (–1.0)	Short-term & current long-term debt
Long-term loans	Loans (–1.0)	Long-term debt
Short-term bonds	Bonds (–1.0)	Short-term & current long-term debt
Current long-term bonds	Bonds (–1.0)	Short-term & current long-term debt
Long-term bonds	Bonds (–1.0)	Long-term debt
Other current assets	Other operating resources	Other current assets
Other long-term assets	Other operating resources	Other long-term assets
Other current liabilities	Other financial resources (–1.0)	Other current liabilities
Other long-term liabilities	Other financial resources (–1.0)	Other long-term liabilities
Deferred long-term asset charges	Other financial resources	Deferred long-term asset charges
Deferred long-term liability charges	Other financial resources (–1.0)	Deferred long-term liability charges
Minority interest	Other financial resources (–1.0)	Minority interest
Common stock		Common stock
Other basis value		Other basis value
Retained earnings		Retained earnings

Table 3-2. Accounting Values for the Generic Property Items

Generic Property Item Name	December 31, 2002 Accounting Value	December 31, 2001 Accounting Value	December 31, 2000 Accounting Value
Coins	$1,192,000,000	$1,031,000,000	$572,000,000
Currency	$3,575,000,000	$3,093,000,000	$1,714,000,000
Checking accounts	$4,766,000,000	$4,123,000,000	$2,285,000,000
Savings accounts	$11,916,000,000	$10,308,000,000	$5,713,000,000
Direct raw materials	$2,658,000,000	$3,882,000,000	$4,438,000,000
Indirect raw materials	$664,000,000	$971,000,000	$1,110,000,000
Products	$6,645,000,000	$9,705,000,000	$11,096,000,000
Services	$0	$0	$0
People	$0	$0	$0
Equipment	$27,294,000,000	$14,897,000,000	$14,639,000,000
Facilities	$45,490,000,000	$24,827,000,000	$24,398,000,000
Information	$7,689,000,000	$6,921,000,000	$0
Goodwill	$10,265,000,000	$10,006,000,000	$10,810,000,000
Short-term monetary investments	$16,825,000,000	$790,000,000	$1,161,000,000
Long-term monetary investments	$5,044,000,000	$183,661,000,000	$162,975,000,000
Accounts receivable	$192,011,000,000	$13,283,000,000	$19,582,000,000
Accounts payable	$91,281,000,000	$53,513,000,000	$63,156,000,000
Short-term loans	$0	$1,201,000,000	$0
Current long-term loans	$0	$0	$0
Long-term loans	$123,134,000,000	$99,946,000,000	$86,858,000,000
Short-term bonds	$0	$1,201,000,000	$0
Current long-term bonds	$0	$0	$0
Long-term bonds	$78,806,000,000	$63,966,000,000	$55,589,000,000
Other current assets	$0	$0	$0
Other long-term assets	$34,748,000,000	$14,177,000,000	$27,737,000,000
Other current liabilities	$0	$8,331,000,000	$0
Other long-term liabilities	$60,949,000,000	$71,053,000,000	$66,476,000,000
Deferred long-term asset charges	$0	$22,294,000,000	$14,870,000,000
Deferred long-term liability charges	$8,964,000,000	$4,305,000,000	$0
Minority interest	$834,000,000	$746,000,000	$707,000,000
Common stock	$1,032,000,000	$1,020,000,000	$1,002,000,000
Other basis value	–$4,249,000,000	$9,224,000,000	$18,612,000,000
Retained earnings	$10,031,000,000	$9,463,000,000	$10,700,000,000

Period Ending:	December 31,2002	December 31,2001	December 31,2000
Property	$6,814,000,000	$19,707,000,000	$30,314,000,000
Materials	$31,416,000,000	$33,113,000,000	$26,928,000,000
Cash Reserves	$21,449,000,000	$18,555,000,000	$10,284,000,000
Coins	$1,192,000,000	$1,031,000,000	$572,000,000
◆ coins	$1,192,000,000	$1,031,000,000	$572,000,000
Currency	$3,575,000,000	$3,093,000,000	$1,714,000,000
◆ currency	$3,575,000,000	$3,093,000,000	$1,714,000,000
Bank Deposits	$16,682,000,000	$14,431,000,000	$7,998,000,000
◆ savings accounts	$11,916,000,000	$10,308,000,000	$5,713,000,000
◆ checking accounts	$4,766,000,000	$4,123,000,000	$2,285,000,000
Raw Materials	$3,322,000,000	$4,853,000,000	$5,548,000,000
Direct Raw Materials	$2,658,000,000	$3,882,000,000	$4,438,000,000
◆ direct raw materials	$2,658,000,000	$3,882,000,000	$4,438,000,000
Indirect Raw Materials	$664,000,000	$971,000,000	$1,110,000,000
◆ indirect raw materials	$664,000,000	$971,000,000	$1,110,000,000
Final Goods	$6,645,000,000	$9,705,000,000	$11,096,000,000
Products	$6,645,000,000	$9,705,000,000	$11,096,000,000
◆ products	$6,645,000,000	$9,705,000,000	$11,096,000,000
Services	$0	$0	$0
◆ services	$0	$0	$0
Resources	($24,602,000,000)	($13,406,000,000)	$3,386,000,000
Operating Resources	$125,486,000,000	$70,828,000,000	$77,584,000,000
Financial Resources	($150,088,000,000)	($84,234,000,000)	($74,198,000,000)

Figure 3-7. Tree-table view of the generic property items in the property hierarchy

Period Ending:	December 31,2002	December 31,2001	December 31,2000
Balance Sheet	$0	$0	$0
Total Assets	$370,782,000,000	$323,969,000,000	$303,100,000,000
Current Assets	$240,252,000,000	$47,186,000,000	$47,671,000,000
Cash and Cash Equivalents	$21,449,000,000	$18,555,000,000	$10,284,000,000
◆ currency	$3,575,000,000	$3,093,000,000	$1,714,000,000
◆ coins	$1,192,000,000	$1,031,000,000	$572,000,000
◆ savings accounts	$11,916,000,000	$10,308,000,000	$5,713,000,000
◆ checking accounts	$4,766,000,000	$4,123,000,000	$2,285,000,000
Short-Term Investments	$16,825,000,000	$790,000,000	$1,161,000,000
◆ short-term monetary investments	$16,825,000,000	$790,000,000	$1,161,000,000
Accounts Receivable	$192,011,000,000	$13,283,000,000	$19,582,000,000
◆ accounts receivable	$192,011,000,000	$13,283,000,000	$19,582,000,000
Inventory	$9,967,000,000	$14,558,000,000	$16,644,000,000
◆ services	$0	$0	$0
◆ products	$6,645,000,000	$9,705,000,000	$11,096,000,000
◆ indirect raw materials	$664,000,000	$971,000,000	$1,110,000,000
◆ direct raw materials	$2,658,000,000	$3,882,000,000	$4,438,000,000
Other Current Assets	$0	$0	$0
◆ other current assets	$0	$0	$0
Long-Term Assets	$130,530,000,000	$276,783,000,000	$255,429,000,000
Total Liabilities	$363,968,000,000	$304,262,000,000	$272,786,000,000
Current Liabilities	$91,281,000,000	$64,246,000,000	$63,156,000,000
Long-Term Liabilities	$272,687,000,000	$240,016,000,000	$209,630,000,000
Stockholders' Equity	$6,814,000,000	$19,707,000,000	$30,314,000,000
Basis Value	($3,217,000,000)	$10,244,000,000	$19,614,000,000
Retained Earnings	$10,031,000,000	$9,463,000,000	$10,700,000,000

Figure 3-8. Tree-table view of the generic property items in the balance sheet hierarchy

To differentiate the groupings from the items, the hierarchy nodes are indicated using folder icons and the items are indicated using asterisk icons (this convention is used throughout this book). Several nodes are shared between the property and balance sheet hierarchies, such as goodwill, accounts receivable, and accounts payable, and the same set of generic property items is displayed in two different hierarchies. This shows how both nodes and items can be defined once and used in different hierarchies. Using this approach, important corporate reports can be generated using a hierarchical data structure and tree-table views.

Corporate Hierarchies

Having described hierarchies in general, the specific ones needed for lean corporations are now presented. These include the organization structure, program structure, and other hierarchies.

The organization structure is the most important corporate hierarchy; this is where command-and-control is accomplished. A good foundation will lead to success, while a poor foundation will lead to failure.

Organization Structure

The organization structure subdivides the corporation into manageable operating units, so it follows that the organizational structure also represents the management reporting structure for the corporation. All lean corporations have organization structures that are analogous to that used by virtually all college and professional football teams, which are scaled-down versions of corporations that have implemented the fundamental features of the lean philosophy. This analogy has been pointed out by several authors and developed to varying degrees. It is fully developed in this book.

Football teams are the ideal analogy for corporate organization structures because they are both task and process oriented. Recall that tasks are activities performed by one person. Processes are created by linking together tasks. In football, each player must execute his task in harmony with the other players' tasks to form a play. Tasks include blocking, running, passing, and so on. Each task must be executed to a high degree of precision, but also synchronized together as a whole. The organization structure that is most effective in doing this is a hybrid type which includes both horizontal (task-oriented) and vertical (process-oriented) groups. This structure is shown generically in Figure 3-9 and specifically for the football team analogy in Figure 3-10.

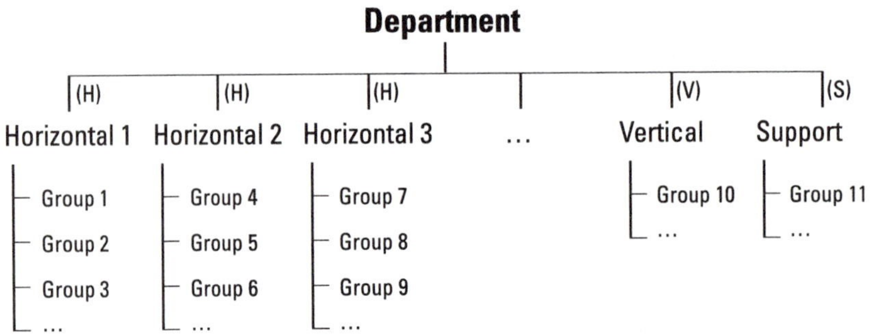

Figure 3-9. Lean organization structure for a department

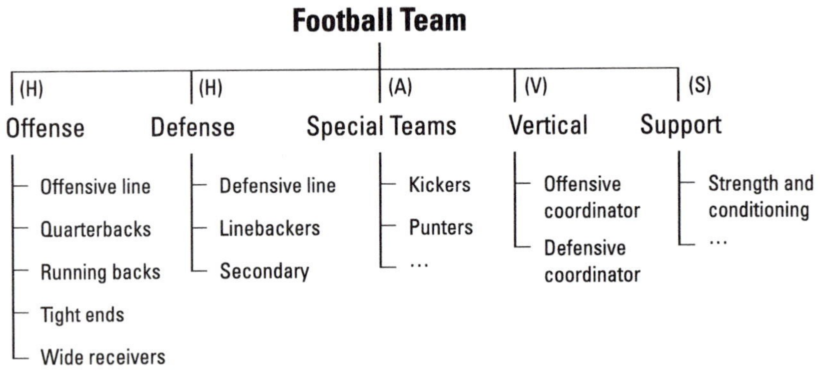

Figure 3-10. Lean organization structure illustrated using the football team analogy

The lean organization structure consists of five types of groups: horizontal, vertical, support, and two upper-management groups (designated Type-A and Type-B). In organization charts, these groups are indicated by the letters H, V, S, A, and B, respectively. Nodes that do not represent groups, but are shown for sorting purposes only, are indicated using the null symbol (∅). All groups have one manager, and each manager is responsible for only one group.

- **Horizontal groups** are functionally oriented. They focus on developing the tasks.
- **Vertical groups** are process oriented. They are responsible for combining the tasks into effective processes.

- **Support groups** are auxiliary groups that provide specialized services for the other groups.
- **Type-A groups** are upper-management groups that have some direct vertical-related (process-related) responsibilities in addition to managing their subordinate verticals groups.
- **Type-B groups** are upper-management groups that have only indirect vertical-related (process-related) responsibilities through the management of their subordinate vertical groups.

In the football team analogy, the horizontal groups develop basic schemes (blocking schemes, pass coverage schemes, and so on), the vertical group develops those basic schemes into plays, and the support groups assist the other groups. Note that the football organization hierarchy defines the groupings according to the definitions presented previously; namely, the groupings and items are separate. For example, the groups are named based on collections (such as defensive line, linebackers, secondary, and so on). Items are the individual players. This allows players to be assigned to different groups.

Also, the groupings are nonoverlapping and minimize coupling. This is best illustrated in the defense, which is organized into three groups. These groups have small degrees of coupling between them with the defensive line and secondary being effectively uncoupled so that they can execute their tasks independently. For example, it makes no difference to the defensive line if the pass coverage is zone or man-to-man; their tasks are unaffected. Nor does is matter to the secondary whether the defensive line uses a bull rush or stunt. All that matters is that each group executes its tasks in a precise and effective manner.

A feature of the lean organization structure that may not be apparent is that the vertical groups allow multiple program teams to be created and run in parallel. This has relatively little to do with football. Creating multiple program teams is needed only when there is more than one process being executed at the same time. In business, this is usually the case. A functionally oriented department will often support several different product programs with many workers supporting several different product programs at the same time. The vertical managers effectively become temporary managers of these workers. When their tasks are finished, the workers report back to their direct supervisor for new assignments.

Sometimes, nonvertical group managers have some direct vertical-related (process-related) responsibilities. For example, a head football coach may also be the offensive or defensive coordinator in rare situations. In this case, the head coach is the manager of a Type-A group. Under normal situations, where all the process-related responsibilities are handled by the offensive and defensive coordinators, the head coach is the manager of a Type-B group. Special Teams is another example of a Type-A group, because the coach is responsible for both developing the tasks (kicking, blocking, and so on) and combining them into plays (kick-offs, kick returns, and so on). Distinguishing between Type-A and Type-B groups allows the process responsibilities to be clearly identified. This is demonstrated in the "Program Structure" section later in this chapter.

The lean organization structure shown in Figure 3-9 corresponds to a department. A typical department consists of two to seven groups (90–200 people) distributed in horizontal, vertical, and support groups. Each group consists of twenty to fifty people and is subdivided into sections that consist of four to twelve people who perform similar work. Each section is assigned a leader. The section leader is usually the most experienced and/or respected worker in the section. The sections within the department typically are highly coupled, meaning that their tasks are highly interrelated. However, each person has specific responsibilities, and unless the members accept these responsibilities, the section cannot be effective. In my experience, many corporate managers are unaware of the importance of accepting responsibilities. Instead, they reward workers for doing other people's jobs, but this is not lean. This would never happen in football. If a player moves out of his position and makes a bad play—or even a good play—he is chastised. The coaches realize that the execution of the system creates superior performance. This is the basis for the saying, "It is the players with the best team, not the team with the best players, that win championships."

Expanding the lean organization structure to larger organizations is straightforward; you simply extend the hierarchy upward. Departments represent the building blocks of corporations. The department level is the highest level for horizontal groups; all higher level groups are collections of Type-A and Type-B groups plus small vertical and support groups. The higher level Type-A and vertical groups are responsible for program management. Each level above the department level consists of two to five Type-A and/or Type-B groups in addition to the vertical and support groups. Thus, corporations of 50,000 to 150,000 people require five levels above the department level. This organization structure is shown in Figure 3-11.

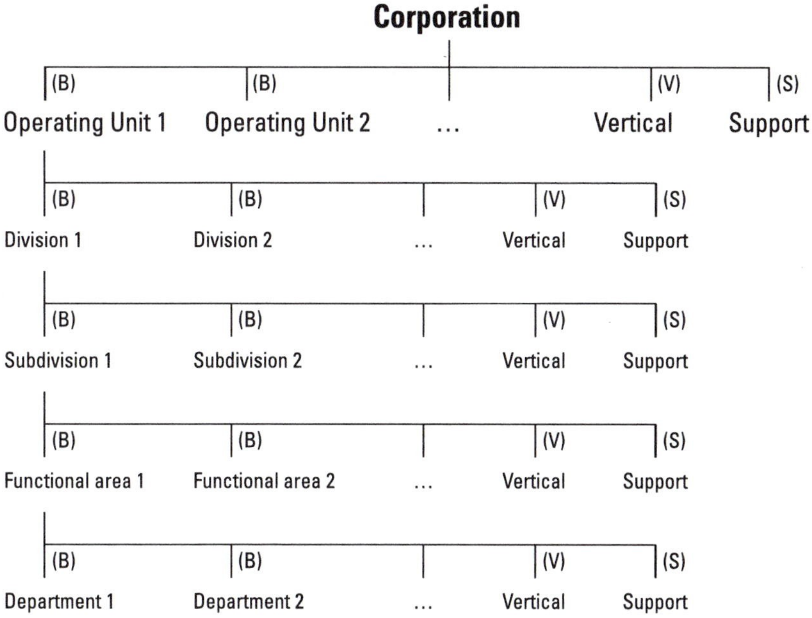

Figure 3-11. Lean corporate organization structure

All lean corporations have the type of organization structure shown in Figure 3-11. In addition, the groupings' sizes and direct reporting structure is the same as that used by military organizations, as shown in Table 3-3.

Table 3-3. Military and Corporate Organizational Units

Level	Military Organizational Unit	Composition	Size (People)	Commander	Commander Type
8	Army	2–5 Corps	52,000–160,000	General	Officer
7	Corps	2–5 Divisions	26,000–65,000	Lieutenant General	Officer
6	Division	8–11 Battalions and support groups	10,000–16,000	Major General	Officer
5	Brigade	2+ Battalions	3,000–5,000	Brigadier General	Officer
4	Battalion	2+ Companies	500–900	Lieutenant Colonel	Officer
3	Company	2+ Platoons	90–200	Captain	Officer
2	Platoon	2+ Sections	20–50	Lieutenant	Officer
1	Section	4–12 Soldiers	4–12	Staff Sergeants	Enlisted
Level	**Corporate Organizational Unit**	**Composition**	**Size (People)**	**Manager**	**Manager Type**
8	Corporation	2–5 Operating units	52,000–160,000	President and CEO	Executive
7	Operating Unit	2–5 Divisions	26,000–65,000	Vice Chairman	Executive
6	Division	8–11 Functional areas	10,000–16,000	Executive Vice President	Executive
5	Subdivision	2+ Functional areas	3,000–5,000	Group Vice President	Executive
4	Functional Area	2+ Departments	500–900	Executive Director	Executive
3	Department	2+ Groups	90–200	Department Head	Manager
2	Group	2+ Sections	20–50	Group Manager	Manager
1	Section	4–12 Workers	4–12	Section Leader	Leader

Level 1 in Table 3-3 represents the lowest formal level of the corporate organization structure. It is led by section leaders who assist the group managers. Section leaders are like captains of a football team, and group managers are like the coaches. The first official level of management begins at Level 2. This is indicated by the double line. This is the same structure as military organizations, where the separation is between enlisted personnel and officers. Departments are usually functionally oriented; therefore, the majority of the workers are located in the horizontal groups. The associated vertical and support groups have smaller numbers of people. The verticals are responsible for coordinating the activities of the other groups with the higher levels. The support groups assist the horizontal and vertical groups. All levels above the department level are responsible for process and product management. This is indicated by the dashed line. The result is a lean organization structure, where standardized work is implemented at the department level and lower. This creates a flat organization structure that allows each department to be reengineered from the bottom up.

The organization structure is the management structure of the corporation. Each node has one and only one manager who reports to one and only one supervisor. Thus, the lean organization implements a direct reporting structure. It defines nonoverlapping areas of management that minimize coupling. Shared responsibility is not allowed: Every worker reports to one and only one manager. All other reporting structures are indirect and represent customer–supplier relationships, not manager–employee relationships. These other reporting structures may be likened to a matrix organization. However, do not confuse the customer with the boss. Workers should have one and only one boss but can have many customers. Customers may, in fact, behave as bosses, but only because the worker's real boss has assigned a part or all of the worker's time to be scheduled by the customer directly; your real boss can change this decision at any time. If the distinction between boss and customer is not made, you will run into problems. Workers will pit one against the other, just like kids do with their parents, or they will choose to work only on projects they like.

Every employee should know who his or her boss is. Fortunately, it is easy to tell, because your boss is the person who controls your pay and can fire you. This is what gives your boss control over your activities. Every employee should also know how he or she fits into the big picture. This is done using the organization chart. The organization chart displays the corporation's employees in the organization structure. It should be made visible to all employees. You may be surprised at how few or how many levels there are between you and the CEO. This can give you motivation to climb the corporate ladder but, at a minimum, shows how you fit in. I have read recent books indicating the death of the organization chart, so that people respond to the question "whom do you work for?" with a response like "that doesn't mean much around here." If I came across a company like that, I would immediately sell all my stock. An unorganized company produces self-appointed experts; that is, all employees think they are their own bosses and can do whatever they like. Don't fall into that trap. A clearly defined chain-of-command is and will always be a necessary condition for successful organizations.

The most important aspect of the lean organization structure is that the horizontal and vertical managers report to the same supervisor at the department level, but they have different levels of responsibility. The department head has a specific level of responsibility. The subordinate group managers have lower responsibility levels. The vertical managers are one level lower in responsibility level than the department head. The horizontal and support group managers are two or more levels lower in responsibility level than the department head. This makes the horizontal and support groups subordinate to the vertical managers for product and process management. However, this is a customer–supplier relationship, not a manager–employee relationship. This means that the vertical managers cannot fire the horizontal managers. They can suggest to the department head that this be done. It is the responsibility to the department head to determine if the problem is with the horizontal managers (performance of the tasks) or whether it is really a problem with the vertical managers (integration of the tasks into processes). Support group managers are one or more levels below the vertical and horizontal managers they support. This is also a customer–supplier relationship.

You should now see the direct analogy to college and professional football teams. The head coach is equivalent to the department head. The offensive and defensive coordinators are one level below the head coach in responsibility. The positional coaches are two levels below the head coach in responsibility. The head coach can fire the coordinators and positional coaches. The coordinators cannot fire positional coaches (and vice versa). Positional coaches are subordinate to the coordinators for the management of team play. The natural advancement for a coach is from a positional coach to a coordinator, then to a head coach. This mirrors the organization and advancement of managers in lean corporations.

The relationship between the groups at the department level should now be clear. Next, the relationships between groups in the higher organization levels are developed. All levels higher than the department level consist of collections of Type-A and/or Type-B groups and additional vertical and support groups that are responsible for product and process management. A collection of several departments is called a functional area. A collection of several functional areas and their associated vertical and support groups is called a subdivision. This type of grouping continues upward as indicated in Figure 3-11. A functional area consists of two to five departments. A level-4 vertical group will usually consist of one to ten process managers and their assistants. A level-4 support group usually consists of one to five support subgroups, each with eight to twenty people. Therefore, the typical size of a subdivision is 3,000 to 5,000 people (200 to 900 for each of the two to five functional areas, plus ten to fifty for the level-4 vertical group and 90 to 200 for the level-4 support group). Note that the size of the vertical and support groups is highly dependent on the number of product programs performed by the corporation.

As was the case for departments, the vertical group managers in the higher organization levels are one level below that of their supervisor. This places their responsibility at the same level as that of the other non-support group managers in the same organization level. This is different than is the case for departments, where verticals were one level higher than the other groups in responsibility. As a consequence, the vertical managers are always one level higher in responsibility than the vertical managers in each successively lower level in the organization structure. This creates a chain-of-command through the vertical groups that spans all levels of the corporation as illustrated in Figure 3-12. This is exactly what is needed to create and enforce the responsibility of the vertical managers in corporations and military organizations. The support group managers are still one or more responsibility levels below that of the other groups in their level.

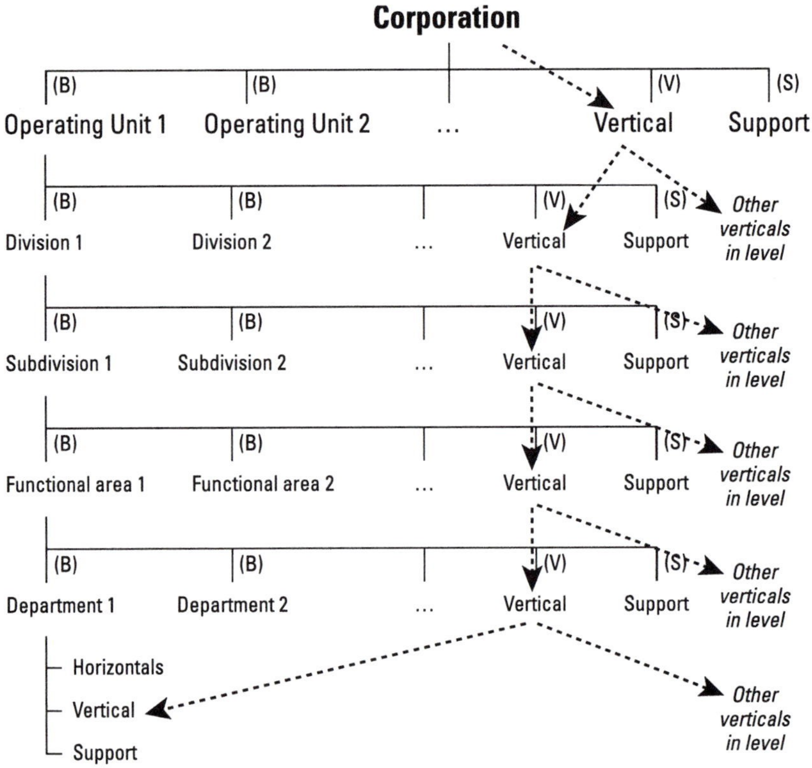

Figure 3-12. Chain-of-command for program management teams

Figure 3-12 shows a program management structure that proceeds through the vertical groups only. Remember that vertical (process) management can be through the direct manager and subordinate vertical managers (Type-A group) or through the subordinate vertical managers only (Type-B group). The managers of Type-A groups are referred to as "wearing two hats," because they effectively have two different jobs: managing the people in their groups and managing the processes they perform. Most organizations have a combination of these two types of upper-management groups. A good example of this is the U.S. Department of Defense, which has the organization structure shown in Figure 3-13. This structure is collapsed to show only the reporting structure of the Army down to the Division level. The chain-of-command for an active army is illustrated as a vertical reporting structure.

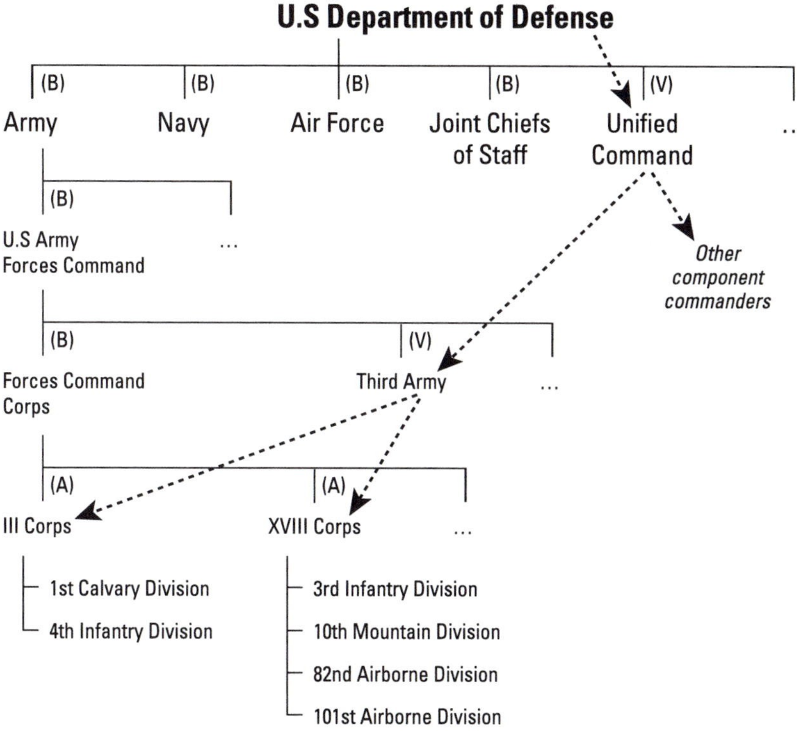

Figure 3-13. Chain-of-command for the U.S. Army

The chain-of-command (in Figure 3-13) has four vertical reporting relationships. The first is from the Secretary of Defense (manager of the Department of Defense) to the commander in the

Unified Command, who is assigned Third Army for a specific mission. The second is from the commander in the Unified Command to the commander of Third Army. The third is from the commander of Third Army to the Corps commanders assigned to the mission. The fourth is from the Corps commanders to the individual Division and Brigade commanders. When active armies are created, these vertical reporting structures become the direct reporting structures. When active armies complete their mission, they return to their original organization structure. This allows each Division and Brigade to train as a unit and to be combined with other Divisions and Brigades in varying configurations to form armies that are tailored for their missions.

Program Structure

The program structure represents the vertical reporting structure for the entire corporation. It necessarily follows the hierarchical relationships of the vertical and Type-A groups in the organization structure. The direct supervisor of each level in the organization structure establishes the number of vertical managers needed. This is another example of the use of local knowledge for the management of lean organizations. The direct supervisor can organize their group as Type-A or Type-B. Subordinate vertical groups consist of one or more vertical managers and their assistants, if needed. Each vertical manager reports to one or more vertical manager(s) in higher levels. This is a true matrix-type structure, where each manager can report to several different higher level managers. Again, recognize that this is a customer–supplier relationship, not a manager–employee relationship.

The program structure is created by assigning specific responsibilities to the vertical managers. First, a list of programs is developed. Then, vertical managers are assigned to specific areas of the program in a top-down manner. This is done using a simple mapping, where vertical responsibility is cascaded down the organization structure through each vertical manager. Figure 3-14 shows the generic format for a program structure that corresponds to the organization structure shown in Figure 3-11.

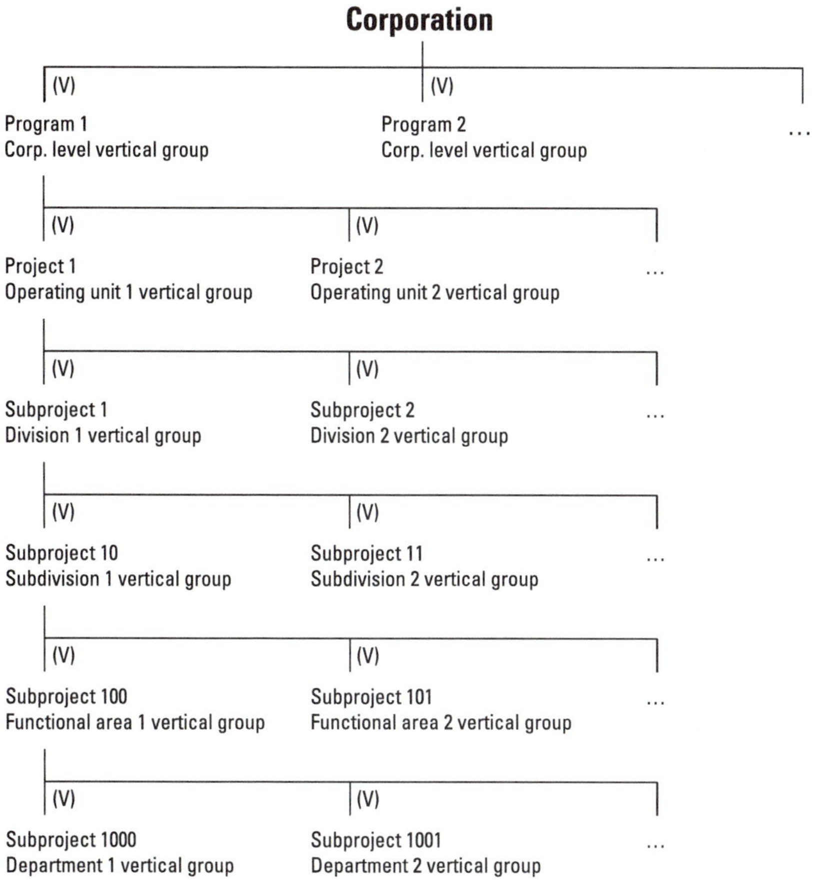

Figure 3-14. Lean corporate program structure

The organization structure always defines the levels in the program structure. These levels are then divided into vertical tiers that support specific products/processes. This is why they are referred to as vertical reporting structures.

To further demonstrate the concept of program structures, the U.S. Department of Defense is used again as an example. The program structure is generated from the vertical reporting relationships implemented in the organization structure, as shown in Figure 3-13 for the command of an active U.S. Army. To more clearly show the chain-of-command, it can be displayed as a program structure. This is shown is Figure 3-15 for Operation Desert Storm.

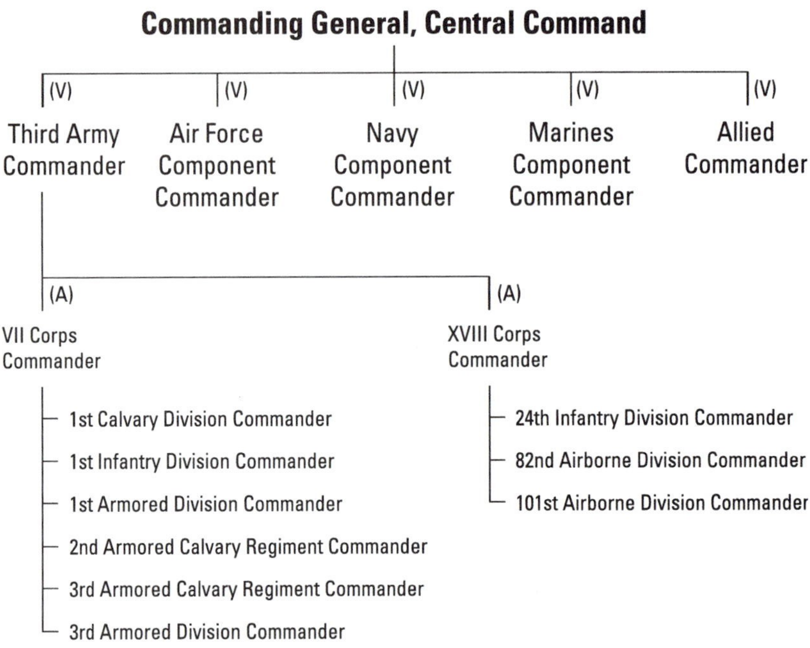

Figure 3-15. Operation Desert Storm chain-of-command shown as a program structure

By using an organization structure with both functionally oriented and vertically oriented groups, the Department of Defense has implemented a lean organization structure for the management of active armies. This doesn't mean that there is no waste or that the organization couldn't be improved. What it does mean is that the organization structure is much more efficient than having fixed force, standing armies deployed at all times.

Program structures for corporations should now be easy to visualize. The number of vertical managers in each level depends on the number and complexity of the specific product programs to be managed. Generally, each vertical group contains two to twenty people that consist of vertical managers and their assistants (if needed). Only the vertical and Type-A groups that are involved in a specific program are shown in the program structure. Horizontal, support, and Type-B groups are not shown. This reinforces the separation between the task owners and process owners. The task owners become members of program teams while they are performing their tasks. They are released from these teams when their tasks are completed. Everyone who works on a given program contributes to its success. Thus, they are all recognized for their contributions. It may even be a good idea to indicate all the programs that workers have contributed to on their entries in the organization chart. This would be analogous to the pins that are displayed on military uniforms to indicate the campaigns an officer served on. This not only would establish pride and visible connections to the product, it would also allow everyone to see which programs their peers have worked on, thus facilitating the transfer of lessons learned from one worker to another.

The vertical and Type-A managers establish program teams based on the requirements of their programs. These requirements relate to tasks that are defined using IDEF0 process models. Each program uses a different number of tasks with different scheduling to achieve its objectives. The IDEF0 process models define the linkages between these tasks, the resource requirements, the task durations, and—most importantly—the controls. As you proceed down the program structure, the products and processes are subdivided into smaller, more manageable units. The amount of detail at each level increases as you proceed down the hierarchy. This allows the higher levels of management to set objectives in general terms and have them implemented in specific terms by the subordinate managers. The program structure is also the primary path for the establishment of program financing. Budgets are established that are based on the content of the program. These are balanced at each level of the program hierarchy to maximize benefits and minimize the risks.

Other Hierarchies

Some of the other hierarchies needed to manage corporations are as follows:

- Property hierarchy
- Product hierarchy
- Output hierarchy
- Requirement hierarchy

Chapter 4

Decoupling Systems and Processes

Business processes and systems are usually large and complex, so the key to managing them is to divide them into smaller, less complex pieces that interact in simple, understandable ways. To do this, the underlying systems and processes must be organized so that coupling between the elements (subsystems and components; subprocesses and tasks) is minimized. The resulting systems and processes are then represented as hierarchies to enforce their organization structures and to facilitate their management. This chapter describes what coupling is, how it is minimized, and how coupled systems and processes are managed.

Understanding How Systems and Processes Are Coupled

To understand how systems and processes are coupled, you must first understand what coupling is. Coupling occurs when changes in one element of a system or process produce changes in another element of a system or process. (A process consists of all the work tasks that are performed in order to produce an item or provide a service.) Systems are coupled primarily through the interactions and connections between subsystems and components. Processes are coupled through the input–output linkages between the work tasks and the use of shared properties.

Coupling is a concern because it usually produces unwanted side effects. It is almost always preferable to have uncoupled systems and processes, so that each one can be modified without affecting the others.

Minimizing System Coupling

Coupling in systems should be minimized so that each element (subsystem or component) can be designed independently without affecting the other elements. This reduces the time it takes to design a system by reducing the amount of interactions between the elements. Most complex products are decomposed into modules that minimize the coupling between the modules. For example, automobiles are decomposed into the body, chassis, engine, transmission, and so on. These modules have relatively few connection points between each other, thus limiting the coupling between them. This allows these modules to be designed and managed efficiently.

Coupling in systems is minimized by analyzing the connections between subsystems and components. The easiest way to minimize coupling is to try dividing the system at different locations to create different sets of subsystems and components. Then the coupling between the subsystems and components is assessed and the best decomposition is determined. To assess coupling, the interactions between subsystems and components are evaluated, either through the use of mathematical models or through personal judgment. When using mathematical models, the interactions are assessed by determining the sensitivities of the subsystem's or component's design parameters to subsystem- and component-level responses. For example, changing the stiffness of one part in an assembly may affect the operating loads and stresses in another part. Often, the design of a part can be changed to minimize this interaction. This is the basic idea behind decoupling systems.

Fewer Connection Points Equals Less Coupling

When personal judgment is used to decouple systems, some knowledge of the interactions between subsystems must be known. A good rule is as follows: The fewer connection points between subsystems, the lesser degree of coupling. Most people know this intuitively and divide systems based on this rule. For example, most vehicle manufacturers have separate engine and transmission engineering organizations. These subsystems have relatively few connections between each other and the other subsystems in the vehicle, so it makes sense to divide the system in this manner.

Generally, there is a strong relationship between systems and processes, so the manner in which one is decoupled often applies to the other. In this book, the emphasis is on business processes and optimizing them using lean principles. Decoupled systems are usually created as a side effect. This is achieved through the organization structure that is aligned to support the resulting optimized business processes.

Example of Decoupling a System

A good example of decoupling a system is the use of separate engine and transmission electronic control modules in vehicles. These modules are designed using a common interface so that different engines can be mated to different transmissions without having to design new control modules. This greatly simplifies the design effort and allows each control module to be designed separately, and then configured at the system level for optimum vehicle performance.

Minimizing Process Coupling

Because coupling in processes is the main source of inefficiency and waste, it should be minimized. For example, any process that consists of a series of tasks performed by several people can be made more efficient by having one person perform all the tasks. The reason that this is more efficient is that no time is lost waiting for the next person to start his or her task or in trying to understand what was done during a previous task.

Lean corporations effectively decouple their processes by reengineering their processes so that as much work as possible can be conducted simultaneously (in parallel) instead of sequentially (in series), thus reducing the amount of time it takes to perform the processes. There are two steps to decoupling processes:

1. Determine the existing process coupling using an IDEF0 process model.
2. Redesign the process to minimize coupling using business process reengineering concepts.

Finding and Redesigning Process Coupling

The determination of existing process coupling is done using an IDEF0 process model. Each work task is modeled in terms of inputs, outputs, resources, and controls. (The details for creating these models are presented in Chapter 6.) Then, the coupling between tasks occurs through the input–output linkages and the usage of shared properties. Because detailed task models are used, the coupling within the process is easily evaluated.

The redesign of processes to minimize coupling is done using business process reengineering concepts, specifically, the concept of process threads. A process thread is a series of tasks that is performed by the same person within a given process. Each process should be designed to have multiple process threads that are executed in parallel, with each thread running continuously throughout the process. This minimizes both the total duration of the process and the number of people needed to execute the process (The details for designing process threads are presented in Chapter 7).

Example of Decoupling a Process

One example of decoupling a process is how pit stops in automobile racing are designed. Each pit crew member is assigned a specific job (such as tire changer, fuel loader, and so on) and is given his or her own equipment to do the job. Each pit stop job is run as a process thread, meaning that each pit crew member executes his or her job in parallel with the others. The result is that pit stops are completed in the minimum amount of time with the minimum amount of the people.

Minimizing Coupling Throughout the Corporation

The concept of minimizing coupling also applies to management structures and employee roles and responsibilities. As with processes and systems, the idea is to isolate changes in one area from the others. This means that management structures should be designed based on the organization of the process and systems that they control. Specific contact points (interfaces) need to be created and enforced, leading to the implementation of clear and direct command-and-control. Information flow between management areas can be used to assess organizational coupling. The objective is to have the majority of information flow within a given area and to minimize the need for information flow across other areas. Employee roles and responsibilities should be aligned to support this objective. This usually means that employee jobs shift from being functionally oriented to being process oriented.

Example of Decoupling a Project Team

Consider the highly coupled project team organization structure shown in Figure 4-1.

This type of organization structure is often used when projects span two different organizations (such as different corporate divisions). The organization structure is highly coupled because there are co-managers at each level and because the workers are assigned to more than one group.

Using the concepts in this book, the project's organization structure violates two principles of the lean philosophy:

- Clearly define roles and responsibilities.
- Optimize processes and systems.

To repair the situation, responsibility should be split between the two project managers. Each manager then receives three workers from each organization (workers 1 through 6 are from one organization and workers 7 through 12 are from the other organization) to assign to his or her groups. To optimize the system, coupling in the organization structure is minimized by having each worker assigned to a single group. The choice of three groups of two people makes the most sense, because each organization then has equal representation (one worker from each organization). Each manager chairs each of his or her three groups and acts as the interface between the groups to coordinate and balance competing issues. The resulting uncoupled project team organization structure is shown in Figure 4-2.

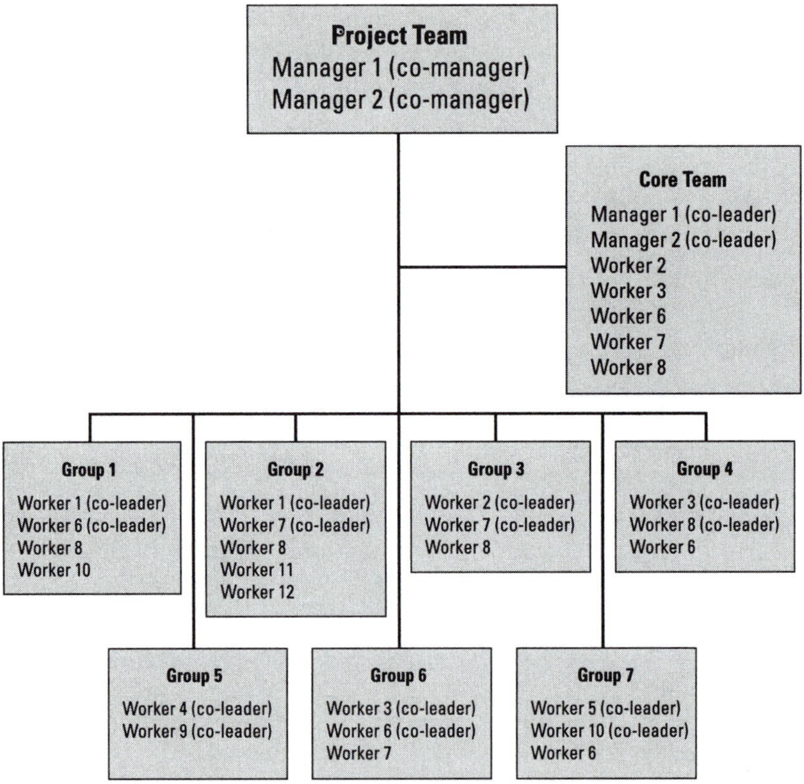

Figure 4-1. Highly coupled project team organization structure

Example of Decoupling Employee Roles

Product engineering organizations have designers, release engineers, analysis engineers, development engineers, and noise and vibration engineers—all different people. Having all these roles complicates the ability to balance competing issues. Each person wants to optimize the design based on his or her own area of responsibility. For example, noise and vibration engineers want changes to improve noise and vibration regardless of the effect on cost or structural integrity. Analysis engineers want a durable part but may give little consideration to packaging and manufacturing concerns. Designers are concerned with manufacturing and packaging.

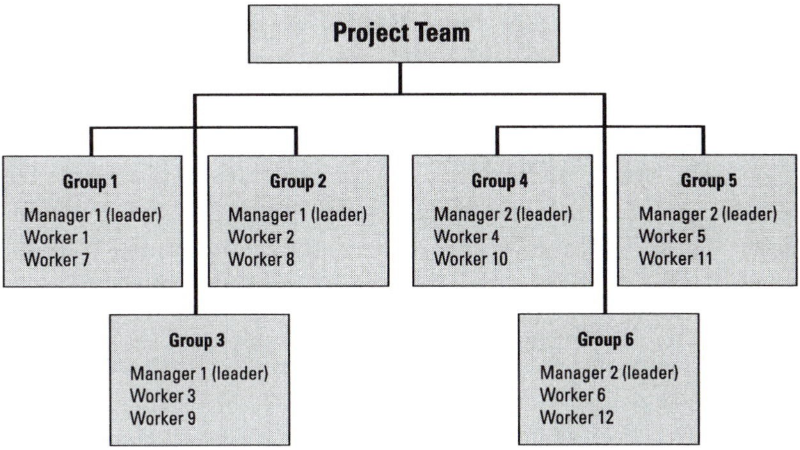

Figure 4-2. Uncoupled project team organization structure

The decoupled approach is to have one person do all these things. The role of project engineer allows all aspects of component design to be handled by one person. This person knows all the issues involved and makes intelligent compromises, and the result is increased efficiency and quality.

The concept of a project engineer is not new. In the late 1930s, the Pratt and Whitney Corporation instituted such a system in which their project engineers acted more like chief engineers. Each was concerned with all aspects of the business, including engineering, sales, manufacturing, quality, and service. This approach was implemented in various degrees and contributed to the success of that company. Today, lean organization structures are designed based on this concept.

Managing Coupled Systems

Large, complex systems can be decoupled only to a certain degree. What remains are coupled entities that must be managed effectively. To do this, you must understand the nature of subgroup interactions and the specialized methods for managing them. These topics are presented in the following sections.

Subgroup Interactions

When you divide systems into smaller groups, you do so to make the systems easier to manage. The idea is that you solve several smaller, easier problems instead of one large, more complex problem. The way the system is divided determines the ease with which the problem is solved. The main issue, then, is how to handle the interactions between subsystems. To facilitate this, consider how the fundamental properties of subsystem interactions are defined:

- Subsystems interact only at connection points (boundaries).
- The effect of one subsystem on another can be fully accounted for using boundary information.
- Boundary information retains the important characteristics of the original subsystem but uses a simplified (less detailed) representation.
- Boundary information can be determined both from analytical models and physical tests.

The fundamental properties of subsystem interactions are described in the following sections.

Subsystems Interact Only at Connection Points (Boundaries)

The first property, that subsystems interact only at connection points (boundaries), allows clearly defined interfaces to be created between subsystems that are independent of the internal configurations of the subsystems. This separates the interface from the implementation, which allows the subsystem's internal configurations to be modified without affecting the connections between subsystems.

Fully Account for The Effect of One Subsystem on Another

The second property, that the effect of one subsystem on another can be fully accounted for using boundary information, allows each subsystem to be designed by representing the effects of the connected subsystems at the boundaries only. The details of the connected subsystems are not important; only the effects that they have on the subsystem of interest are important.

Boundary Information Uses a Simplified (Less Detailed) Representation

The third property, that boundary information retains the important characteristics of the original subsystem but uses a simplified (less detailed) representation, allows complex external systems to be modeled using simpler methods. This greatly reduces the effort needed to generate these models.

Boundary Information Can Be Determined from Analytical Models and Physical Tests

The fourth property, that boundary information can be determined both from analytical models and from physical tests, allows analytical models and physical hardware to be validated and combinations of both items to be used to predict system performance.

The preceding properties of subsystem interactions allow an effective way to conduct system integration. The methods that were designed to do this are called substructuring methods. Understanding and applying these concepts can dramatically improve the product development process. Unfortunately, these concepts are probably the most difficult ones in this book. They are presented only in general terms here, so please do not worry if you do not understand them completely. These are advanced subjects that can be learned later—or you can hire experts to do this.

Substructuring

Substructuring is a class of specialized methods used in structural analysis, whereby systems are subdivided into smaller subsystems to facilitate the design of complex systems. Substructuring is important to corporations because they are large, complex entities. The way you handle these complex structures is to break them down into manageable pieces. Substructuring provides a systematic approach for doing this.

Substructuring was developed in the 1960s as an alternative way of solving large mathematical models by dividing the system into multiple subsystems, which are represented using boundary information (boundary matrices and forces). The system is then solved in terms of the subsystem boundary responses. Each subsystem model can be solved separately by applying the boundary responses to the individual subsystem models.

To show how substructuring is done, first consider the traditional approach of solving a large system using a mathematical model. All components are modeled and assembled into a system model, and then the system model is solved. This approach is completely acceptable, but it has limitations. The problem is that as the model size grows, the solution time increases exponentially. So a one-million-degrees-of-freedom model may take 1 hour to solve while a two-million-degrees-of-freedom model may take 4 to 8 hours. Now, if each component manufacturer wants to determine the effect of a component change on system performance, the same model must be run multiple times. This is not efficient.

With substructuring, the system model is divided into several subsystems. Each subsystem has connections to the other subsystems but only at a relatively small number of points. Then, you conduct analysis using the following four steps:

1. **Condense each subsystem to represent its characteristics at its boundaries.** This can be done by representing the subsystem using a simple model or by using static or dynamic reduction methods. Understanding the details for this step is important only to the people who are conducting the method, so it is not described in detail here.

2. **Assemble all these condensed models into a system model.** This system model is designed to calculate the system-level performance only. Information at the subsystem level is retained only in general terms.
3. **Solve the system model for the system responses and subsystem boundary responses.** This determines the interactions between the subsystems. These interactions can be represented at the boundary of each subsystem.
4. **Solve the detailed models for each subsystem using subsystem boundary responses.** Then analyze in detail each subsystem by each horizontal group to determine the detailed performance of its components.

Substructuring requires that mathematical models be created for all subsystems. These mathematical models can be created based on the laws of physics, on measured data, or on a combination of the two. Models that are based on measured data are called empirical models, and while they are useful at predicting the effects of system changes, they do not lend themselves to a better understanding of the physics involved. Analytical models that are based on the laws of physics do lend insight into the governing physics and are usually effective for the design of products. One of the most powerful analysis methods today is the finite element method, which can be used to model a wide variety of physics. It is the subject of the following section.

The Finite Element Method

The finite element method creates complex mathematical models of physical systems out of a simple set of basic elements. These elements include beams, bars, plates, and solid elements that are designed based on the physical phenomenon being modeled. Some examples of these elements are shown in Figure 4-3.

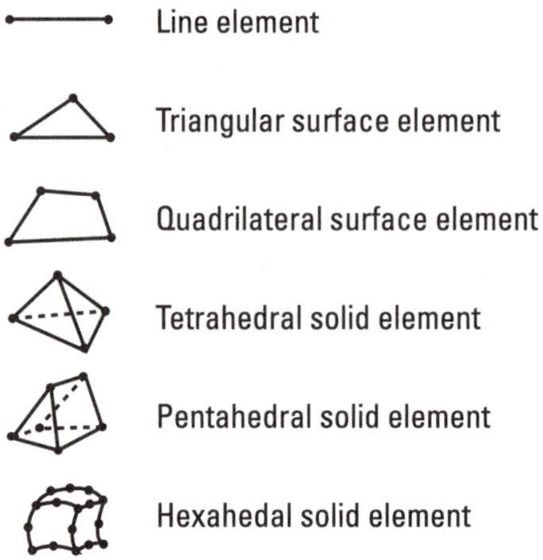

Figure 4-3. Basic types of finite elements

Each finite element has boundary nodes that can be varied in their positions to correspond to the geometry of the item being modeled. The elements are connected together at the nodes. Complex systems are created by connecting many finite elements together, and as the complexity of the system increases, the number of elements needed to describe it increases. A typical finite element model of an automotive powertrain structure is shown in Figure 4-4.

Figure 4-4. Finite element model of an automotive powertrain structure *(From SAE paper 2001-01-1503: Reprinted with permission of the General Motors Corporation)*

Loads and constraints are applied to the finite element models, and the responses are calculated. These responses include deflections, stresses, vibration levels, and so on. Designs are evaluated based on these responses and modified to achieve the design requirements.

The use of substructuring allows each subsystem or component to be assigned to a different design team. After that, a separate system integration group is used to assess system performance and establish subsystem and component design targets. This was first done on airplanes and spacecraft in the 1970s, and then on automobiles in the 1980s. Today, many large systems are engineered using this approach in many different industries.

Systems Engineering

Systems engineering, as the name suggests, is the methods and procedures used to integrate subsystems and components into systems. The ability of a company to produce great products is related directly to its ability to conduct system integration. In fact, many companies of the future will be only system integrators; in other words, they will not make any of the components in their products. They will buy components from suppliers and integrate them into systems, a practice that is already commonplace in the computer industry. Automotive and other industries may follow in the same manner.

The main idea behind systems engineering is that all aspects of subsystem and component design are based on their effect on system performance, thus creating a direct link to satisfying the needs and wants of the customer and eliminating waste by optimizing the system instead of the individual parts. The two keys to conducting systems engineering are as follows:

- Being able to represent the key attributes of each subsystem using a reduced model
- Determining the optimal values of these attributes based on their effect on system performance

Representing the key attributes of each subsystem using a

reduced model is done using substructuring. The horizontal groups build the component models and supply them to their associated vertical groups. The vertical groups combine the subsystem models into a system model and determine the baseline results. These results are compared to the system level requirements and optimized. The optimized system results are rolled down to the horizontal groups in terms of design requirements (see Chapter 5). The horizontal groups modify their components (if necessary) to meet these requirements.

The systems engineering approach effectively eliminates feedback loops in the design process. However, because the mathematical models are not perfect and each group cannot meet its requirements precisely, the results will not be exact. For this reason, one or more iterations of the entire systems engineering procedure may be needed.

The first time through the procedure establishes the baseline results and determines the feasibility of meeting the system performance requirements. This is important in determining the scope of the changes that are needed. Major changes must be implemented at this point before the component designs become established. The idea is to establish a superior system design that will meet its requirements with good subsystem and component designs instead of relying on superior subsystems and components to achieve this. Design effort is balanced between components, subsystems, and systems. This is the same strategy used in football, where practice time is split between developing individual skills, unit skills, and team play.

The goal of a lean corporation is to execute the systems engineering approach once, and then proceed directly into production. However, this is usually not possible for complex systems, and some amount of testing and validation is needed. The first time through the systems engineering procedure creates design targets for all subsystems and components. The second time through the procedure determines the success at meeting these design targets based on the mathematical models. This second run-through is presented in the product's performance reviews and is often called a virtual build phase. All lean corporations should have one virtual build phase; that is, the first build phase that is conducted.

Testing and validation is conducted in the second build phase. This phase is conducted in essentially the same manner as the first phase, except that hardware is used instead of mathematical models. In the lean philosophy, you need to identify defects immediately. This is done by first testing the components, then the subsystems, and finally the system. Each item is tested to verify that it meets its specific requirements. Subsystem tests are not run until the components are validated; system tests are not run until the subsystems are validated. This approach allows problems to be identified as early as possible.

Component and subsystem tests must be done under simple, consistent boundary conditions. It is not a component test if the component must be attached to another subsystem, because the results will pertain only to that subsystem. Generally, two types of boundary conditions are used for component tests.

- **Free-boundary conditions** means that no constraints are applied to the connection points. For free-boundary conditions, you measure responses at the connection points.
- **Fixed-boundary conditions** means the item is constrained to zero motion at all the connection points. For fixed-boundary conditions, you measure forces.

Either type of boundary condition can be used for validation. Generally, free-boundary conditions are used for stiff structures like cast brackets, stiff covers, and powertrain assemblies. Fixed-boundary conditions, on the other hand, are used for flexible structures like stamped mounting brackets, flexible covers, and engine/transmission mounts.

Correlation of the mathematical models is done during the second phase, and the sources of any discrepancies are identified. The causes of these discrepancies are identified and corrected to continuously improve the modeling and test procedures. Measured results are added to the performance reviews to indicate the results that are achieved. Because a system engineering approach is used, the performance of the system should be reasonably close to that desired. The remaining effort in the second phase involves identifying and solving any remaining performance-related issues. New mathematical models are created and used for this purpose.

The third phase is used to validate the manufacturing system. The main goal of this phase is to validate the manufacturing variation that was assumed in the mathematical models. Statistically significant sample sizes are produced using production intent tools and processes. This allows the performance reviews to include the effects of variation. Chapter 5 describes how variation is included in performance reviews and how the optimal values of the key attributes based on system performance is done using the requirement roll-down process.

Using the systems engineering approach described in this section is a true example of a paradigm shift. Therefore, it will almost certainly be resisted. As with all aspects of the lean approach, it should be implemented from the bottom up. Start with a single component and/or subsystem and implement the approach. Then expand to other areas. Balance and optimize the system using the reduced models. Limit the amount of detail at each level in the program structure to that corresponding to the level of management (high levels being more general, and lower levels being more detailed). This prevents micromanagement and allows the vertical groups to provide design direction in terms of general requirements, while allowing the subsystem or component supplier to determine the details of how the requirements are achieved.

Managing Coupled Processes

Most processes have some degree of coupling, so managing them effectively is important. Fortunately, traditional process management techniques can be used (see the works cited in the bibliography if you are not familiar with traditional process management techniques). The key to successful implementation of these techniques is that definition of the hierarchies that are needed. These include the work breakdown structure (WBS) and organizational breakdown structure (OBS). In addition, the WBS is also used to impose controls on the work tasks. This is done through the use of controlling tasks.

Work Breakdown Structure (WBS)

The WBS organizes work tasks in relation to the people who manage the work. In this book, the WBS is determined directly from the program structure (see Chapter 8 for a detailed presentation on the creation of the WBS). The WBS is used to manage the materials needed to execute a process. Each node in the WBS has one person assigned to it who is responsible for managing the associated materials corresponding to his or her assignment. This establishes clearly defined command-and-control over the materials.

Organizational Breakdown Structure (OBS)

The OBS organizes work tasks in relation to the organizational groups that perform the work. In this book, the OBS is determined directly from the organization structure (see Chapter 8 for a more detailed presentation on the creation of the OBS). The OBS is used to manage the resources needed to execute a process. Each node in the OBS has one person assigned to it who is responsible for managing the associated resources corresponding to his or her assignment. This establishes clearly defined command-and-control over the resources in the same manner as the WBS does for materials.

Controlling Tasks

Controlling tasks are defined to run in parallel to all the tasks they control. These tasks implement several features of the lean philosophy:

- They establish clearly defined owners of each task's controls.
- They are implemented using a hierarchy where control is implemented from the top down.
- They are responsible for the associated performance reviews and bill of materials.

Each node in the WBS has a corresponding controlling task associated with it. This controlling task can be considered the standardized work task corresponding to each vertical manager. Controlling tasks are different than regular tasks in that they are not sequenced using input and output relationships. Instead, controlling tasks are designed to run in parallel to the tasks they control. This is shown in Figure 4-5.

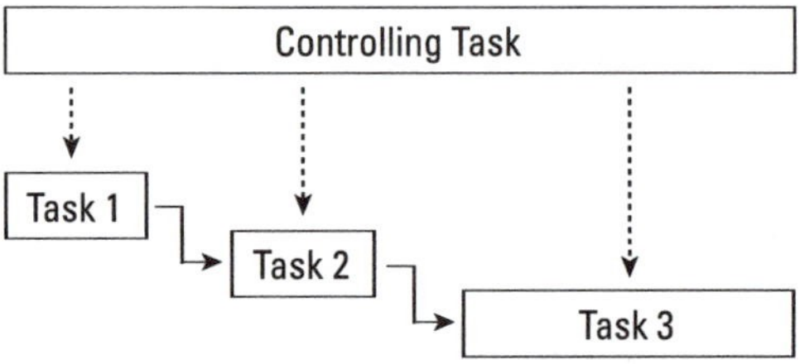

Figure 4-5. Controlling task

By definition, controlling tasks have access to all outputs from the tasks they control. Controlling tasks are documented using the same IDEF0 task models as regular work tasks. See Chapter 11 for some examples of IDEF0 task models for controlling-type tasks and a detailed presentation on how they are used to manage business processes.

Chapter 5

Requirement Roll-Down Using the Design for Six Sigma Approach

In a lean corporation, all design decisions are made based on how they benefit the customer. These decisions are weighed with respect to other decisions, leading to trade-offs, and this balancing act defines the design process. Performance attributes are prioritized at the system, subsystem, and component levels. Setting the priorities at the system level is usually straightforward: Trade-offs, such as vehicle acceleration versus fuel economy, are based on market research, which indicates the needs, wants, and expectations of customers. Priorities at the subsystem and component levels are then determined from the system-level priorities. Establishing these priorities is achieved by using requirement roll-down.

Requirement Roll-Down Basics

Requirement roll-down is the establishment of design requirements at each level of the program structure. These requirements are the primary means by which product quality is ensured. In my experience, corporations are good at setting requirements at the system level, but they are weak in relating these requirements to subsystems and components, mainly because of the extra time and effort required to relate them.

Some people believe that requirement roll-down is wasted effort. However, if you do not know how the attributes of a subsystem or component affect system performance, you cannot optimize the system. Therefore, you are necessarily introducing waste into the product or process and are not implementing a lean system. Without requirement roll-down, you cannot determine the ideal process or design, because the underlying relationships between component, subsystem, and system attributes are unknown. The only thing that you can do is to optimize the individual items, which leads to over-designed or under-designed components and suboptimized subsystems and systems.

The remaining sections in this chapter present a procedure for requirement roll-down that is consistent with the lean philosophy. The procedure relates system-level performance to subsystem- and component-level attributes, thereby allowing the subsystems and components to be designed based on system-level performance. This procedure is needed to produce optimized systems. Customer satisfaction is achieved by including product variation into the requirement roll-down process. The Design for Six Sigma (DFSS) approach is used. To fully understand the Design for Six Sigma approach, see the works cited in the bibliography.

Design Requirements

Design requirements are constraints that are applied to design attributes to ensure that the desired performance levels are achieved. They start off as design targets and end up as specifications. However, the idea that you cannot start the design process until the values of all requirements are set is incorrect. In fact, the entire design process is the establishment of the requirement values. With an engine, for example, there is always a requirement for horsepower and torque. As the engine is being designed, these design targets are balanced with respect to other requirements, such as vehicle acceleration and fuel economy. When the engine design is finalized, horsepower and torque values become specifications.

In lean corporations, design requirements need to have the following characteristics, each of which is described in the following sections:

- They must be measurable.
- They must use simple boundary conditions.
- They must facilitate requirement roll-down.
- They must be physics based.

Design Characteristics Must Be Measurable

The first characteristic, that requirements must be measurable, is the only way to verify that the requirement is being met. Ideally, the measurement is nondestructive and does not modify the part at all, so that the same parts can be used in component, subsystem, and system tests. This multiple testing allows the effects of component variation to be correlated to subsystem and system variation. Having measurable requirements also allows the mathematical models and test procedures to be correlated and continuously improved.

Design Characteristics Must Use Simple Boundary Conditions

The second characteristic, that requirements must use simple boundary conditions, is needed so that the measured attributes are a function of the subsystem or component itself and not of the supporting system. This characteristic allows the physical properties (mechanical impedances, vibrational natural frequencies, and so on) of the subsystem or component to be determined under consistent and repeatable conditions. Different designs can then be compared in an objective manner. Also, simple boundary conditions are needed to implement the substructuring methods presented in Chapter 4.

Thus, either free-boundary (low stiffness supports) or fixed-boundary (high stiffness supports) should be used for testing mechanical items. For example, when testing the noise radiation of stamped covers (engine timing chain covers, valve covers, and so on) they are fastened to stiff, heavy fixtures that approximate their actual operating environment. Conversely, when testing the noise and vibration of powertrain systems, they are supported on flexible mounts that approximate their actual operating environment. The selection of which boundary conditions to use is dependent on the subsystem or component of interest. For flexible subsystems or components, fixed-boundary supports are usually used. For stiff subsystems or components, free-boundary supports are usually used.

Design Characteristics Must Facilitate Requirement Roll-Down

The third characteristic, that requirements must facilitate requirement roll-down, is needed so that all design decisions can be made based on how they affect the customer. This means that all the subsystem and component requirements must be related to system-level requirements. Then, all subsystems and components can be designed based on how they affect the customer. By having all subsystem and component requirements related directly to system requirements, these items can be designed simultaneously (in parallel) instead of sequentially (in series), thus reducing the design process duration.

Design Characteristics Must Be Physics Based

The fourth characteristic, that requirements must be physics based, is needed to gain insight into the physical phenomenon that governs system performance. Grounding the design in physics identifies the ideal system and determines the type and extent of modifications needed to improve the system. Understanding the physical phenomenon is done using math models, which determine the sensitivity of each design attribute with respect to each system-level requirement. Only the most sensitive attributes are modified to achieve the desired system performance. This approach is referred to as the Pareto approach, named after Vilfredo Pareto, who theorized that for all systems there is only one (or a few) significant factors that affect its performance. This theory is known as the 80–20 rule: Eighty percent of the results are produced by only twenty percent of the factors.

Design requirements that are related to product performance are displayed on product performance reviews. Other requirements that do not affect system performance are not shown on product performance reviews. These other requirements are important but are treated separately. Examples include material type, color, and so on. These controls are then given to the supplier or manufacturer, which is responsible for meeting and verifying that components meet these conditions.

Product Performance Reviews

Product performance reviews (sometimes called design reviews) are evaluation documents that assess the performance of a product relative to design targets. Most corporations have their own product performance reviews that are based on years of experience. These reviews include sets of important performance requirements that must be balanced to meet customer expectations. Lean organizations have one product performance review for each node in the program structure, with each product performance review also being a hierarchy. This structure is shown generically in Figure 5-1.

Figure 5-1 shows only three levels: system, subsystem, and component. The actual number of levels is dictated by the number of levels in the program structure. Each vertical group manages one or more system or subsystem performance review, based on its responsibility in the program structure. Component performance reviews are managed by their corresponding horizontal groups. Each performance review includes no more than about one hundred requirements that are organized into ten to twenty areas. Each area represents an important aspect of product performance. Each performance review should be no more than four to five pages in length. This corresponds to approximately twenty-five requirements per page.

A system-level performance review is used to establish an overall numerical rating for the product design. All areas and individual requirements in the system-level performance review are assessed using rating scales that represent the design's benefits to customers. The overall rating is determined by weighing each subsystem and component rating according to the relative importance of the item, and then summarizing the results. The weighing factors are based on customers' needs and wants.

Subsystem and component performance reviews use simplified rating scales. Each item is assessed only as to whether it is an area of concern, which is at least partially a judgment call. Usually, three conditions are used that represent high (red), medium (yellow), and low (green) degrees of concern. They are based in part on how closely the achieved results relate to the design targets. Detailed rating scales are not used for subsystem and component performance reviews; this reinforces that it is the system performance, not subsystem or component performance, that is of primary concern.

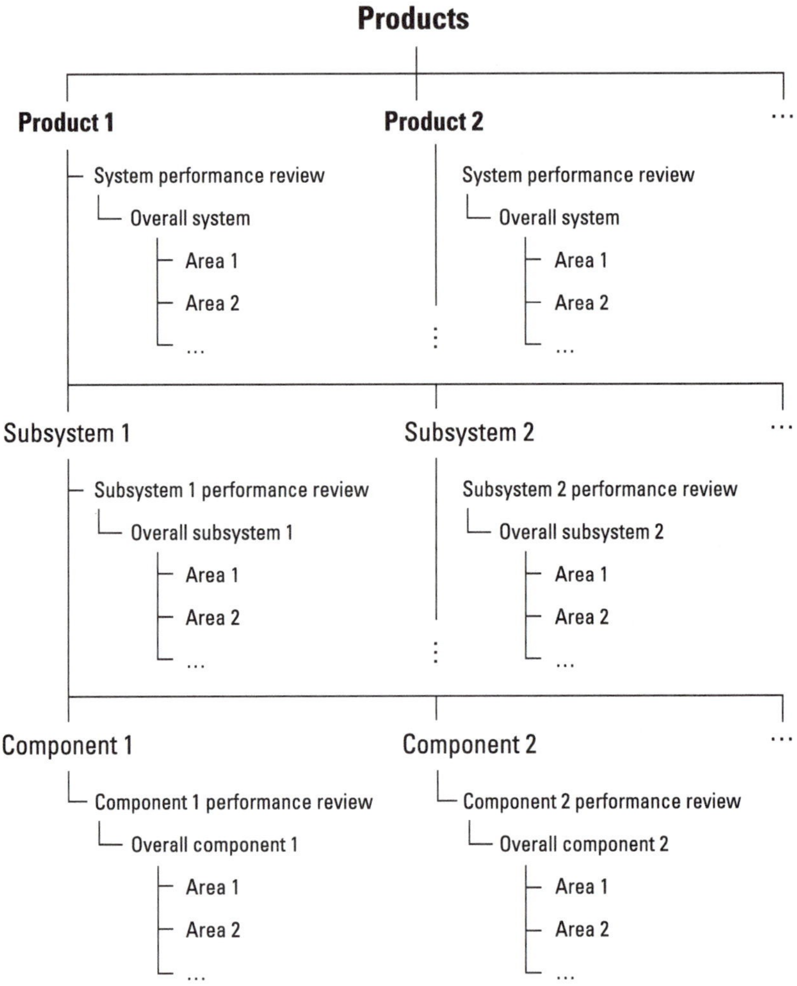

Figure 5-1. Product performance review structure

It is also important to consider product performance reviews that are reported in product rating publications. Many potential customers rely strongly on these reports, so make sure products score well in these assessments. Most publications give overviews of their assessment process, and even give their exact assessment criteria.

In all cases, assessment procedures can be reverse-engineered from given data to a reasonable level of accuracy. Then, past and current products can be assessed and the performance levels needed for future world-class products can be predicted and used as design requirements. A typical system-level product performance review for a car is shown in Figure 5-2.

Vehicle Performance Review	Target Value	Actual Value	Rating
Overall vehicle			80
Performance			86
Acceleration			94
• 45-65 mph time	5	5.7	93
• 1/4 mile speed	90	85	92
• 1/4 mile time	16	16.4	92
• 0-60 mph time	8	8.3	95
• 0-30 mph time	2.9	3	98
Braking and Handling			78
• braking and handling	90	78	78
Comfort			84
Ride Quality			77
• ride quality	90	77	77
Noise			85
• noise	90	85	85
Passenger Comfort			90
• passenger confort	90	90	90
Convenience			84
Service and Range			84
• oil change interval	5,000	4,000	86
• driving range	350	300	82
Safety Equipment			78
Features			81
• anti-lock brakes	90	78	78
• stability Control	90	80	80
• traction control	90	85	85
Accident Avoidance			75
• accident avoidance	90	75	75
Crash Protection			78
• offset	90	77	77
• side	90	80	80
• front	90	77	77
Fuel Economy			65
Overall fuel economy			65
• highway fuel economy	30	21	65
• city fuel economy	20	15	65
Reliability			83
Powertrain Reliability			95
• powertrain reliability	90	95	95
Body Reliability			65
• body reliability	90	65	65
Chassis Reliability			89
• chassis reliability	90	89	89
Value			80
Purchase Price			96
• loaded price	33,000	35,000	93
• with typical options price	29,000	30,000	95
• base price	25,000	25,000	100
Operating Cost			68
• operating cost	500	900	68
Depreciation			76
• depreciation	72	60	76

Figure 5-2. System-level product performance review for a car

The overall rating is based on seven areas: performance, comfort, convenience, safety equipment, fuel economy, reliability, and value. To simplify the discussion, I concentrate here on the performance and fuel economy areas. The performance area is subdivided into two subareas: acceleration and braking/handling. The fuel economy area is subdivided into only one group: overall fuel economy. A uniform assessment of all items is conducted using a 100-point scale. The performance at each level of the hierarchy is determined as the average of the subareas' ratings. The overall rating is determined numerically and is then assigned a grade based on the scale, shown in Table 5-1.

Table 5-1. Car Assessment Grading Scale

Rating	Grade
≥ 90	Excellent
80–89	Very good
70–79	Good
60–69	Fair
≤ 59	Poor

Rating Systems

Integral to product performance reviews are the rating systems that are used for their assessments. Subsystem- and component-level performance reviews usually use simple rating systems that indicate whether the design targets have been met, based on a combination of objective and subjective judgments. System-level performance reviews use detailed rating systems that allow each requirement to be assessed based on its benefit to the customer.

Subsystem- and component-level rating systems are based on whether the design targets are met. These targets are simple mathematical relations, such as minimum values, maximum values, in-range, out-of-range, and other criteria. The results are assessed by comparing the actual value to that of the target using some level of judgment to determine whether the results are acceptable.

Generally, the results are assessed in terms of high (red), medium (yellow), and low (green) levels of concern, which usually corresponds to "not meeting the requirement," "not meeting the requirement but judged acceptable," and "meeting the requirement," respectively. The color codes may be used to visually display this information in performance reviews. More detailed rating systems are not used with subsystems and components, because the emphasis is placed on optimizing the overall system. In other words, meeting each individual subsystem and component design target is not as important as meeting the overall system performance goals.

System-level ratings use numerical scales that assess performance based on the benefits to the customer. A rating structure from 0 to 100 is a good choice, because the rating structure has enough resolution to be useful without being excessive. Every requirement then must have its performance variables expressed as a function of the rating system.

Establish a rating criterion that is based on market research. Don't assume that the evaluation of performance is always monotonic (always increasing or decreasing). You must allow for so-called sweet spots. For example, vehicle acceleration is usually a non-monotonic rating function; customers will be dissatisfied if the vehicle accelerates too quickly or too slowly. You must take this into account in the market research by making sure that both positive and negative responses are solicited.

As with everything else, ratings are subject to variation. When you present a rating function, you are showing the mean values of the ratings as a function of some independent variable. Rating functions also have standard deviations associated with them. These standard deviations can be included in the rating, but for simplicity, it is neglected in this book. A sample system-level requirement rating function is shown in Figure 5-3.

The numerical rating for each requirement is weighted and summarized into an overall score for the system. This score allows for trade-offs and balancing during the design process. The overall score is given a grade using a scale such as the one shown in Table 5-1. Generally, the grades (see Table 5-1) are expressed using three to five categories.

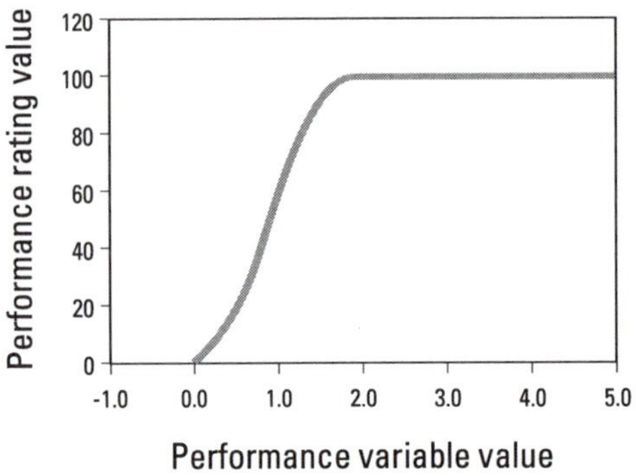

Figure 5-3. System-level requirement rating function

Note that the use of relative assessments is not recommended. An example of a relative assessment is the comparison of one design to another without knowing the performance level that is needed to produce an acceptable design. This is often called an A-to-B comparison. Although, the comparison may accurately indicate the relative difference between the designs, it does not indicate the level that is needed to produce the desired system performance and customer demands. This causes a significant amount of wasted effort. For example, a design of a component may have been adequate from the start, but it was "improved" to make it comparable to the design of another component. Improving the design of the first component was unnecessary, and the resources used to improve the design could have been used for a component that actually has an inadequate design. Also keep in mind that improving a subsystem or component design does not always lead to improved system performance. One component design may be better than another in relation to one aspect, but when assembled into a system, the difference in the overall system may be negligible or the performance could actually be worse. Therefore, avoid relative assessments in product and process engineering.

Design for Variation

Understanding how variation affects system performance is critical to customer satisfaction. Companies are usually good at engineering systems using deterministic approaches, such that all parameters are modeled at their mean (average) values, and the system performance is determined by those mean values. The effects of variation, however, are not directly analyzed. Instead, they are compensated for by applying a safety factor—determined through experience—to the design targets. The same safety factors are usually applied to different designs of the same type. This produces reasonable results, but almost always produces systems with varying levels of performance. This is because all components and subsystems have some level of variation, and variation on the component and subsystem level contributes to system variation in different degrees, depending on the design of the system. This means that systems with comparable mean values of performance can have significantly different levels of variation. This is illustrated in Figure 5-4.

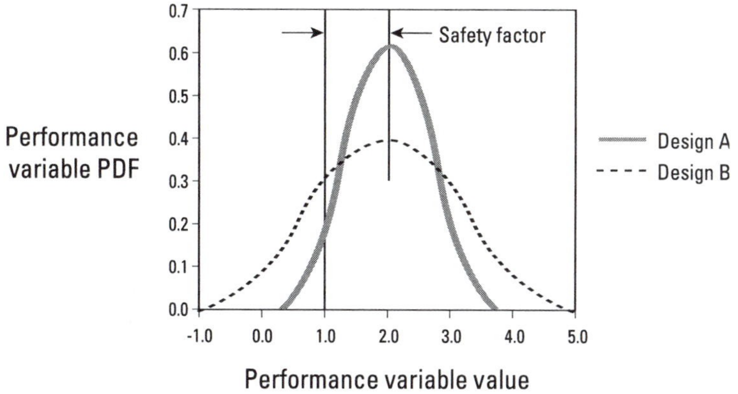

Figure 5-4. Variation of system performance

Figure 5-4 shows the probability density functions (PDF) for a particular performance variable, corresponding to two different designs that have the same mean value but difference levels of variation. These curves indicate the expected variation in the performance values, corresponding to the population of all units produced. Narrow distributions produce results that are have smaller levels of variation. Wide distributions produce results that have larger levels of variation. The percentage of units that have performance values that occur in any range is equal to the corresponding area under the curve between the two limits of the range. For symmetrical distributions, 50 percent of the units have performance values that occur above the mean value and 50 percent below the mean value. The area under the entire curve is always equal to 1.0.

For some systems, a distinct value of system performance identifies the regions of acceptable and unacceptable results. This is shown in Figure 5-4 as a value of 1.0. If all units with performance values below this level are considered defective, the number of defects per unit (DPU) is calculated as the area under the PDF curve below this limiting value. Multiplying this by one million gives the number of defects per million opportunities (DPMO). The number of defects for design B is much greater than that of design A, as indicated by the large difference in the areas of their respective regions below the limiting value of 1.0. This shows why two designs with the same mean values and safety factors can have significantly different levels of defects.

Often, designs have regions where performance is unacceptable, both below a lower limit and above an upper limit. In this case, the number of defects is calculated by adding the numbers corresponding to each region. If, in Figure 5-4, an upper limit was placed at 3.0, the number of defects per million opportunities would be two times more than the case with only one unacceptable region (because the areas of each region are equal). For nonsymmetrical PDF curves and/or nonsymmetrical lower and upper limits, the number of defects in each region may vary. The total number of defects per million opportunities is simply the addition of the defects corresponding to the two regions.

To help visualize the number of defects and to create a standardized way of assessing performance, a value called process sigma can be determined. Process sigma is the number of standard deviations between the mean value and a single lower limit of a normal distribution that produces the same number of defects as the original process. This allows all processes to be rated using a common parameter. See Figure 5-5.

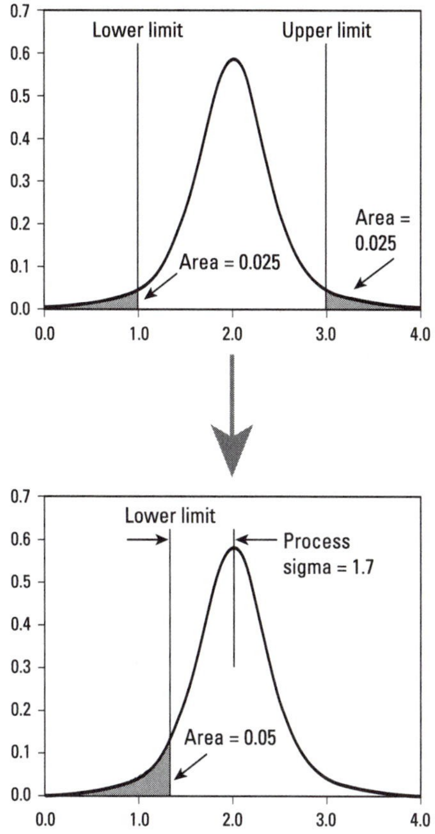

Figure 5-5. Process sigma

To account for variation that is not included in the statistical models, an adjustment value is applied to process sigma, and the resulting DPMO is calculated. The standard adjustment value reduces process sigma by 1.5 before the DPMO is calculated. The adjustment value of 1.5 is widely used in industry but should be evaluated for applicability in each situation. Reducing the process sigma by the adjustment value takes short-term results from analyses or tests and converts them into predicted long-term capabilities. Hence, the value of process sigma before subtracting the adjustment value is called short-term process sigma. The value of process sigma after subtracting the adjustment value is called long-term process sigma. The basic idea is that processes tend to have more variation over longer time periods than over shorter time periods. The adjustment value is used to account for this effect. The process sigma and DPMO values corresponding to an adjustment value of 1.5 is shown in Table 5-2.

Table 5-2. Process Sigma and DPMO

Process Sigma	DPMO
1.5	500,000
2.0	310,000
2.5	160,000
3.0	67,000
3.5	23,000
4.0	6,200
4.5	1,300
5.0	230
5.5	32
6.0	3.4

By convention, process sigma is reported as short-term and DPMO as long-term. Therefore, a six sigma process is expected to produce 3.4 DPMO (assuming a 1.5 sigma adjustment value that results in a long-term sigma value of 4.5). The Design for Six Sigma (DFSS) approach uses process sigma as the primary indicator of process performance. The "six sigma" in the DFSS approach refers to a process sigma value equal to six (3.4 DPMO). Processes that exhibit six sigma performance are usually world-class in performance level. That is why the DFSS approach is becoming so popular and why it is critical to achieving customer satisfaction. The requirement roll-down process uses the DFSS approach. This is presented in the "Requirement Roll-Down Process" section later in this chapter.

The use of DPMO and process sigma generally allows a better representation of the effects of system design, as related to customer satisfaction, than does the use of mean values and safety factors. However, the calculation of DPMO and process sigma requires that variation be estimated and modeled when synthesizing new designs. Reasonably accurate models of variation can be determined through empirical data. For geometric parameters, estimates of variation can be made from the tolerances on these parameters. Usually, a mean value is given with a tolerance, such as 1.0 ± 0.009. Depending on the process, an assumption can be made as to the process capability, using the data in Table 5-2.

For example, if a 4.5 sigma process is assumed, there are 1,300 defects per million opportunities. A random variable with this performance level could be modeled as a normal distribution with a mean value of 1.0 and a standard deviation of 0.0028 (where defects are assumed to occur outside the tolerance region: 1.0 ± 0.009).

Each random variable is represented using one of several simple models (among the most widely used models are the uniform and normal distributions). The distribution type determines how the random variable is expected to vary from occurrence to occurrence, with respect to the item and time.

- Variation with respect to item represents part-to-part variation, which is analyzed using multiple samples.
- Variation with respect to time can be viewed as noise. Noise can be modeled by identifying the key factors that cause the variation, such a temperature, humidity, and so on, and representing those factors using random variables. This type of variation is analyzed by selecting appropriate test conditions and time lengths.

The effects of variation are added to performance reviews by including process sigma or DPMO as design requirements. These requirements are assessed in the same manner as any other design requirements. Subsystem- and component-level requirements are assessed directly by comparing their target values to those actually achieved. System-level requirements are assessed using a rating function that indicates the performance achieved based on a numerical rating scale.

Performance Assessment

The performance of a design is assessed through requirements that are shown on performance reviews. Most assessments are done using one of the following criteria:

- **Mean value:** Assessments using mean values do not consider variation.
- **Safety factor:** Assessments using safety factors indirectly consider variation through established empirical data and/or historical relationships between safety factor values and defect rates.
- **Process sigma value or process DPMO value:** Assessments using process sigma and DPMO directly consider variation and allow defect rates to be predicted.

Also note that mean values and safety factors generally apply only to monotonic rating systems, where defects occur only below or above a single specified limit. Process sigma and DPMO apply to both monotonic and nonmonotonic rating systems, where defects can occur both below a lower limit and above an upper limit. Therefore, the use of process sigma or DPMO is usually a better method of assessment and generally leads to higher product quality than the other assessment types. The drawback is that additional effort is needed to estimate and model variation. As corporations become lean, they transition from the use of mean values and safety factors for assessments to process sigma and DPMO. This is done using the requirement roll-down process.

Requirement Roll-Down Process

The requirement roll-down process is used to establish the target values for each requirement in each level of the performance review structure. Before this can happen, the content and scope of the product program needs to be developed from the top down. First, the product manager and staff determine the program objectives, which are set only at the system level. All effort conducted in the product program is related to achieving these objectives. The objectives are given to each subordinate vertical group which, in turn, determines which subsystems and components need to be created or modified. Each group then conducts a design failure mode and effects analysis (DFMEA). This analysis identifies a list of functional requirements needed to achieve the objectives and the potential failure modes that could occur.

Each failure mode is assessed based on the degree of severity, occurrence, and ability to be detected/prevented. A rating scale from one to ten is used for each area, and then an overall rating (calculated by multiplying the three ratings together) is assigned to the item. This number is referred to as the risk priority number (RPN), which is then used to assess the risk associated with each failure mode. The potential causes and mechanisms for each failure mode are identified, and methods of detecting and preventing these are determined. The detection/prevention options are formalized into design requirements that can be assessed through analyses or tests. This creates a link between the system-level objectives and the subsystem and component requirements.

The methods for assessing the requirements are selected from the standardized work tasks, which are represented using process models. This allows program cost, timing, and risk to be evaluated. The process for the DFMEA is shown in Figure 5-6.

The DFMEA process is conducted at each level of the program structure. This results in system-, subsystem-, and component-level performance requirements that are assessed using standardized work tasks. The requirements and tasks are designed to implement the roll-down of requirements. This means that all subsystem- and component-level requirements are related directly back to system-level requirements, using the substructuring approach described in Chapter 4.

The requirement roll-down process is based on the Design for Six Sigma (DFSS) approach. Two important issues are the keys to the DFSS approach. The first is that everything is related back to the customer. Second, calculations are done to determine the number of satisfied customers, taking variation into account. There are ten steps in the requirement roll-down process, as follows:

1. Identify the system attributes that are critical to the quality of the system.
2. Identify the factors that are expected to affect the system attributes.
3. Determine the relation between the factors and the attributes in the form of mathematical models.
4. Estimate the mean values and standard deviations for the factors.
5. Run the model to see whether the design is acceptable. If the design is acceptable, go to Step 8. If the design is not acceptable, go to Step 6.
6. Conduct a sensitivity study to determine the factors that are most sensitive to the attributes.
7. Reengineer the system to be less sensitive to the critical factor or control the critical factor better.
8. Correlate the model and rate its accuracy level.
9. Verify the results using hardware.
10. Document the specifications and modeling procedures.

The requirement roll-down process implements the DFSS approach at each level in the program hierarchy. This process allows the system-level requirements to be related to subsystem and component attributes. Having each level of the program structure relate its attributes to the system level allows subsystem- and component-level processes to be run in parallel. In contrast, the traditional approach to requirement roll-down requires that system-, subsystem- and component-level processes be run in series. The result is that the roll-down process using the DFSS approach is more efficient than the traditional approach and also tends to produce better optimized systems. The reason is that the traditional approach tends to optimize at the subsystem level, while the approach based on DFSS does not. This difference is demonstrated in Chapter 12.

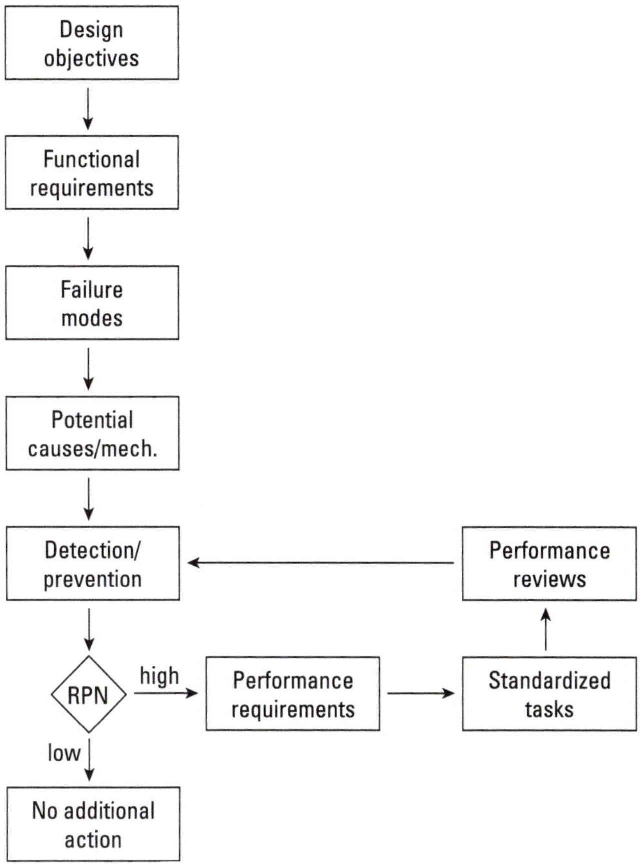

Figure 5-6. DFMEA process

Design Verification Process

The requirement roll-down process is used to establish design requirements for all subsystems and components. The design verification process is done to verify the results. The process proceeds from the bottom up to eliminate waste. Components are verified first, then subsystems, and lastly, the system. Any defective designs that do not perform as intended are caught before they are assembled into subsystems and systems. This way, defects are easier to identify.

An example of the design verification process is the assessment of the noise and vibration performance of engine-mounted accessories (for example, alternators, power steering pumps, and so on). The accessory components are verified first. They are mounted on flexible supports that simulate free-boundary conditions, and their radiated noise and vibration levels are measured. The results are compared to their performance requirements. If they meet their performance targets, they are assembled into the engine subsystem. Then the accessory subsystem's noise and vibration is measured and compared to the engine requirements. If they meet their targets, they are assembled into the vehicle system and tested to verify the performance of the vehicle. This creates an extremely effective method of product validation, because any problems with components and/or subsystems are identified as early as possible.

PART III

Making Your Business Processes Lean

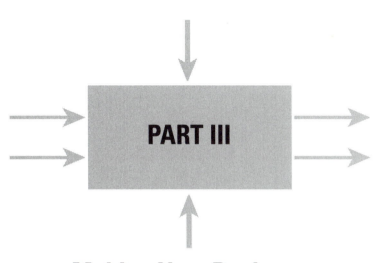

Chapter 6

Discovering Your Business Processes

The preceding four chapters show how to establish a framework for the creation of a lean corporation. This chapter shows how to begin the transformation from your current corporate state to a lean state. It all begins with the discovery of your current business processes. I use the term "discovery" because these business processes are often not well defined, so discovering them is not a trivial task. Often, the people who execute the processes—especially in large corporations—do not understand them. How can the people who execute the processes not understand them? Well, all people know is that work shows up, they do it, and they give some results to somebody. This means work is duplicated and non-value-added. But people become so busy with the day-to-day work that they don't see the large and complex business processes in which they work. Their discovery requires a specialized approach.

The Discovery Process: A Top-Down Versus a Bottom-Up Approach

The traditional way to discover business processes is to use a top-down approach, which means that the processes are described in general terms and progressively expanded into more detailed elements. Smaller, less complex processes can be efficiently discovered using the top-down approach. What you find; however, is that at some level of size and complexity, the top-down approach begins to fail. It fails because the person or small group defining the processes lacks the detailed knowledge of the tasks involved to sequence them correctly. I believe this is one of the main reasons why a significant number of reengineering efforts fail.

Fortunately, there is another way to discover business processes: a bottom-up approach. This approach starts with the simplest elements that make up the process, and then progressively combines them together. The key to the bottom-up approach is that it requires only local knowledge. This means that you need to know only your elements and those elements that you interact with. Then, the entire process is created by linking together all the interacting elements.

You can discover your business processes using a bottom-up approach in several ways. The approach that is presented in this book is an evolutionary process, starting with a small number of groups and expanding to others. Each group is responsible for defining its own tasks. Tasks are then linked together though their input–output relationships.

Note that all inputs are outputs of other tasks within the defined process or are externally supplied items called external inputs. Some outputs are linked to requirements; requirements are selected based on program content and risk assessment and are made visible using performance reviews. After the requirements are selected, the resulting business processes are created through their linkages to work tasks. All aspects of the work can be tracked and managed using this approach. The ultimate goal is to include all organizational units into the system, thereby creating a lean corporation.

The most important aspect of the bottom-up approach is that outputs are identified first, then inputs, followed by the procedure. Starting with outputs (the end product) automatically focuses you on the end result and clearly defines the scope of the task. Inputs, which define what is needed to produce the outputs, are identified after the outputs. The procedure—the method that determines how the inputs are transformed into outputs—is defined last.

Together, the inputs and outputs define an interface, while the procedure defines the implementation. Separating the interface from the implementation has several advantages.

- It allows the processes to be quickly prototyped, because only the interfaces need to be developed to create the processes. After the processes are validated, the effort to create the implementations is justified.

- It facilitates continuous improvement, because implementations can change without affecting the interface.

These are both fundamental features of the lean philosophy and are the basis for the discovery and reengineering of business processes.

A Step-by-Step Look at Business Process Discovery

Business processes are discovered using the bottom-up approach of identifying the outputs first, then inputs, followed by the procedure. However, additional steps are included that correspond to organizational and other items that are needed. In Chapter 2, a corporation is represented using the business process model shown in Figure 2-3, a model that includes inputs, outputs, resources, and controls. So steps to identify the resources and controls are needed. Project management steps (such as the formalization of the project and the establishment of formats and hierarchies) are also needed. The resulting twelve-step procedure for business process discovery is as follows:

1. Determine which business processes to discover.
2. Formalize the project.
3. Establish formats and hierarchies.
4. Document the outputs.
5. Document the controls.
6. Document the tasks.
7. Create the master lists.
8. Select inputs.
9. Identify and validate the processes.
10. Document the resources.

11. Document the procedures.
12. Close the project.

Each step is described in detail in the following sections. To make the discussion easier to understand, the standardized terminology used in this chapter is defined as follows:

- A **task** is a unit of work performed by one person and defined in terms of inputs, outputs, resources, and controls using the process model shown in Figure 2-3 (see Chapter 2). Tasks are the lowest level of work breakdown that is tracked in a program.
- An **output** is an item that is produced by the execution of a task. Outputs are inputs to successor tasks, are compared to requirements in performance reviews, or are delivered to the customer(s) of the process. This later type of output is often called **external deliverables**.
- An **input** is an item that must be supplied to a task for it to be executed. Inputs are the responsibility of the process manager, not the person who performs the task. Inputs are either outputs of other tasks or items delivered from external suppliers. The list of all external inputs needed for a project is called the **bill of materials**.
- A **resource** is used to transform inputs into outputs. Resources include people, equipment, facilities, and so on. They do not include any items that are considered inputs (such as materials). Resources are the responsibility of the person who performs the task.
- A **control** is a condition that a task or output must satisfy. Controls are used to ensure that the cost, timing, and quality objectives of the project are met. External controls are imposed on the person who performs the task. Internal controls are imposed by the person who performs the task.

- A **procedure** is a set of instructions describing how a task should be performed. Procedures should include the internal quality checks and the specifications for the generated outputs. Every task must have a documented procedure if it has an impact on product quality.
- A **performance requirement** is a type of control that is applied to outputs and is listed on product performance reviews. Performance requirements relate customer needs and wants into measurable attributes. They are the primary means of ensuring that high quality products and services are created from the business processes.

Step 1: Determine Which Business Processes to Discover

The first step is to determine which business processes to discover and to obtain the proper levels of management support. Because a bottom-up approach is used, all that is needed is to determine which organizational groups to select to document their tasks. After these tasks are documented, the business processes are created by linking the tasks together using their input–output relationships. Support must come from the direct managers of the groups involved. Indirect support rarely works, as described later in this section.

The motivation for discovering your business process usually comes from the vertical groups that are responsible for creating great products. However, they rely on the efforts of the horizontal and support groups to do so. Verticals control the budget and must decide how much to spend and where, based on program content and risk assessment. They are the owners of the business processes and benefit the most from their discovery. Horizontal and support groups are the owners of the tasks that make up the business processes. They are less likely to support business process discovery because it is extra work and because documenting their tasks exposes both the efficient and inefficient features of their work. This resistance is caused by the culture of the corporation. As a corporation becomes lean, this resistance disappears. Workers realize that documenting their tasks is an important step in identifying areas of inefficiency and waste.

Ultimately, someone must decide that discovering their business processes is a good idea. Usually a manager or a director makes this decision, or it might be a priority of an executive, perhaps even the CEO. If you are not in a position to make the project happen, you must convince the people who are. A convincing argument is that the definition of business processes is becoming mandatory in many industries. For example, the automotive industry has adopted a quality management system called ISO/TS 16949:2002. To be certified under this standard an organization must:

- Identify the processes needed for the quality management system and their application throughout the organization.
- Determine the sequence and interaction of these processes.
- Determine criteria and methods needed to ensure that both the operation and control of these processes are effective.
- Ensure the availability of resources and information necessary to support the operation and monitoring of these processes.
- Monitor, measure, and analyze these processes.
- Implement actions necessary to achieve planned results and continual improvement of these processes.[1]

Discovering your business processes may be required for certification, and the approach presented in this chapter can be an effective way of doing this.

1. ©International Organization for Standardization (ISO). This material is reproduced from ISO/TS 16949:2002 with permission of the American National Standards Institute on behalf of ISO. No part of this material may be copied or reproduced in any form, electronic retrieval system or otherwise or made available on the Internet, a public network, by satellite or otherwise without the prior written consent of the American National Standards Institute (ANSI) 25 West 43rd Street, New York, NY 10036.

Copies of this standard may be purchased from the ANSI, 212-642-4900, http://webstore.ansi.org.

After a mandate to discover your business processes is obtained, you decide which ones to discover. Consider the following suggestions:

- A good starting point is at the department level or lower. This is a maximum of 100 to 200 workers distributed in two to five groups. When success is achieved, other groups can be added into the system.
- Find groups with significant interactions with each other but few with outsiders. The resulting processes have many linkages between tasks (which demonstrate the effectiveness of the discovery process) but are relatively moderate in size so they are easier to discover.
- Start with groups that have their processes already partially documented.
- Identify any "broken processes." These are processes that someone believes isn't functioning well.
- Look for support groups that conduct similar work such as analysis groups, test labs, and so on.
- Select important processes: ones that are either time or cost critical.
- Select hidden processes that you want to make visible.

After the groups are selected, you must obtain the required levels of management support at a level above all the groups involved. If a department is selected, the department head is the required level of management support. The best situation is to have a person from the associated vertical group become responsible for managing the discovery process and the department head responsible for ensuring the tasks get done. This separation of the responsibility is very effective. The manager of the discovery process decides what needs to be done, and the department head sets and enforces the deadlines. This allows for reasonable deadlines that still allow the department to keep functioning while its processes are being discovered.

Getting the correct level of management support is a critical factor in successfully discovering your business processes. Because the approach is bottom-up, many people are involved, but only at small levels; approximately one to three people per group, 10 to 20 percent of their time, for 2 to 3 months. Management must be willing to have their people devote this amount of time to this effort. Trying to conduct process discovery as a second job is a recipe for failure. If management is not willing to support the discovery process at this level, it is probably not worth attempting. However, more and more managers and executives are becoming increasingly interested in process discovery. They realize that it has the potential to save their department and their corporation millions of dollars.

Step 2: Formalize the Project

The second step is to formalize the business process discovery project. This includes documenting the project scope, selecting a project manager, establishing a timeline, and formalizing a project proposal.

Document the Project Scope

The scope generally depends on the level of management support. Some managers will want to conduct a small pilot project using just one section (ten to twenty tasks). This can be done to demonstrate several key aspects, such as program planning, resource management, and performance reviews. However, only internal links will be shown, so the processes may look overly simplified. Generally, a more meaningful project is to do at least one group (thirty to sixty tasks) or an entire department (100 to 300 tasks). Also, selecting a group(s) with many linkages within its sections better demonstrates the value of process discovery.

The project scope should define which groups will be included in the project and what deliverables will be produced. (The deliverables of the project are just the specific items that will be produced. They include the data that are generated during the execution of the twelve-step procedure and any other specific items that have been agreed upon.) Each group that is included in the project should have one person identified for each section (usually the section leader) who is responsible for documenting his or her section's tasks according to the formats defined by the project manager. An effective approach is for each section leader to delegate a few tasks to each of the section members. That way, the work is distributed in an efficient manner; it also facilitates the task ownership that will be needed in the future.

Select a Project Manager

This person will be responsible for the entire project. The project manager will need to devote 25 to 50 percent of his or her time to the project or have an assistant. The project manager establishes what needs to be done, but the manager cannot make it happen; this is a responsibility of the group managers and department heads who must establish the priority of the project. Selecting a project manager who has experience with the groups involved is helpful but not required. What is more important is that the project manager must be willing to learn and apply the procedure of business process discovery that is presented in this book. Luckily, this is not too difficult.

Establish a Timeline

Usually, 2 to 4 months are needed for most business process discovery projects (ones with 100 to 300 tasks). A typical timeline is shown in Figure 6-1.

Realize that the actual duration for conducting the steps may be as little as half a day to a few days. One to two weeks are given so that the people involved in the project can continue some of their normal day-to-day activities.

Remember that many people will do their work at the last minute or not at all. Doing work at the last minute is okay, but not doing it at all is usually a test of the management commitment to the project. As a side note, if you're the project manager, keep after the people responsible for discovering their processes. But before escalating nonconformance issues to management, give the delinquent people another chance. I usually tell them how many people have completed their work to exert a little peer pressure on them to do theirs. If this doesn't work, move on with the people who have completed their work and make the delinquent people come to you to catch up. Or let management exert the pressure on them. And while you may occasionally want to extend deadlines, do this as a last resort, because you'll set a precedent. It is important to complete the project in a timely manner, so finish the project with the people who have completed their work on time.

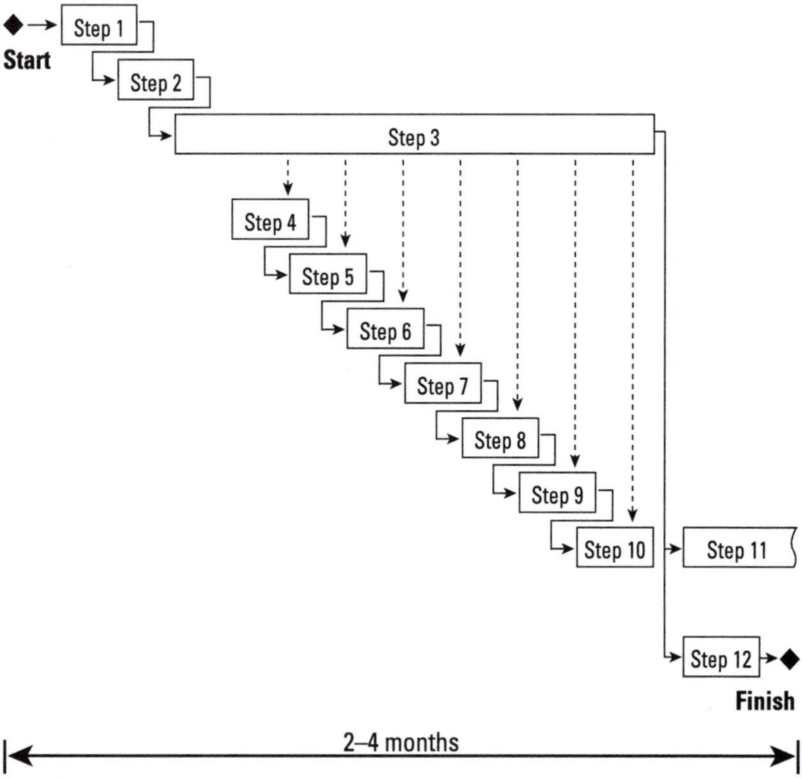

Figure 6-1. Typical timeline for a business process discovery project

Formalize a Project Proposal

A project proposal needs to be developed and approved by management. The proposal should clearly define the goals, scope, resources, and timing of the project. The goals of the pilot project should be to demonstrate the effectiveness of the discovery process and to show the benefits of using the resulting processes for business management. Then, if these goals are achieved, you can put the system into production usage, adding other groups over time. Being able to start small and grow large is an important feature of the discovery process.

When the project proposal is ready, present it to management. Negotiate any changes that are requested and get the approval of the project. Once the project is formalized and approved it can be started.

Step 3: Establish Formats and Hierarchies

The third step is for the project manager to establish the formats and hierarchies needed for business process discovery. Formats establish a common way for all people to document their information. Hierarchies allow this information to be managed efficiently. It is an important step that shows the people involved that the project is important. If this step is done poorly, it will have to be redone later, which negatively affects morale and gives people a reason to resist.

For projects, I recommend using Microsoft® Excel spreadsheets for data entry, because Excel is on nearly every computer and people are familiar with it. The formats are just the column headings and the selection lists, which are specified as templates. Examples of the templates that are used for process discovery are shown in Chapter 10.

Develop numbering conventions by encoding information into the numbering schemes to help people decipher the items. Be forewarned, however, that people have strong feelings about numbering schemes (theirs is the best and yours is wrong!). Try to find numbering schemes that are already used within the corporation. If you have to modify or extend these existing numbering schemes, call them a different name and tell people they are for internal use only. Don't worry about making your numbering scheme consistent throughout departments at this time, because that can be very difficult. If you are forced to join a committee to make the numbering schemes consistent, and consensus isn't reached in one or two meetings, withdraw from the committee and use your own numbering scheme. Eventually, some smart executive will impose a standard numbering scheme.

There are no perfect numbering schemes, so pick a good one and move on. About the best I've seen is to select one hierarchy that seems to be the most appropriate for the item, and then embed this information into the numbering scheme. Tasks are most associated with who owns them, and you can embed the ownership information into the task numbering scheme. For example, if the group name is Vehicle Performance Group, its tasks can be numbered as VPG.1, VPG.2, and so on. Outputs are associated with tasks, so embed task numbers in output numbers. For example, the first two outputs of task VPG.1 could be numbered as VPG.1-1 and VPG.1-2. Using this approach, outputs are numbered by appending a hyphen and a number to the task number.

The various hierarchies that are needed are discussed in Chapter 3. Most corporations have many hierarchies already established for different purposes, so start there. The hierarchies you need depend on the scope of the project; see Table 6-1.

Table 6-1. Hierarchies Needed for Different Project Scopes

Project Scope	Organization Structure	Product Hierarchy	Output Hierarchy	Requirement Hierarchy	Resource Hierarchy	Program Structure
Business Processes	X	X	X			
Performance Reviews	X	X	X	X		
Resource Management	X	X	X	X	X	
Program Management	X	X	X	X	X	X

The first hierarchy to create is the organization hierarchy. Include all the groups involved in the project, and then determine their direct levels of management up to the level where one person is above all participants. This is the person who must support the project. Always make sure you have strong support at the correct levels. Then create the other hierarchies that are needed, as they are needed.

After all the formats and hierarchies are defined, create the instructions. These instructions should specify the purpose, timeline, and deliverables for each step. Start with the general instructions given in the following sections and modify them, as needed.

Step 4: Document the Outputs

The fourth step is to document the outputs. The program manager issues the instructions for this step, while the section leaders perform the activity. Outputs are the items that are created from the execution of a task. Each section leader will own his or her tasks and outputs. Sections leaders can add, modify, and delete tasks and outputs as they see fit. However, outputs are useful only if other people use them. Therefore, outputs should be created based on what the users need and want. For now, define outputs based on what is currently being produced. This will determine the baseline processes that will be reengineered, and having an accurate baseline is important to predict efficiency gains of reengineered processes. You can use predicted efficiency gains to justify any investments that are needed to implement the new processes.

The section leaders should create a preliminary list of their tasks and assign outputs to each one. Each task and output must have a unique number and name: The number is specified by the numbering scheme and is designed to be unique, while the name is just a short description of the item. Section leaders are responsible for creating their unique item names. These names should be reasonably specific so that they can be distinguished from one another when assembled into the master lists. Outputs are characterized using the hierarchies specified by the project manager. This organizes them into related groupings and makes it easier to find specific outputs.

Outputs can be either physical items or electronic items. Physical items include components, subsystems, and assemblies that are produced from the execution of the task. Electronic items are computer files that include single values, plots, matrices, tables, and so on. The typical data required for each output are as follows:

- Output number
- Output name

- Output type
- Output units
- Primary hierarchy node
- Secondary hierarchy nodes

After all the outputs are specified, their associated controls are defined.

Step 5: Document the Controls

The fifth step is to document the controls. Controls are used to ensure that the cost, timing, and quality objectives of the project are met. The controls that are related to cost and timing are automatically created during program management and need not be defined in the task model (for example, cost controls come from material and resource costs and timing controls come from start and end dates of the tasks). Only the controls that are related to quality need to be defined in the task models. These consist primarily of the performance requirements that are applied to outputs and are listed in performance reviews. Thus, not every output has an associated requirement.

It should be noted that the term "requirement" is used here to refer only to requirements that are listed as controls in task models, called external requirements. But there will always be many other requirements that are not listed in task models. These other requirements are referred to as internal requirements, such as the requirement that a procedure should be followed or that an output should be delivered in a specified format or condition. You need only define the external requirements, because these are the requirements that the process manager uses to control the quality of the product that is being produced. The typical data needed for each requirement are as follows:

- Requirement number
- Requirement name
- Requirement type

- Requirement units
- Target value
- Primary hierarchy node
- Secondary hierarchy nodes

Historical values of requirements are created as processes are executed. This allows new designs to be compared to previous designs. Additionally, competitor designs can be evaluated and used for reference.

Step 6: Document the Tasks

The sixth step is to document the tasks by organizing related outputs together. In Step 4, a preliminary list of tasks was created. In this step, that list is reviewed and revised, if necessary. Business processes are created by selecting the requirements that correspond to program objectives. This determines the associated outputs and tasks that must be performed. Therefore, tasks should be organized with respect to these requirements. Generally, this means that tasks should have outputs that all relate to a single node of the requirement hierarchy. Selection of this node then identifies the task and outputs for inclusion into the program plan. Often, it is necessary to modify the requirement hierarchy to produce a good mapping of the outputs to requirements.

A good rule of thumb is that sections should have around ten to thirty tasks, each with five to twenty outputs. If a section has more than thirty tasks, it should probably be divided into two separate sections. If a task has more that twenty outputs, related outputs can be combined together. Each task should also have a specified duration, which is an estimate of how long it takes to perform the task when it is performed without interruption during normal working hours (such as worker-days).

Guidelines for Dividing Outputs into Tasks

The decision on how to divide outputs into tasks is subjective. Consider the following guidelines as you decide how to do this:

- **Tasks usually have durations of several days or weeks.** The reason that they are defined is because they utilize a significant amount of time and resources.
- **Do not make each output a task.** This distorts the time estimates. Usually, several outputs can be created from the same amount of effort. These should be combined together into a single task.
- **Decision-type tasks are not included.** Control is done using specially defined controlling tasks that are defined in Chapter 4.
- **Feedback loops are not utilized; development phases are used instead.** This allows multiple executions of the tasks to occur during a program.
- **Create tasks based on the ideal case, where all inputs and resources are available at the start.**
- **If outputs are generated at significantly different times during the execution of the task, then the task should be divided into two or more tasks.**

The Typical Data Required for Each Task

The typical data required for each task are as follows:

- Task number
- Task name
- Task type
- Task duration
- Primary hierarchy node
- Secondary hierarchy nodes

Staying with the Documentation Process

The organization of outputs into tasks is probably the most difficult part of the business process discovery. Most people will struggle with this to some degree. But don't be discouraged. The reason that people struggle is that they do not fully understand their processes. Forcing everyone to define their work in this manner is how business processes are discovered.

Step 7: Create the Master Lists

The seventh step is the creation of the master lists. This is done by the project manager. Master lists include all items of a given type. Master lists of tasks, outputs, and requirements are needed and are used for two purposes:

- The master lists are used to review each group's information and to determine if changes are needed. Often, the names are not specific enough, or there is inconsistent data.
- The output master list is used to select inputs to the tasks.

Section leaders supply the project manager with their Excel spreadsheets containing the task data. The project manager reviews the data and assembles it into the master lists, and all the items in the master lists are assigned numbers so that they can be identified. Use the numbering schemes that were developed in Step 3. If there are many items (over 100), organize them into sections using the hierarchy node names associated with the items.

Review the task information carefully. After the master lists are generated and distributed, the task information becomes coupled. Changing this information then affects more than one person, so be sure the project manager reviews the task information carefully. After the master lists are created, they are sent back to the section leaders with instructions on how to select the inputs.

Step 8: Select Inputs

The eighth step is the selection of the inputs for each task. Inputs are the items that must be supplied in order to perform a task, but they do not include the resources that are used to do the task. This distinction is based on the responsibility for the items. Inputs are the responsibility of the person who supplies them. Resources are the responsibility of the person who performs the task. To illustrate this step, consider a mechanical test that is conducted to validate a component. The component is an input. It is supplied by an upstream work task or an external supplier per the direction of the process manager. Any equipment, facilities, and/or supplies needed to run the test are supplied by the person who performs the test. This distinction is necessary to produce efficient tasks. Generally, only inputs that are needed, but are not readily available, are defined. They primarily include the items that require significant time or money to create. Thus, they must be scheduled and synchronized with the tasks that use them. The idea is to use this as an opportunity to transfer responsibility for the items. So, if an item is not listed as an input, the person who performs the task is responsible for getting it. Also, inputs determine when tasks can be started. If no inputs are listed, it is assumed that the task can start immediately. Therefore, it is recommended that each task have at least one input.

Internal and External Inputs

All inputs come from outputs of other tasks or from external suppliers. These are called internal and external inputs, respectively. Internal inputs come from groups that have defined their work using task models. These are all the groups included in the project and any other groups that were part of previous projects. External inputs come from groups that do not have their work defined using task models.

Task owners select their inputs and document them on their Excel spreadsheets. Internal inputs are done first and are selected from the master list of outputs. Items selected from the master list of outputs automatically define their supplier, the owner of the task that produces the output. Inevitably, not all inputs will be listed on the master list of outputs and will, instead, need to be created by identifying the responsible owner. Some of the missing inputs will be items that can be supplied by internal groups; these should be created as internal inputs. Others will be items that can be supplied only by external groups; these should be created as external inputs.

The Input–Output Negotiation Meeting

Identifying the input owners is done by having the task owners negotiate their inputs and outputs. This can be done efficiently using an input–output negotiation meeting. The objective of the meeting is to find owners for all the inputs that are needed and are not on the master list of outputs. You do this by identifying potential owners and seeing whether they are willing to produce the item. If they are willing, that item is added as an output to an existing or new task and given an output number and name. The item is then listed as an input on the requestor's task; it becomes an internal input. If no one is willing to produce the item, it is created as an external input. Note that you want one person to document external inputs during the meeting. Choose someone who is knowledgeable about the corporation's organization structure (usually a vertical manager or the project manager) so that the supplying group can be tentatively identified. By having one person document the external inputs, you avoid creating duplicate inputs for the same item.

All of the section leaders (owners of the tasks) should be present at the meeting so that all of the tasks' inputs and outputs can be negotiated, if needed. If many tasks are involved, more than one person from each section may be included. In this case, however, you must clearly divide the responsibilities. Either divide by type—one person negotiates all outputs, one negotiates all inputs—or divide by tasks—each person negotiates both inputs and outputs but only for his or her designated tasks. The fewer people involved in the meeting, the better: One person can typically handle the negotiation of ten to twenty tasks.

There are only three important rules in conducting an input–output negotiation meeting:

- **Existing tasks and outputs cannot be deleted; only new ones can be created.** After the meeting, task owners can delete any outputs or tasks that are not being used (that is, they are not inputs to any other tasks).

- **Each output that is added must be assigned a number according to the specified numbering scheme.** This number must be listed on both the user's task model (as an input) and the supplier's task model (as an output).
- **If you are responsible for negotiating outputs, you must stay for the entire meeting (bring something else to do in case you are not needed).** If you are responsible for negotiating inputs only, you can leave the meeting after you have all your inputs documented.

The input–output negotiation meeting ends when all the needed inputs have their owners identified. After the meeting, the task owners update their Excel spreadsheets and send them to the project manager. Then the processes are identified and validated.

Step 9: Identify and Validate the Processes

The ninth step is to identify and validate the business processes. This is done manually or by creating a simple software application for this purpose. The procedure is as follows:

1. **A set of requirements is selected that corresponds to the program objectives.** These requirements determine the needed outputs of the business process through the requirement-to-output mapping (or the needed outputs of the business process can be selected directly).
2. **The needed outputs then determine the needed tasks corresponding to the business process.** The needed tasks have inputs that are either outputs of other tasks or external inputs. The inputs that are outputs of other tasks determine the predecessor tasks. The external inputs become the bill of materials (BOM) corresponding to the business process.

3. **Different processes are created by selecting different sets of requirements and/or outputs.** The resulting processes are evaluated and modified as needed by changing the inputs, outputs, and other attributes associated with the individual task's IDEF0 models. This allows the business processes to be identified and validated.

A good starting point is to look at each group's internal linkages by selecting all the group's outputs and creating the corresponding process. Linkages between the group's tasks are evaluated and modified, as needed. The project manager then works with the section leaders to modify any tasks, outputs, or inputs that are needed. Usually, the initial processes generated are reasonably accurate. However, they almost always require some amount of changes. Remember that you are only capturing the current processes; you're not yet trying to reengineer them. The current processes are used to quantify the improvements of the reengineered processes.

When evaluating processes, make sure the tasks are sequenced in a reasonable order. Identify any feedback loops and remove them. This requires that one or more inputs be removed from one or more tasks. An effective way to break feedback loops is to replace some internal inputs with external inputs. In this case, the external inputs become the initial values of the items.

Additional constraints can be applied to tasks to affect their sequencing. These are called discretionary constraints because they are not required by the input–output relationships. Discretionary constraints disrupt the natural flow of the process, so use them sparingly. If you end up using a lot of discretionary constraints, you probably have poorly defined tasks. One exception is when discretionary constraints are used to balance resource utilization. However, this should be done when the processes are being executed (run-time), not when the processes are being discovered (design-time, the focus of this chapter). Chapter 8 discusses this issue in detail.

After each group's internal linkages are validated, validate the overall process corresponding to the outputs. This process includes all the tasks that have been defined. The main purpose is to validate the linkages between the groups, so be sure to validate both internal and external linkages.

After the overall process is validated, the requirement-to-output links are validated. Up to this point, outputs were selected to create processes. Now, requirements are selected to create processes. This is how most businesses processes are created. Requirements are used to translate customer needs and wants into measurable attributes. Depending on the program content, many different business processes are created. Processes should be created that correspond to several different levels of program content. In product engineering, these can be a new product design, a major product upgrade, and/or a minor product upgrade. The product content corresponding to these are then determined in terms of requirements. Then the business processes are created. The resulting processes should be reasonably accurate, because the input–output linkages were already validated. What may be needed are modifications to the linking of the outputs to the requirements. These should be reviewed and modified, as needed. After this is done, the discovered business processes are validated. These become the baselines for which improvements will be measured. Next, the task resources are documented so that resource management can be conducted.

Step 10: Document the Resources

The tenth step is to document the resources needed to perform each task. This is the responsibility of the project manager and the task owners (section leaders). The project manager establishes the resource hierarchy. This is done using the concepts presented in Chapter 2. The task owners determine the resource items that they need to perform their tasks. These resources should be defined generically using the minimum functionality that is required for the given task. These generic resources are then converted to specific resources when the tasks are executed.

Every task requires one resource to be selected from the people hierarchy. This defines the skills needed to perform the task.

Only one selection is allowed because all tasks are defined as activities that are performed by one person. Additional resources are assigned to tasks, as needed. The idea, again, is to document the resources that are difficult to obtain or are expensive to use. Usage cost for these resources are estimated so that the cost of performing the tasks can be predicted, and resources are managed by the people who use them. An owner is identified for each resource based on who uses the resources the most. This is done because these people are most knowledgeable about the items and have a vested interest in them; it also facilitates continuous improvement in procedures.

If you're familiar with responsibility assignment matrices, consider this. Because of the way tasks are refined in this book, the people resources do not need to be defined using a responsibility assignment matrix, because this matrix is automatically defined by the task model. A responsibility assignment matrix indicates all the people involved in a task and their responsibilities, and five roles are typically defined: participant (P), accountable (A), review required (R), input required (I), and sign-off required (S). Here, I use the ANSI/PMI 99-001-2000 naming conventions. For lean corporations, there are no participants and only one person is accountable for each task. People resources are the most expensive (and valuable) assets and must be utilized efficiently, thus tasks are designed so they can be performed by one person. The other roles are determined automatically. The input required roles are determined by the selected inputs. The review required and sign-off required roles are determined by controlling tasks (see Chapter 4). Therefore, responsibility matrices are used, but they are implemented in a lean fashion.

Cost estimates for each resource should be made in terms of cost/hour of use and can be done at any level of detail. Typically, rough estimates are done initially and are assigned to the generic items. The cost/hour of specific resources can be assigned these same values. Later, the actual costs of specific resources can be used. Ultimately, one goal of a lean corporation is that the financial statements can be determined directly from this data. However, this is a sizable task and is not necessary for most projects.

The typical data needed for each resource are as follows:

- Resource number
- Resource name
- Resource cost/hour use
- Primary hierarchy node
- Secondary hierarchy nodes

After the resources are defined, you can calculate cost estimates for each program plan. This is an important capability that is used to balance program cost and risk. Next, the procedures are documented.

Step 11: Document the Procedures

The eleventh step is to document the procedures. This is what creates the standardized work that is the foundation of lean corporations. The task owners are responsible for this step. Each task should have a documented procedure with instructions on how it should be performed. These instructions should be detailed enough that with less than half a day of training, qualified people can perform them. The procedures should be patterned after the quick-start instructions that are shipped with many products. The idea is that they are short (under ten pages) and simple.

Keep in mind that you want to document the current procedures as they are being performed. Do not reengineer them yet; that comes later. Be sure the procedures also list any assumptions or constraints used. Often, the only way to improve procedures is to eliminate or change these assumptions and constraints. The typical content of a procedure document is as follows:

- Procedure number
- Procedure name
- Procedure type
- Procedure owner
- Procedure flow chart

- Procedure constraints/assumptions
- Procedure description
- Output formats
- Primary hierarchy node
- Secondary hierarchy nodes

As discussed in Chapter 1, the work instructions should be documented by the workers who perform the tasks. This empowers them to take control of their own portions of business processes and helps them identify weak features in their procedures, leading directly to improvements. Understanding the constraints and assumptions associated with the work procedures is also needed when the business processes are reengineered, which is presented in Chapter 7.

Step 12: Close the Project

The last step is to close the project. At this point, each of the project objectives should have been addressed, but don't wait until all the procedures are documented to close the project, because this can take months. Schedule a meeting with the group managers and department heads to review the results. Then write a short report to document the results and close out the project. Management should then assess the success of the project and decide what steps to take next. Assuming the project is considered a success, additional groups can be added or the newly discovered processes can be reengineered.

Chapter 7

Reengineering Your Business Processes

In Chapter 6, the procedure for discovering your business processes is presented. The main benefit is that discovered processes become visible and, as a consequence, can be evaluated and reengineered. This chapter gives an overview of how business processes are evaluated and reengineered after they are discovered. The focus is on the optimization of the overall process using the fundamental principles of the lean philosophy. To do this, the current process is evaluated and then the ideal process is envisioned by identifying and eliminating all sources of waste.

This chapter begins with an overview of reengineering, discussing the underlying principles of reengineering, and comparing and contrasting them with those of the lean philosophy. The remainder of this chapter focuses on the reengineering of large, complex business processes using the lean philosophy. The techniques used for process evaluation are presented first, followed by the techniques used for process redesign.

Overview of Reengineering

Reengineering refers to the concepts presented by Hammer and Champy in their book *Reengineering the Corporation*. They define reengineering as "the fundamental rethinking and radical redesign of business processes to achieve dramatic improvements...." Reengineering has one governing principle: Management structures must be organized around business processes. This produces changes in the business processes themselves: in jobs and structures; in management and measurement systems; and in values and beliefs.

Reengineering changes business processes so that tasks are

performed in their natural order. Processes have multiple versions, and each version is customized to its purpose. Checks and controls are reduced, and reconciliation is minimized. Jobs and structures change from being task-oriented to being process-oriented. Several jobs are usually combined into one. Jobs change from one-dimensional to multidimensional. Work is performed where it makes sense. The organization structure shifts from functional departments to process teams.

Management styles and measurement systems also change. Workers are empowered to make product and process decisions. Case managers are created to provide a single point of contact for each issue. Managers become coaches instead of supervisors, and executives change from scorekeepers to leaders.

Corporate values and beliefs change from a focus on the individual to a focus on the team. Job preparation changes from training to education. Performance measures and compensation shift from effort to results. Advancement criteria changes from performance to ability, where performance dictates pay while the development of new skills and abilities dictates promotions.

Reengineering as an Application of the Lean Philosophy

Reengineering has a lot in common with the lean philosophy. In fact, reengineering can be considered as an application of the lean philosophy, as shown in Table 7-1.

The only major differences between reengineering and the lean philosophy are in the organization structure and in the implementation. Reengineering uses a mostly vertical organization structure. This means that the direct reporting is done through the vertical groups, and few or no horizontal or support groups exist. The advantage of a mostly vertical organization structure is that everyone is process oriented. The disadvantage is that standardized work is difficult to establish, because workers who perform similar activities usually report to different managers. Alternatively, the lean philosophy uses a hybrid organization structure that contains vertical, horizontal, and support groups. The advantage of the lean philosophy's hybrid organization structure is that it allows both

Table 7-1. Reengineering as an Application of the Lean Philosophy

Reengineering Features	Lean Philosophy Features					
	Process-oriented	Clearly defined roles & responsibilities	Optimized processes and systems	Focus on the customer	Transparency	Continuous improvement	Flexibility
Steps are performed in natural order	X		X				
Processes have multiple versions	X						X
Checks and controls are reduced			X			X	
Reconciliation is minimized			X			X	
Several jobs are combined into one			X				
Jobs change from simple to multidimensional			X				
Work is performed where it makes sense	X		X				
Work units changes from functional departments to process teams	X						
Workers make decisions		X					
A case manager provides a single point contact		X		X			
Managers change from supervisors to coaches		X					
Executives change from scorekeepers to leaders		X					
Values change		X		X			
Job preparation changes from training to education						X	
Focus on performance measures					X		
Compensation shifts from activity to results				X			
Advancement criteria change from performance to ability		X					

standardized work to be implemented and processes to be managed in an effective manner. This type of hybrid organization structure is used for virtually all college and professional football teams, as described in Chapter 3.

The difference in the implementations of reengineering and the lean philosophy is based on how they are conducted. Reengineering is implemented from the top down, while the lean philosophy is implemented from the bottom up. This difference has a significant impact on the outcome of the redesigned business processes. Because reengineering is top down, it tends to work best on small, simple processes that can be understood by one or a small group of people. Because a small number of people are involved, radical changes are easier to achieve. The lean philosophy is bottom up, so it tends to work better on larger, more complex processes that cannot be understood by one or a small group of people. Because many people are involved, radical changes are more difficult to achieve. The approximate region where each approach is expected to perform best is shown in Figure 7-1.

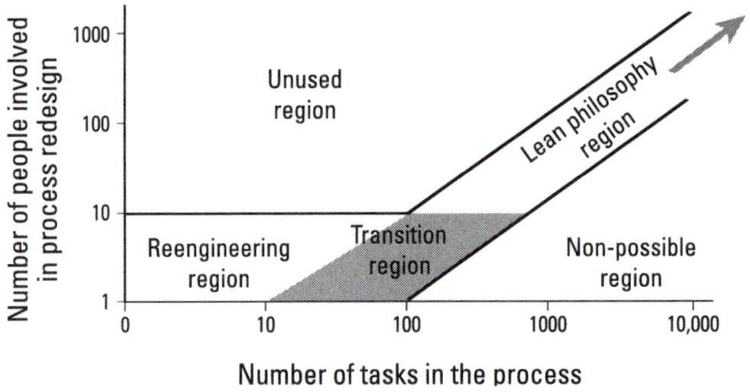

Figure 7-1. Regions where reengineering and the lean philosophy work best

Reengineering performs best when the number of people involved in process redesign is less than 10 and the number of tasks is less than 100. The lean philosophy performs best when the number of tasks involved is greater than 100. Typically, one person per 20 to 30 tasks is needed when discovering business processes using the lean philosophy.

The expectation for reengineering is usually radical change. The expectation for the lean philosophy is usually continuous improvement. However, either approach can be used to implement radical change and/or continuous improvement. This is a management decision, not a limitation of either approach.

Finding Techniques for Process Evaluation

The techniques used for process evaluation are as follows:

1. Create the baseline process.
2. Assess quality, time, and costs.

Each technique is described in the two following sections.

Creating the Baseline Process

A baseline process is created to represent the current business process. This is done by selecting all the requirements or outputs that correspond to the business process objectives for a specific program. Then, the tasks that produce the selected outputs or the outputs that are mapped to the selected requirements are determined along with all their predecessor tasks based on their input–output linkages. This is done manually or by creating a simple software application for this purpose. Often, the process that corresponds to all the identified outputs is selected as the baseline process. Then, the baseline process contains all the work tasks that are defined.

The only problem you may encounter when creating the baseline process is the existence of feedback loops. Feedback loops occur when outputs from one task are selected as inputs to one or more predecessor tasks. This is shown in Figure 7-2. Because tasks owners are free to select inputs from any task, feedback loops may be created.

Feedback loops imply that a series of tasks is repeated. Each repetition is called an iteration, and the number of iterations is not known up front. Usually, a criterion (control) is used to determine when to stop iterating. Furthermore, the starting task in a feedback loop is not automatically defined. It can be any one of the tasks included in the feedback loop, as shown in Figure 7-3.

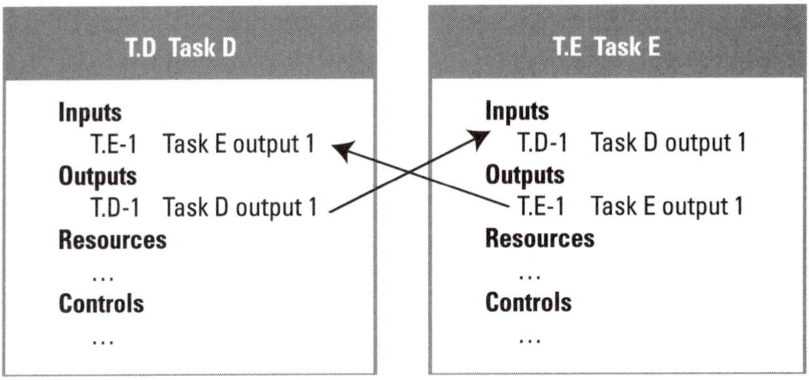

Figure 7-2. Example of a feedback loop

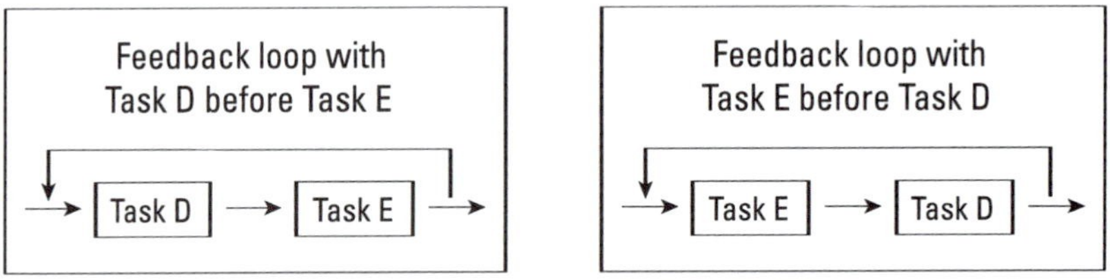

Figure 7-3. Different starting tasks for a feedback loop

For complex processes, the selection of different starting tasks for a feedback loop can have a significant effect on the overall process; see Figure 7-4.

In Figure 7-4, Process 1 has Task D as the starting task in the feedback loop and Process 2 has Task E as the starting task in the feedback loop. Even for this simple example, the effect of the starting task in the feedback loop is significant. This example illustrates that vastly different processes can be created by selecting different starting tasks for feedback loops.

Removal of feedback loops is done by selecting the starting task in the loop and removing all inputs to this task that are outputs from the successor tasks. An effective way to break feedback loops is to replace some internal inputs with external inputs; in this case, the external inputs become the initial values of the items. Also review the tasks that have been selected as the starting point for feedback loops—select an alternative starting task for feedback loops, and review the resulting processes.

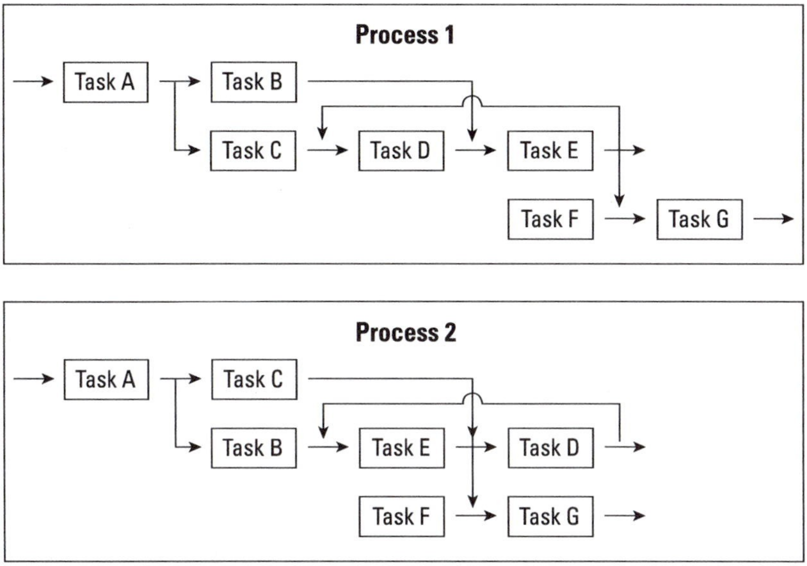

Figure 7-4. Effects of different starting tasks in feedback loops

A more rigorous handling of feedback loops is done during process redesign. This is shown in the "Process Redesign" section later in this chapter.

After the feedback loops are addressed, do a reality check to see whether the baseline processes makes sense. The baseline processes are usually pretty accurate but are not usually completely correct. Studying the processes and the point at which feedback loops occur allows you to modify the input–output relationships to achieve a better representation of the baseline process. But keep in mind that all you are doing at this point is defining the current process, not reengineering it. The process manager should try several renditions to see which ones best characterize the current process. These versions should then be discussed with the tasks owners. The task owners can often suggest other updates that further improve the accuracy of the baseline processes. After this is done, the process manager assesses the cost, quality, and timing of the processes. This information becomes the baseline for all process improvements.

Assessing Quality, Time, and Costs

The process manager reviews each process and evaluates it with respect to quality, time, and cost, each of which is addressed in more detail in the three following sections.

Quality

Process managers assess quality by using product performance reviews. (The format and content of performance reviews are shown in Chapter 5.) Dramatic increases in quality can be achieved using a set of standardized work tasks and augmenting those tasks with product performance reviews. These reviews make the performance of the product visible and allow program managers to focus efforts on the problem areas. The idea is that you cannot fix a problem unless you know that one exists. In my experiences with program managers, they are never concerned with red (problem) items showing up on performance reviews. They know that these problems will eventually be solved. Their real concern is with problems that do not show up on performance reviews at all. These are the problems they do not know about; ones that will be discovered late in the design process when corrective action is both difficult and expensive.

Time

Time (process duration) is determined by task duration and task linkages. In all companies, time-to-market is critical. (Time-to-market is the total time it takes from the initial concept to the production of saleable units.) It is, therefore, critical to reduce the duration of processes to the minimum amount of time. Because each task has an estimated duration, you can determine the total duration for any program. If feedback loops exist, their effect must be included in the estimate. The calculated total duration of a program then becomes the baseline for comparison of reengineered processes.

Cost

Program cost is dictated by program content. Program content is used to select the requirements and/or outputs needed and, consequently, the tasks to be performed. Program costs are calculated from the cost of materials and resources corresponding to the included tasks.

Material costs are determined by their purchase costs. Some materials may be used for several tasks. For example, the same prototype vehicle may be used by several programs, so the cost of the prototype should be distributed to each program using weighting factors based either on its utilization or excepted production volume of the resulting product. This allows the material costs to be estimated for each program.

Resources are usually cost at dollars per hour. Corporations usually maintain two cost numbers on resources: accounting value and actual value. The accounting value is used to minimize tax expenses and is dictated by the method of depreciation used. The actual value, on the other hand, is used to represent the fair market value of the item, which can be estimated by distributing the purchase cost over the expected useful life of the item. This cost may be adjusted by the percentage of time that the resource is expected to be used during the year. Generally, most resources have adjustments that correspond to 70 to 100 percent utilization rates. Therefore, if a resource is used at its expected utilization rate, the calculated cost of using it is equal to the reduction in actual value. An example is shown in Figure 7-5.

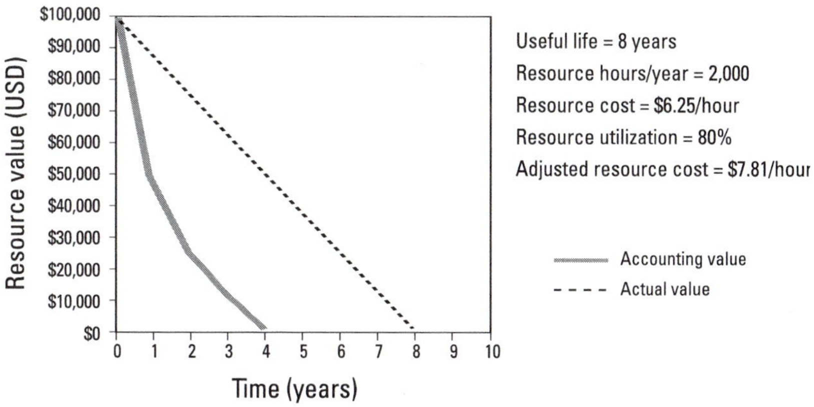

Figure 7-5. Resource cost estimation

By estimating material and resource costs, you can estimate the total cost of the baseline process. This becomes the baseline for which reengineered processes are compared. More detail on material and resource management is presented in Chapters 8 and 12.

Process Redesign

In the lean philosophy, the focus is on optimizing the processes, not the tasks. This is a systems engineering approach, in which the overall system (or process) is engineered; thus processes are redesigned using the fundamental features of the lean philosophy, while tasks are redesigned only to support process optimization. Ideal processes are envisioned, and an attempt to implement them is conducted. The techniques used are as follows:

1. Eliminate or isolate feedback loops.
2. Eliminate non-value-added tasks.
3. Optimize the critical path.
4. Optimize process threads.
5. Revise tasks.
6. Develop new tasks.
7. Add controlling tasks.

Each technique is described in the following sections.

Eliminate or Isolate Feedback Loops

Because feedback loops are a form of waste, eliminate them from all business processes, where possible. If they cannot be eliminated, at least isolate them. The reason you iterate tasks (that is, outputs feed back as inputs to earlier tasks) is because you did not achieve the desired results the first time through.

Iterations within a task are acceptable and are often necessary. Iterations between one or more tasks, however, should be avoided, because when iterations occur between tasks, you must transfer information between the people who execute the tasks, and you may have significant wait time until the resource becomes available. Also, any outputs that are supplied to downstream tasks, which are then modified during the iterations, require the downstream tasks to be re-executed. This is another source of waste and frustration to the people who perform the downstream tasks.

Feedback loops involving a small number of tasks can be isolated inside a subprocess. This is demonstrated using Process 1 in Figure 7-4. The result is shown in Figure 7-6. Isolating feedback loops in subprocesses allows iterations to be conducted prior to supplying the outputs to downstream tasks. This prevents the downstream tasks from having to be reexecuted due to changes in these outputs.

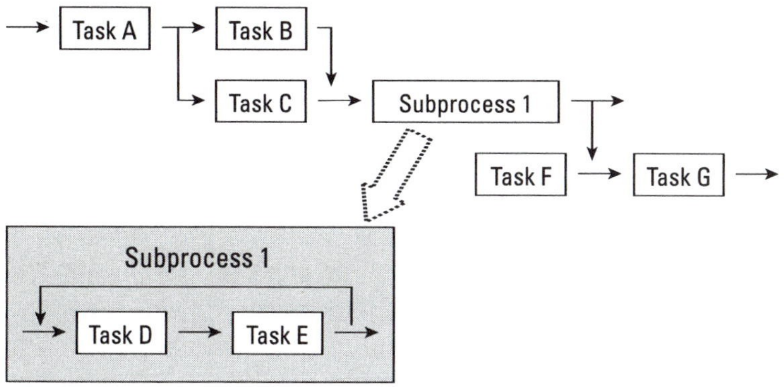

Figure 7-6. Isolating a feedback loop inside a subprocess

The lean philosophy uses the systems engineering approach, so iterations are ideally done only at the system level. This means that the entire process is performed, and the system-level results are assessed. Then, based on the results, a new set of tasks is created and the resulting new processes are performed. Using process models and relating outputs to requirements allow these new processes to be developed quickly.

The job of eliminating and isolating feedback loops goes to the process manager. Unlike the tasks owners who are responsible only for their tasks, the process manager is responsible for the entire process. The process manager is usually from a vertical group and must work with the horizontal and support groups to optimize processes.

Eliminate Non-Value-Added Tasks

Eliminate all non-value-added tasks from the process. Non-value-added tasks are those with outputs that are not used; they must be scrutinized as to their value. They should either be revised to include value-added outputs or be deleted. Significant reductions in process timing and costs can be achieved by eliminating non-value-added tasks.

Often, departments perform work because it has always been done that way or because the department managers feel they will be judged based on the amount of outputs produced. So, they create their outputs whether or not anyone wants them. This happens because process managers do not have full control over their processes or because they do not know how every output relates back to achieving customer needs and wants. In lean corporations, however, every output is related back to achieving customer needs and wants.

The program manager is responsible for deciding which outputs are most important at achieving his or her objectives. By having program managers selecting outputs to be generated, you automatically force the producers of these outputs to develop value-added items. Otherwise, their outputs will not be selected, and their services will not be needed. In this way, non-value-added tasks are automatically eliminated from business processes using this approach.

Optimize the Critical Path

The time it takes to execute a process is determined by the duration of the tasks and whether they are run in parallel or series. Some tasks can finish late without affecting the end date of the process. Other tasks are related such that if they finish late they do affect the end date of the process. These later types of tasks are said to be on the critical path.

Tasks on the critical path are the ones that must be modified to reduce the overall time it takes to execute a process.

To determine whether a task is on the critical path, a parameter called *float* is calculated. Float indicates how much time the task can be delayed before it affects the end date of the process.

For example, consider a process that has two tasks that start at the same time and run in parallel. One task has a duration of 10 days and the other has a duration of 5 days. The process then has an overall duration of 10 days (because the tasks run in parallel). The 5-day duration task has a value of float equal to 5 days, indicating that this task can be finished 5 days late without affecting the end date of the process. The 10-day duration task has a zero float value, indicating that it must be finished on time or the end date of the process will be delayed. A task with a zero float value is said to be on the critical path. Most project management software programs calculate float for you, but seeing how this process works can be enlightening.

To determine the critical path, you do the following:

1. **List all tasks, along with their durations.**
2. **Do a forward pass: You determine the earliest start date a task can have assuming all predecessors start on time and take their estimated durations to finish.**
3. **Add the duration of the task to the earliest start date to determine its earliest finish date.** This is done for all tasks. The latest earliest finish date is equal to the process end date.
4. **Do a backward pass: You determine the latest finish date a task can have without affecting the process end date that was determined from the forward pass.** The latest finish date for each task is calculated by assuming all successors finish as late as possible (without affecting the process end date) and take their estimated durations to finish.
5. **Subtract the duration of the task from the latest finish date to determine its latest start date.** The difference between the latest start date and earliest start date is equal to the float value for the task. This is done for all tasks. If the float value is zero, then the task is on the critical path. Tasks with

float values greater than zero are not on the critical path and can finish late (up to the float value) without affecting the overall process end date. This flexibility can be used to balance resources.

After the critical path is determined, it should be evaluated. Often, one task or a small number of tasks on the critical path have large durations. These tasks should be reviewed to see whether they can be made to be more efficient. Dividing these tasks into two or more may help by allowing some successor tasks on the critical path to start earlier. An example is shown in Figure 7-7.

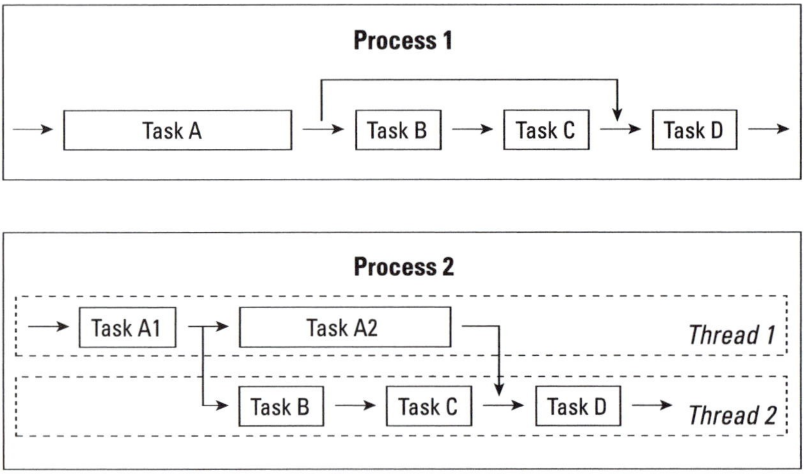

Figure 7-7. Dividing a task on the critical path to produce a shorter process duration

Task A in Process 1 has the longest duration and is on the critical path. If Task A can be divided into two tasks (A1 and A2), with Task A1 supplying inputs to Task B and Task A2 supplying inputs to Task D, the process can be redesigned as shown in Process 2. Reviewing the input–output linkages allows you to conduct this type of process optimization. This can be done only by creating the processes in terms of process models. The twelve-step business process discovery procedure allows this to happen.

Optimize Process Threads

Figure 7-7 shows another feature: the concept of threads. Threads are sequences of tasks that execute in parallel. Process 1 has only one thread. Process 2 has two threads. The ideal case is to have one person execute each thread. Each thread has minimal float, thereby eliminating the tendency for work to expand to the amount of time given. This also facilitates forming a process team with a minimum number of members and in which all members are fully utilized (that is, continuously working on tasks within their threads).

The idea is to have as few people as possible executing a process. This optimizes the use of people resources. Because tasks may span many disciplines, it is essential that they be made simple to perform. In fact, this simplicity is a fundamental feature of the lean philosophy. Making tasks simple to perform requires that the complex details be hidden from the worker. Instead, the worker sees a simple interface that asks for information that is well known to the worker.

This is exactly the same concept used in object-oriented programming. The user just wants to perform some action. The details are unimportant as long as the desired outputs (results) are achieved.

Implementing this type of approach can often be done using Web-based applications. Specialists design the implementation with direct involvement from the users. These specialists are available to train and assist the users, and they conduct nonstandard activities, such as troubleshooting. The result is that the user becomes a product specialist who performs the majority of the work tasks, a dramatic change from the current state. One incredible advantage is that the user learns not only what works, but also why it works.

For example, the design of most components is a balancing process in which several areas of performance are adjusted to produce the best overall design. For structural components, these areas include stiffness, mass, radiated noise, packaging, and so on. If each performance area is analyzed by different people, they cannot balance these areas of performance to optimize the design. Instead, each person optimizes the performance in his or her area, which takes extra time and does not ensure optimal or even acceptable system performance. Having one person analyze all the performance areas allows him or her to understand how each area is related to the others. This allows the person to make intelligent trade-offs in the optimization of the design.

This same idea applies to product testing, too. There is an incredible synergy between test and analysis that is obtained only when the same person does both jobs. Analysis models are always made using assumptions. These assumptions can be validated only by using tests and comparing the analysis results to the test results. During the course of testing, especially when problems crop up, you often learn some aspect of the system of which you were not aware. Finding the source of the problem often leads to a better understanding of the system. Testing also introduces statistical variation into the assessments, which should be taken into account when designing products. Assessing the limitations of tests in terms of repeatability is another important issue. These issues are well understood when the same person conducts both the analysis and test tasks.

Having optimizing process threads requires that workers be trained to perform tasks that are performed in sequence, regardless of the task type. This is needed because handoffs are a significant source of waste. For many processes, only 10 to 25 percent of the time is used to execute tasks. The rest of the time is waiting for resources to become available. Improved resource scheduling helps, but the best solution is to minimize handoffs using process threads.

Coupling between threads occurs where outputs are shared between one or more threads. These are good points to establish milestones. Coupling between threads should be minimized, if possible, using the concepts presented in Chapter 4.

Revise Tasks

Tasks are revised using the scientific method; in other words, the physical phenomenon that governs the task must be determined. This allows the ideal task to be estimated and the efficiency of the current task to be determined. Tasks with low efficiencies are usually easier to improve than those with high efficiencies.

The people who perform the tasks should be responsible for revising them. The task owner is responsible for approving any changes and for challenging the assumptions used.

Tasks can also be revised by combining several tasks into one, or splitting one task into several. Tasks with short durations are candidates for being combined with other tasks. A general rule-of-thumb is that each task should take no less than one day, and tasks should be combined only when they share common nodes in the requirement hierarchy. This usually happens with tasks developed by different groups. Tasks with short durations that do not share common nodes in the requirement hierarchy should be kept separate. In this case, they are probably good candidates for being automated.

Develop New Tasks

New tasks are developed to implement new technology. Usually, program requirements increase—not decrease—over time, and new technologies can be developed to improve both the product and the tasks used to create them. In product engineering, this is the development of new design, analysis, and test tasks. The goal is to have the tasks more directly estimate product performance using the substructuring approach presented in Chapter 4.

Development of new tasks can be done internally or externally, but be sure the workers who perform the tasks are involved in the development process. This is why the establishment of technology development groups in corporations is useful. The most skilled workers can be rotated into technology development groups to allow their knowledge to be extracted and implemented into new procedures. The creation of Web-enabled applications can be done effectively in this manner, automating tasks and allowing nonexperts to perform them. Each task expert is responsible for training and consulting for any special problems that may arise. As with all tasks, the new tasks are documented using process models and may be selected for use by the program managers.

Add Controlling Tasks

Controlling tasks are added to facilitate the management of the redesigned business processes. As described in Chapter 4, controlling tasks run in parallel to all the tasks they control. Every regular task has a single controlling task which is implemented according to the program structure, with one controlling task for each vertical manager assigned to the program. This establishes a clear chain of command, with one person responsible for the management of a given set of tasks.

The addition of controlling tasks to the redesigned business processes allows both the regular (noncontrolling) and controlling tasks to be represented in hierarchical form. This is important to managing large, complex processes where hierarchical management structures are needed. See Chapter 11 for an example of adding controlling tasks to a redesigned business process.

Reengineered Processes

Always compare reengineered processes to the baseline process using the quality, cost, and time assessments discussed in the preceding sections. The result is a fair assessment between the baseline process and any reengineered processes. This is useful when capital expenditures are necessary to implement the reengineered process, because you can make a business case for these expenditures based on the expected improvements in quality and reduction in time and cost that accompany the reengineered processes.

An example demonstrating how processes are reengineered using the lean philosophy is presented in Chapter 11.

Chapter 8
Implementing New Business Processes

This chapter shows you how to implement new business processes after you discover your existing processes and reengineer them. The techniques are based on traditional methods of program management, but lean concepts are applied that enable the processes to be managed efficiently. First, you get an overview of the program management process, including its five subprocesses:

- *Initiation: Establish program objectives.*
- *Planning: Roll-down program objectives to create business processes, create management hierarchies, and determine program assessment reports.*
- *Execution: Perform the work tasks.*
- *Control: Control the process using the controlling tasks defined in Chapter 4, focusing on materials and resource management.*
- *Program closeout: Document the program results and finish all work relative to the program.*

Program Management Process

The traditional approach to program management is described in the Project Management Body of Knowledge (PMBOK®) Guide. This approach is an industry standard (ANSI/PMI 90-001-2000) and is used throughout this book as the basis for managing lean business processes.[1] Programs are managed using five subprocesses:

[1]PMI® does not endorse or otherwise sponsor this publication, and makes no warranty, guarantee, or representation, expressed or implied, as to the accuracy of its content.

initiation, planning, execution, control, and closeout. The five subprocesses interact, as shown in Figure 8-1.

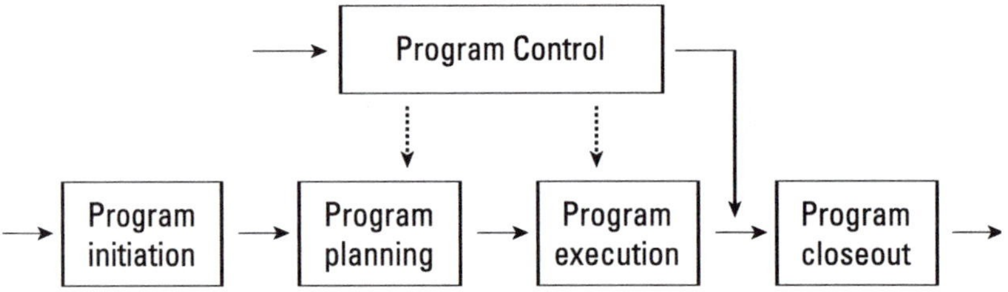

Figure 8-1. Program management process

Program initiation is done first, and then program planning and program execution are run in parallel with program control. Program closeout is done last. Because IDEF0 models are used to model both the regular and controlling work tasks, the overall process is generated and managed in a straightforward manner. This chapter describes each subprocess and the approaches you can use to successfully implement them.

Program Initiation

Program initiation happens first and is the simplest of the five subprocesses. Only one work task is executed during program initiation; it defines the scope of the program, including the role of the program manager, the system-level deliverables, and other related items. Program initiation is done at the highest level of the organization. The assigned program manager then develops a program plan in the next subprocess, program planning.

Program Planning

Program planning is critical to produce successful programs, so plan to spend about ten percent of the time allocated to the program in the planning subprocess. Avoid too much or too little planning. Program planning is like a virtual execution of the business process. Although almost no program ever is executed as planned, the planning process allows the majority of the important tasks to be identified and sequenced appropriately.

Many different work tasks are done during the planning subprocess (see the PMBOK® Guide), but the end result is that a detailed process plan is developed that shows all the work tasks and their inputs, outputs, resources, and controls. These are generated automatically by the IDEF0 process models when the desired requirements or outputs for the process are selected. The only hard part is determining which requirements or outputs to select; do this by establishing and rolling down the business objectives.

Business Objectives

Business objectives are rolled down in the standard top-down manner, and details are added as you progress downward from level to level. The highest level is the business objectives for the corporation, which are developed by the CEO and approved by the Board of Directors. Business objectives are usually made for one year, but then are reviewed and/or modified, as needed, often quarterly or semiannually. Most business objectives for the CEO are related to the corporate financial statements. This makes sense because these statements reflect the performance of the corporation.

These business objectives are then rolled down to each subsequent level in the organization structure hierarchy. Managers review their supervisors' objectives and develop their own proposed objectives. These are reviewed with their supervisors, and the objectives are modified. Changes to both a supervisor's and an employee's objectives are typically made, because synergies are achieved through this process. The business objectives roll-down process is illustrated in Figure 8-2.

Be sure you have no more than ten to twenty business objectives for each person, regardless of level. This enforces the concept that higher-level objectives are more general and lower-level objectives more detailed.

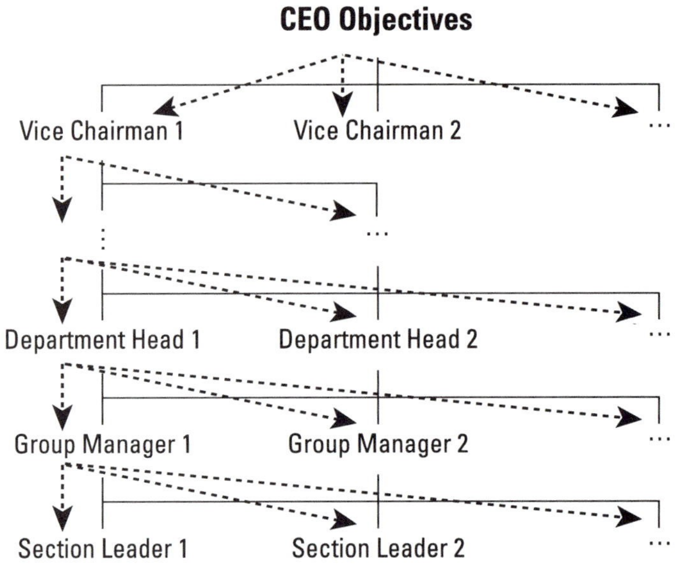

Figure 8-2. Business objectives roll-down process

Business Processes

When the business objectives have been determined, the business processes needed to support these objectives are determined. This process is shown in Figure 8-3.

Each management level determines what work is recommended and develops timing, cost, and risk assessments. Timing and cost estimates are determined directly from the standard work definitions:

- Timing is determined from the task durations and the input–output linkages.
- Cost is determined from the materials and resources needed to perform the tasks.

Risk assessment is conducted using a DFMEA approach (see Chapter 5). Each task is assessed with respect to the severity, occurrence, and detection consequences relative to potential failure modes related to the product being produced. This information is passed back up the organization hierarchy, where timing, cost, and risk are balanced to produce an acceptable plan.

Executive Level	The direct manager of the system-level vertical group gets the program objectives, reviews them with the system-level group managers, and assigns responsibility for each program objective to a system-level vertical manager. ↓	The direct manager of the system-level vertical group balances timing, cost, and risk, and gets program approval. ↑
System Level	Each system-level vertical manager reviews their program objectives with their subordinate subsystem vertical managers, determines the system-level objectives, and assigns responsibility for each system-level objective to a subsystem-level vertical manager. ↓	Each system-level vertical manager determines what work they recommend should be conducted and gives timing, cost, and risk assessment. ↑
Subsystem Level	Each subsystem-level vertical manager reviews their system-level objectives with their subordinate component-level managers, determines the subsystem-level objectives, and assigns responsibility for each subsystem-level objective to a component-level manager. ↓	Each subsystem-level vertical manager determines what work they recommend should be conducted and gives timing, cost, and risk assessment. ↑
Component Level	Each component-level manager reviews their subsystem-level objectives with their subordinate component section leaders, determines the component-level objectives, and assigns responsibility for each component-level objective to a component section leader. →	Each component section leader determines what work they recommend should be conducted and gives timing, cost, and risk assessment.

Figure 8-3. Determination of business processes from business objectives

Planning Horizons

Different planning horizons are used for business processes based on their specific needs. Planning horizons can be broken down into three categories:

- **Long-term:** one to five years
- **Mid-term:** three months to one year
- **Short-term:** one to three months

Each term has different planning characteristics, which are discussed in the following sections.

Long-Term Planning Horizon

Long-term planning is done for growth. Generic resources are used except that instead of using the detailed program plans to determine resource needs, forecasts of future needs are based on previous program requirements. In addition, new technologies and worker skills are continuously reviewed and assessed as to their impact on business processes. Then these resources are obtained and/or developed. Long-term planning is needed, especially for resources that take significant time to obtain, such as a new facility, or where the development of skills requires long-term training. Long-term planning is done mostly at the department level or higher, prior to program execution.

Mid-Term Planning Horizon

Mid-term planning is similar to long-term planning, except that the specific programs are used to determine resource needs. Resources are designated by their roles and usages: Many different people can perform a role, and many different pieces of equipment can perform a usage. The different roles and usages are created as generic resources, which are mapped to specific resources so that their inventory can be determined. The generic resource utilization can be determined directly from the detailed program plans. Mid-term planning is done at the group or department level, prior to program execution.

Short-Term Planning Horizon

Short-term planning is where generic resources are replaced with the specific resources that are used to perform the work tasks. Materials must be scheduled and obtained according to program timing requirements. This is material and resource management at the lowest level. Detailed schedules are needed for the specific people and equipment that are used. Short-term planning is done primarily at the group level, during program execution. See the "Property Management" section for a more detailed discussion.

Budgets

Budgets are used to control cash flows in the corporation, so cash flow statements are the basis for budgets. Cash flow includes operating, investing, and financing activities. These are just consequences of property management, because property consists of materials and resources. (Materials are the items that get acted upon by resources. Resources are the items that act on materials. Managing materials is the responsibility of the vertical managers. Managing resources is the responsibility of the horizontal and support groups.)

All materials and resources have their usage costs estimated (see Chapter 7). Knowing these costs allows the determination of program costs, and the result determines the budgets needed to execute the programs. These budgets are controlled using work orders that restrict usage to the responsible people. Budgets include direct and indirect support: Direct support is money needed to execute current programs, while indirect support is money used for continuous improvement of processes and long-term capability development.

Budgets are implemented using the organization structure. Direct support flows through the vertical reporting relationships. Indirect support flows through the direct reporting structure. These flows are illustrated at the department level in Figure 8-4.

The lean philosophy focuses on reducing expenses; therefore, lean corporations track expenses for each organizational group. These expenses include the cost for materials and resources.

- Material costs are straightforward. They are the costs of the external inputs used in the business processes.
- Resource expenses are determined at their normal usage rates. This usually corresponds to a 70 to 100 percent utilization. This value changes through time as the item loses value through depreciation.

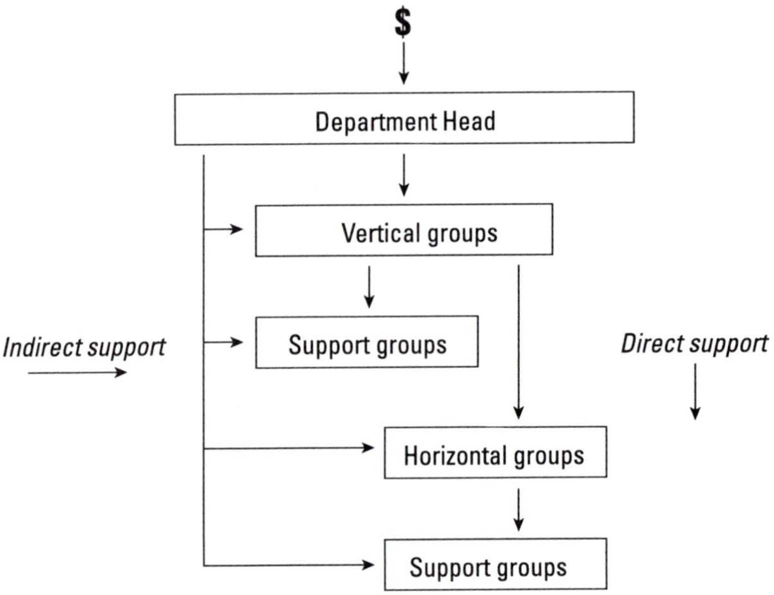

Figure 8-4. Budget flow through the organization

Two depreciation schemes are generally used. One is used for tax purposes (to minimize tax) and the other is used for expenses that give fair value of the item's usage cost. This is needed to ensure that operational efficiency can be evaluated and compared to alternatives such as purchasing or leasing new equipment and contracting out noncritical work.

Scheduling

Scheduling is done on the three planning horizons. Long-term work is projected and arrangements start being made to support that effort. Mid-term work is scheduled using generic roles and resources. Short-term work is scheduled and started.

Business Process Management Hierarchies

Each business process is managed using a work breakdown structure (WBS) along with an organizational breakdown structure (OBS). A WBS organizes work packages in relation to the people who manage the work; it is just the program structure augmented with hierarchy nodes that correspond to managed work packages. A work package is defined as a set of work tasks that are performed by the same organizational group for a specific program. Using this definition, each work package corresponds to one vertical manager and one horizontal or support manager. The vertical manager imposes the controls on the tasks within the work package and schedules the materials needed to perform these tasks. The horizontal or support group manager manages the resources that are used to perform the tasks in the work package. This implements the hybrid organization structure described in Chapter 3 that is used for virtually all college and professional football teams.

The lowest level in each branch of the WBS is a work package. Work packages usually contain ten to one hundred tasks. The levels above the work packages are called subprojects, projects, and programs:

- Subprojects contain two to ten work packages that are managed by one person.
- Projects contain two to ten subprojects.
- Programs contain two or more projects. Corporations usually have ten to twenty programs active at a given time.

Each program is managed independently from the other programs by having different program managers for each program (a decoupled management approach). The general structure of a WBS is shown in Figure 8-5.

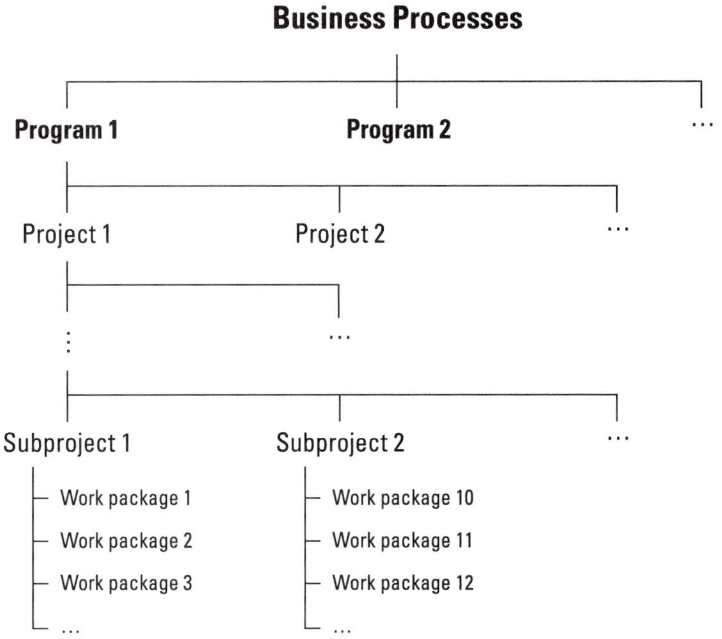

Figure 8-5. General structure of a WBS

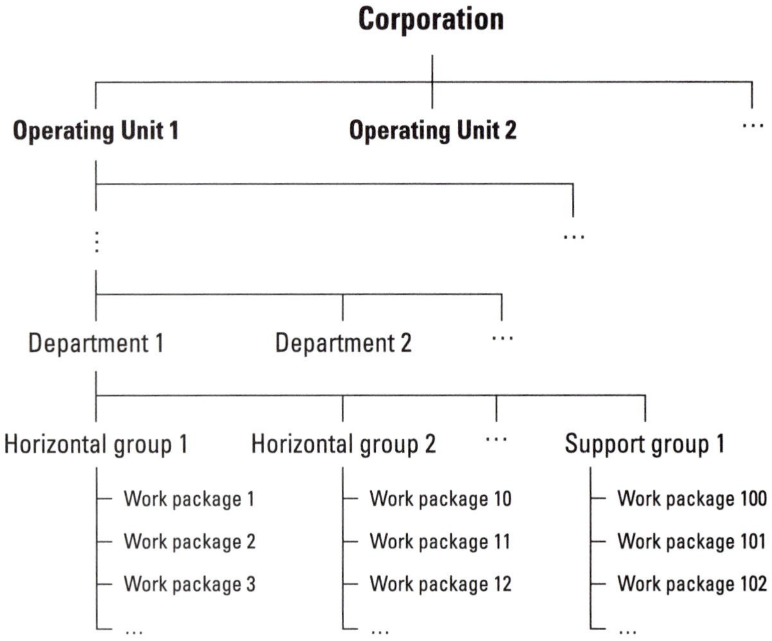

Figure 8-6. General structure of an OBS

An organizational breakdown structure (OBS) is used to organize work packages in relation to the organizational groups that perform the work. The OBS is just the organizational structure, augmented with hierarchy nodes that correspond to the managed work packages. Each organizational group has child hierarchy nodes corresponding to the work packages it performs. This allows the group's resources to be managed across all programs. The general structure of an OBS is shown in Figure 8-6.

Process Assessment Reports

Process assessment reports can be completed with many different formats. These reports follow the conventions established in this book, namely that a report is a specific set of attributes corresponding to a specific set of items displayed in a specific hierarchy. Standard process assessment reports are shown in Table 8-1.

Table 8-1. Standard Process Assessment Report

Program Assessment Report	Report Type	Hierarchy	Items	Attributes	Hierarchy Summary Type
Program Timing Report	Tree-Table View	WBS	Tasks	Timing	Nonlinear
Program Bill of Materials	Tree-Table View	WBS	External Inputs	Timing	None
Program Cost Report	Tree-Table View	WBS	Tasks and External Inputs	Cost	Linear Summation
Program Management	Tree-Table View	OBS	Tasks	Timing	Nonlinear
Performance Reviews	Tree-Table View	Performance Review Structure	Requirements	Assessments	Custom

Process assessment reports are used during the program execution and program control subprocesses to ensure program quality, time, and cost goals are met. Examples of these reports are presented in Chapter 12.

Program Approval

The last step in program planning is program approval. Mid-term planning is done to see whether the required resources are available in the time frame needed. This is done at the generic resource level. The assignment of specific resources is done only during the execution phase. The program is officially approved after resource commitments are obtained. Budgets are allocated for the costs associated with the program. These budgets are used to acquire the resources and materials needed to execute the program.

Program Execution and Control

Program execution and control are closely related, so these two subprocesses are presented in one section. Each task that is executed has a corresponding controlling task. Controlling tasks are used to impose controls on the regular work tasks and to manage the materials that are needed by these tasks. Resources are managed by the organizational groups that are responsible for performing the work tasks. The key to a successful program is the management of materials and resources. Collectively, these are called property.

Property Management

Through property management and the concepts in this book, you can experience drastic savings. Property includes materials and resources, and managing them is dependent on their usage. IDEF0 models define inputs, outputs, and resources based on their use. Any property can be either an input, an output, or a resource for a given task and can be used more than once. For example, the same item can be an output of one task and an input to another. Likewise, a resource can be an output of an acquisition task and also an input to a disposal task. Also, inputs that are not totally consumed by a task may become available after the task is completed. This makes the input available to be shared between tasks, just like resources.

To manage corporate property, all materials and resources are identified as being shared or unshared.

Unshared properties are easy to manage because they are assigned to only one entity. No scheduling is needed and all of the cost of the item can be allocated to the entity itself. An example of an unshared resource is a laptop computer that is assigned to a specific individual. The individual always has access to it and its cost can be amortized into the cost of the individual. An example of an unshared material is any raw material that is completely consumed by a task. Because the material is consumed, it is not available for use after the task is completed. Thus, it is an unshared property.

Shared properties are more difficult to manage than unshared properties because their usage must be scheduled. However, the use of shared properties is the key to minimizing waste. This is why lean corporations must know how to manage this type of property effectively. Shared properties must be scheduled and their costs allocated to the users in some fashion. The use of IDEF0 models allows this to be done relatively easily. An example of a shared resource is a test facility that is used to conduct many different tests. An example of a shared material is a prototype vehicle that is used by many groups.

Shared properties can be inputs, outputs, or resources as determined by the IDEF0 task model. Managing shared properties that are resources is done using traditional resource management techniques. Resource utilization is calculated as a function of time and compared to the number of resources that are available. This is done at the generic resource level. Tasks are resequenced in order to level and balance resource demands by adding discretionary constraints to one or more tasks. This approach is applied in Chapter 7 using process threads, where each thread is optimized so that it can be performed by one worker. Because each program is unique, it needs to be optimized. The optimization is a balancing act between overall process duration and resource requirements. Most project management software packages have resource-balancing capability. A detailed discussion of this topic, therefore, is not presented here (see the works cited in the Bibliography).

Resource Management

Resource management requires mapping resources to work tasks. This is done when the tasks are defined in terms of IDEF0 models and resources are designated by their roles and usages. The different roles and usages are created as generic resources, which are defined using a set of attributes. Both the specific and generic resources are mapped to these attributes. The mapping for specific resources indicates whether the item has the associated attribute. This is illustrated in Table 8-2.

Table 8-2. Mapping of Specific Resources to Attributes

	Attribute 1	Attribute 2	Attribute 3	Attribute 4	Attribute 5	...
Specific Resource A	X		X	X	X	
Specific Resource B	X	X		X		
Specific Resource C	X		X		X	
Specific Resource D		X		X	X	
Specific Resource E		X			X	
...						

A simple example is people resources. The individuals are the specific resources. Their education, training, and experience are the attributes. Generic resources are created to represent the different types of items needed to support the business processes. These generic resources are mapped to the same set of attributes as the specific resources. However, this is done by establishing required and preferred attributes, as shown in Table 8-3.

Required attributes are indicated using the letter R and represent attributes that the generic resource must have. Preferred attributes are indicated using the letter P and represent attributes that are preferred, but not required. If only one attribute of several is required for a generic resource, the attributes are identified by putting a comma and a lowercase letter next to its R or P code. Each lowercase letter identifies a group of attributes for which only one is required or preferred. In Table 8-3, generic resource E has attributes 2 and 3 specified as a group, where only one is required. Attributes 4 and 5 are specified as a group, where only one is preferred. Using the example of people resources, this could be required education, such as a B.S. in Mechanical Engineering (Attribute 2) or a B.S. in Industrial Engineering (Attribute 3), while a preferred education could be an M.S. in Mechanical Engineering (Attribute 4) or an M.S. in Industrial Engineering (Attribute 5).

Table 8-3. Mapping of Generic Resources to Attributes

	Attribute 1	Attribute 2	Attribute 3	Attribute 4	Attribute 5	...
Generic Resource A	R					
Generic Resource B	R	R				
Generic Resource C	R		R			
Generic Resource D	R		P	P		
Generic Resource E		R,a	R,a	P,b	P,b	
...						

Resource requirements corresponding to standard work tasks are done at the mid-term level using generic resources. This allows mid-term planning to be done using generic resources instead of specific resources. The amounts of generic resources are determined based on the program content and timing. (It is common to determine resource needs once a year.) The required generic resources are determined and compared to those that are available. Adjustments are then done to meet resource needs, usually at the department level.

When programs are executed, specific resources must be identified. Each generic resource is replaced by a specific resource. Because the generic and specific resources are mapped to the same set of attributes, they can be mapped to each other. The specific resources can also be ranked with respect to the degree that they meet the required and preferred attributes corresponding to the generic resources. This is shown in Table 8-4.

Table 8-4. Mapping of Specific Resources to Generic Resources

	Specific Resource A	Specific Resource B	Specific Resource C	Specific Resource D	Specific Resource E	...
Generic Resource A	R + 3	R + 2	R + 2	R – 1	R – 1	
Generic Resource B	R – 1	R + 1	R – 1	R – 1	R – 1	
Generic Resource C	R + 2	R – 1	R + 1	R – 2	R – 2	
Generic Resource D	R + 3, P	R + 3, P – 1	R + 2, P – 1	R – 1, P – 1	R – 1, P – 1	
Generic Resource E	R + 3, P	R + 2, P	R + 2, P	R + 2, P	R + 1, P	
...						

Table 8-4 uses the specific and generic resources shown in Tables 8-2 and 8-3. A rating code is used to indicate the degree to which each specific resource meets the required and preferred attributes. A code of R indicates that the specific resource meets all of the required attributes corresponding to the generic resource, has no additional attributes, and has no specified preferred attributes. A code of "R + *n*," with *n* representing an integer, indicates that the specific resource meets all of the required attributes corresponding to the generic resource, has *n* (a certain number of) additional attributes that were not specified, and has no specified preferred attributes. A code of "R – *n*," with *n* representing an integer, indicates that the specific resource meets all but *n* of the required attributes corresponding to the generic resource.

For generic resources that have preferred attributes, the number of preferred attributes for the specific resource is indicated using a code of "P–*n*" that is added after the required attribute rating code and separated by a comma. The maximum preferred rating is a "P," which indicates that all of the preferred attributes are met. A preferred rating of "P–*n*" indicates that all but *n* of the preferred attributes are met.

The relative ranking of the rating codes are as follows:

R – *n* < R – 1 < R < R + 1 < R + *n*	No preferred attributes specified
R – *n* < R – 1 < R, P – *n* < R, P – 1 < R, P < R+1, P < R + *n*, P	Preferred attributes specified

This type of rating, although admittedly cryptic and confusing, allows resource managers to rank the specific resources as the degree to which each specific resource is qualified to be used as the generic resource. This extra information (as opposed to just using qualified and not-qualified ratings) allows resource managers to optimize the use of resources by reserving the specific resources with the highest ratings for the most critical tasks, and vice versa. Also, specific resources with ratings of R–1 or R–2 may be elevated to a rating of R by scheduling the required modifications or additional training prior to when the generic resource is needed.

Resources and attributes are organized into hierarchies. The specific resources are items that are put into the resource hierarchy (see Chapter 2). Generic resources and attributes are organized into separate hierarchies that are primarily used to sort the items. There are usually only several hundreds of generic resources and attributes. Thus, only two to four levels in each hierarchy are needed. Most corporations already have some type of organization structure for these items. All that is needed is to formalize them into hierarchies and implement the rating system just discussed.

Materials Management

Materials are managed by the controlling tasks, using the same techniques as shared resources. Up to this point, all inputs have been selected from the master list of outputs. This produces a one-to-one mapping between inputs and outputs. Therefore, all that is needed is the management of outputs. Output utilization is determined, leveled, and balanced, as needed. This is done in exactly the same way as for resources. (See the preceding section.)

To provide additional flexibility in business processes, generic inputs can be created that allow one of several different outputs to be used based on availability. This is done by mapping the generic inputs to two or more outputs and rating them in order of preference. This mapping is shown in Table 8-5.

Table 8-5. Mapping of Generic Inputs to Outputs

	Output 1	Output 2	Output 3	Output 4	Output 5	...
Generic Input 1	R, P	R, P – 1				
Generic Input 2	R, P – 1	R, P				
Generic Input 3	R, P – 2		R, P		R, P – 1	
Generic Input 4		R, P – 2		R, P	R, P – 1	
Generic Input 5		R, P–1			R, P	
...						

The rating scheme used is the same as the one used for generic resources, except that the ratings are specified directly instead of being calculated. The highest rating used is R, P. The lowest rating used is R, P – *n*. Usually, only two or three outputs are mapped to a generic input, and often only one is given the R, P rating, which indicates that it is the preferred choice. This is useful when conducting product development in phases. Depending on the development phase, different items may be preferred. For example, measured results may be preferred to calculated results in the later design phases. Also, the most current levels of hardware may be preferred, but older versions can be used if the preferred hardware is not available.

As a side note, Microsoft® Project 2000 defines two types of resources: work resources and material resources. Work resources are shared properties, and material resources are unshared properties. The reason Microsoft® Project treats materials as resources is because they are managed using the same techniques. The reason that materials and resources are treated differently in this book is to enforce the separation of management responsibility for the items. Materials are the responsibility of the vertical manager, while resources are the responsibility of the person who performs the task. This allows the corresponding business process to be managed effectively.

Program Closeout

The last subprocess in program management is program closeout, which occurs after all the tasks in the execution subprocess are finished. A final accounting of the program cost is made, accounting budgets are closed, and program outputs are delivered to their customers. Any remaining resources and materials are released to be used on other programs. The final program documentation is completed and stored for future reference.

This is also the time to conduct an assessment of the success of the program. Document the lessons that were learned and modify the program management process to include any improvements that can be implemented immediately. Also plan for mid-term and long-term process improvements. Efforts then shift to other active and new programs.

An example of implementing your business processes is shown in Chapter 12.

Chapter 9
The Lean Corporation

This chapter presents the last steps in creating a lean corporation: expanding process models to all the areas within the corporation. For simplicity, it is assumed that a corporation consists of only four areas: product engineering, manufacturing, financial, and sales and service. Each of these areas is reviewed in generalities to show how its high-level processes are interrelated. Additionally, the product engineering area is shown in greater detail to demonstrate how the previous chapters' concepts support the creation of lean corporations.

Lean Corporation Organizational Structures

As indicated in Chapter 3, lean corporations utilize the hybrid organization structure shown in Figure 3-11. Each level in the corporate organization structure may have Type-A, Type-B, vertical, horizontal, and support groups, depending on the business processes. Money flows primarily from vertical groups to horizontal and support groups to sustain business processes. Responsibility and authority is clear and direct.

The generic format of the lean corporate organization structure with each of the four areas explicitly identified is shown in Figure 9-1.

At the top of the organization structure are the stockholders, who elect the Board of Directors. The Board of Directors elects the Chairman of the Board and the Chief Executive Officer (CEO); often, the same person serves as both the Chairman of the Board and the CEO. The box labeled "Corporation" is where the CEO is located. The corporation is a Type-A group, which indicates that the

CEO is responsible for both vertical and horizontal management. The level below the CEO contains operating units, corporate financial, and support groups. The operating units are self-contained entities that produce and sell products and/or services. For product-related organizations, each operating unit has a product engineering, manufacturing, financial, and sales and service area. Operating units are usually Type-B groups, because they contain separate vertical management groups. The highest level vertical group is the corporate financial group, which is responsible for managing all corporate finances. This group distributes funds to the other groups at the corporate level. These funds are then distributed according to the reporting structure defined in the corporate organizational structure. The corporate level support groups consist of departments like information technology, research and development, legal, and so on. These support groups are organized using the lean organization structure and are generally themselves divided into horizontal, vertical, and support groups.

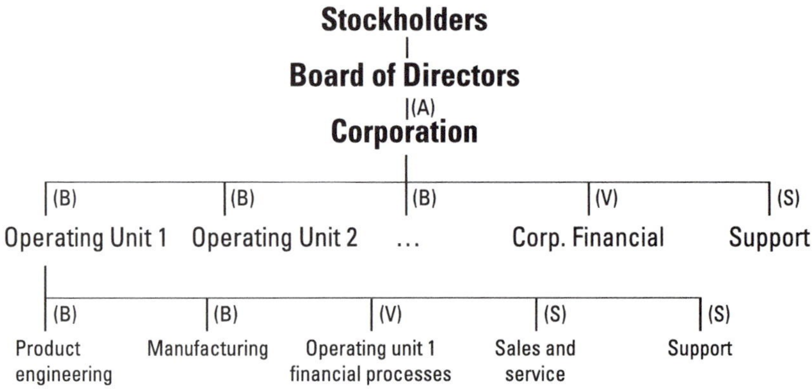

Figure 9-1. Lean corporation organization structure

The corporate organization structure also dictates how the business processes are managed. Keep in mind that the program structure is determined directly from the organization structure. The relationships between the vertical groups define the business process management chain-of-command. The horizontal and support groups define and execute the business subprocesses and tasks. Thus, the corporate business process can be represented in IDEF0 format directly from the organization structure. The lean corporation program structure corresponding to the lean organization structure is shown in Figure 9-2.

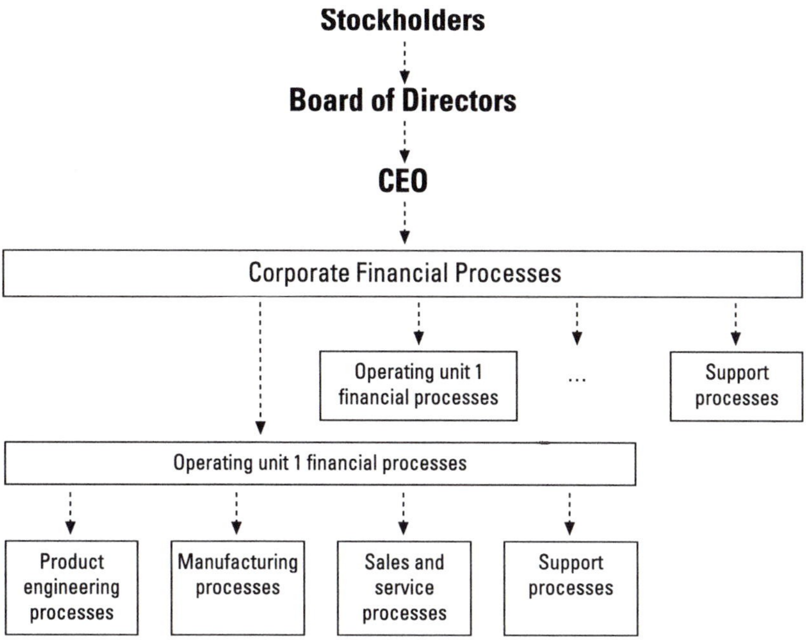

Figure 9-2. Lean corporation program structure

The four major corporate areas fit into the lean corporation program structure, as shown in Figure 9-2. Each is described in the following sections.

Financial

The financial area of the corporation is distributed throughout the organizational structure. Financial groups are vertical groups, because they control cash flow throughout the corporation. Money is made available to support operations using budgets and accounts. The detailed breakdown of these budgets is determined through the program planning process. Each group then receives its budgeted money and purchases materials and resources directly. The financial groups only negotiate discounts with suppliers in terms of percentages.

Accounts are funded through cash reserves. Capital expenditures are usually financed. The financial groups acquire loans and issue debt instruments such as bonds. These are financing activities. Investment activities include purchasing bonds, stocks, and mutual funds. The corporate-level finance group also issues and buys back stocks and distributes dividends.

The work tasks for the financial department are discovered using the same procedure presented in Chapter 6. Potential tasks are as follows:

- Trade bonds/fixed income.
- Trade stocks.
- Trade mutual funds.
- Transfer money/shares.
- Create/delete accounts.
- Acquire loans.
- Distribute dividends.
- Issue bonds.
- Issue stocks.
- Receive payments.
- Issue payments.

After all tasks are defined in terms of process models, you can discover the financial business processes. The financial business processes are represented using the IDEF0 format, which allows them to be summarized as a hierarchy. This highest level can be represented as a single process, as shown in Figure 9-3.

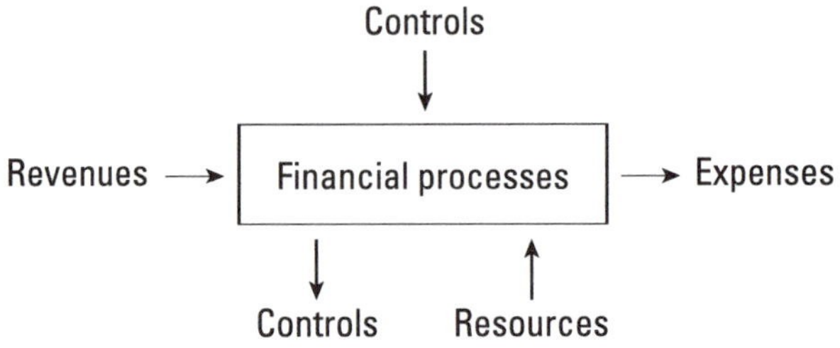

Figure 9-3. Representation of high-level financial business processes

Product Engineering

The product engineering area is organized into a single hierarchy that mirrors the decomposition of the product into systems, subsystems, and components. This is a consequence of minimizing the coupling between groups (see Chapter 4) and facilitates the roll-down of product requirements (see Chapter 5). The product engineering area follows the lean organization structure, with vertical management groups located at each level in the hierarchy. The number of levels in the product engineering organization depends on the complexity of the products being engineered. A generic example of a product engineering organization structure is shown in Figure 9-4.

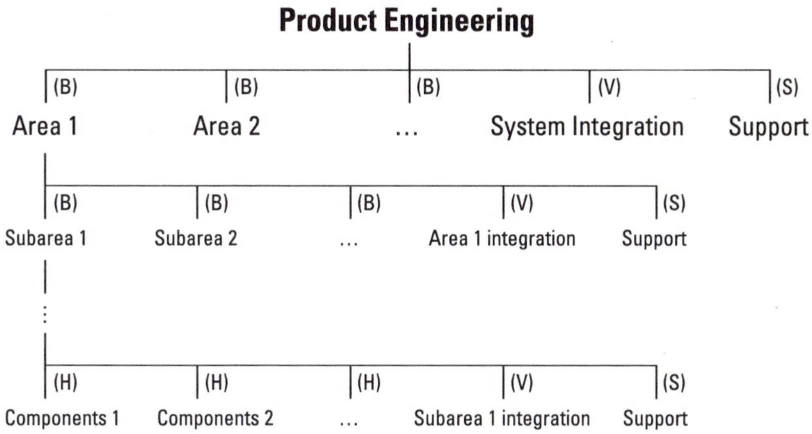

Figure 9-4. Generic product engineering organization structure

The main activity of the product engineering department is the creation of product designs. The work tasks are discovered using the procedure presented in Chapter 6; fortunately, a large number of product engineering activities are well suited for the business process discovery procedure. These include analysis, test, drafting, and other similar activities. Potential tasks are as follows:

- Create product design math data.
- Create product design analysis model.

- Analyze the product design.
- Procure prototype hardware.
- Test the product design.
- Conduct geometric tolerance study.
- Conduct product DFMEA.
- Create product design specifications.
- Conduct cost analysis.
- Select supplier for subsystems and components.
- Validate production processes.
- Track product performance in the field.

Because the product engineering business processes are represented using the IDEF0 format, they can be summarized as a hierarchy. A high-level representation of product engineering business processes is shown in Figure 9-5.

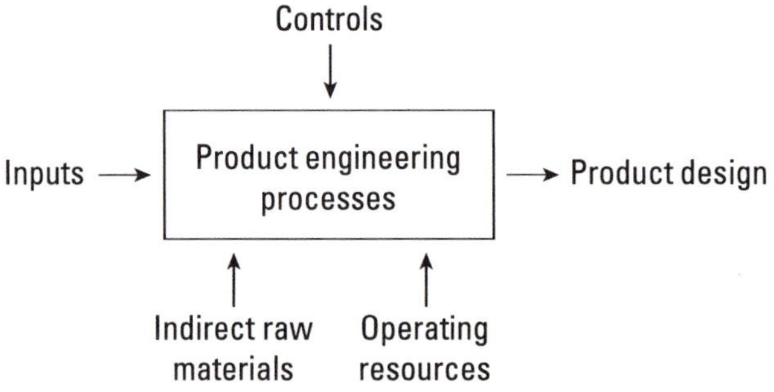

Figure 9-5. Representation of high-level product engineering business processes

Manufacturing

The manufacturing area is organized similarly to the product engineering department. However, instead of being subdivided based on the product structure, it is subdivided based on the manufacturing processes. The lowest level of the organization structure includes the basic operations that are performed. These operations are represented as tasks and sequenced together to form processes.

The people that perform the tasks are responsible for supplying the resources and indirect raw materials. These include equipment and equipment-supporting materials (like machining fluid). It is the responsibility of the process managers to supply the raw materials to be processed into final goods. The manufacturing organization is organized as shown in Figure 9-6.

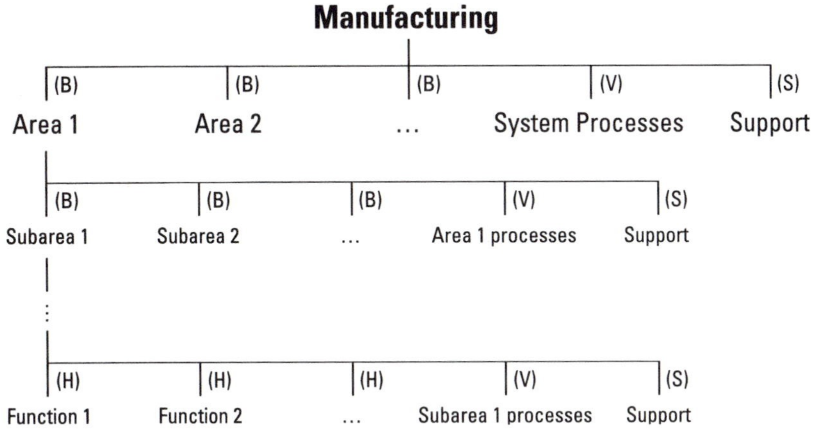

Figure 9-6. Manufacturing organization structure

Manufacturing departments are embedded with product engineering groups at the levels corresponding to the products that are produced. For example, if a company manufactures both vehicles and engines, the resulting organization structure would have two manufacturing departments: one at the vehicle level (system) and one at the engine level (subsystem). This is illustrated in Figure 9-7.

Each embedded manufacturing department is independent and usually corresponds to specific facilities (plants). These facilities are managed using the lean manufacturing philosophy. The standard work tasks for each manufacturing department are modeled in the same way as all other corporate tasks (using IDEF0 process models). Potential tasks are as follows:

- Purchase/lease of equipment
- Purchase of indirect materials
- Assembly operation 1

- Assembly operation 2
- Machining operation 1
- Machining operation 2
- Welding operation 1
- Welding operation 2
- Stamping operation 1
- Stamping operation 2
- Other operations

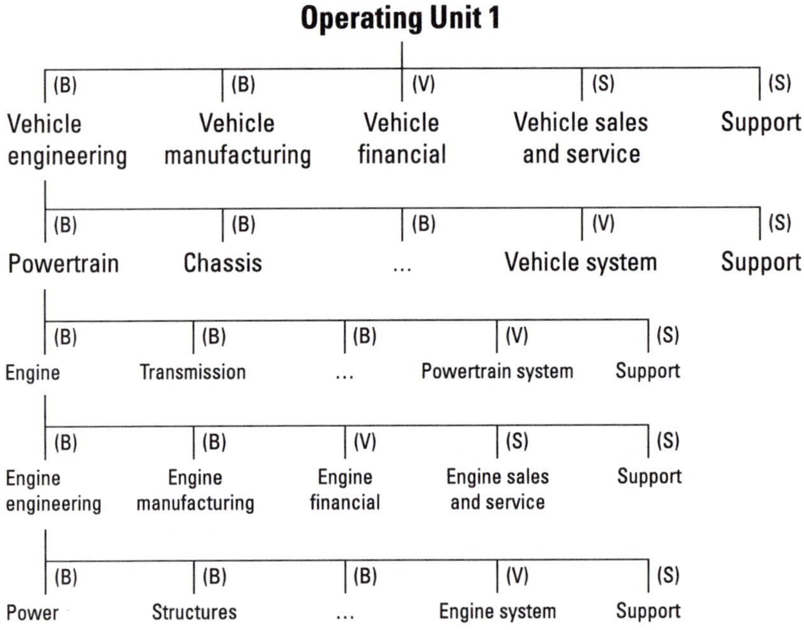

Figure 9-7. Organization structure showing embedded manufacturing departments

Because the manufacturing business processes are represented using the IDEF0 format, they can be summarized as a hierarchy. The highest level can be represented as a single process, as shown in Figure 9-8.

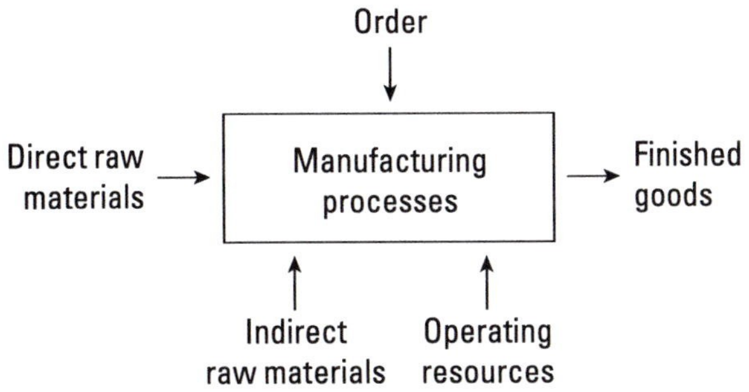

Figure 9-8. Representation of high-level manufacturing processes

Sales and Service

The sales and service area is considered a support group. Each level in the organization structure whose products and/or services are sold has a sales and service group to support this activity. The sales and service groups are embedded into the corporate organization structure in a similar manner as the manufacturing groups. One sales and service group supports one or more manufacturing groups. Large service and sales groups are themselves organized into horizontal, vertical, and support groups.

The standard work tasks for the sales and service department are discovered using the same procedure as for the other areas. Potential tasks are as follows:

- Take order.
- Report status of order.
- Provide product information.
- Provide sales quote.
- Solicit sales.
- Create advertisement.
- Buy advertising media.
- Schedule service.
- Perform service.

After all tasks are defined in terms of process models, the sales and service business processes are discovered. This highest level can be represented as a single process, as shown in Figure 9-9.

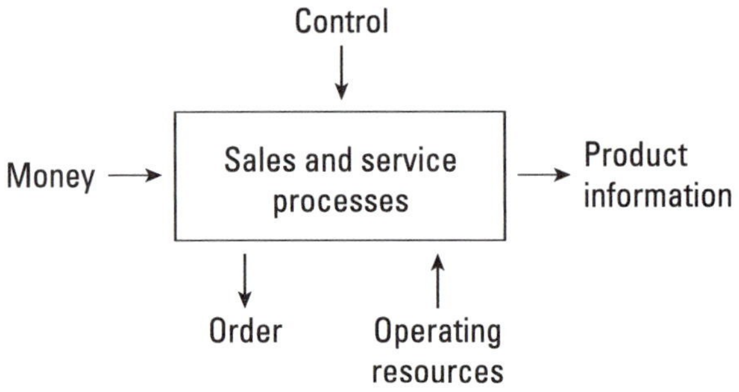

Figure 9-9. Representation of high-level sales and service business processes

Creating a Lean Corporation

The lean corporation is created when all departments have their processes modeled and managed using the fundamental features of the lean philosophy. This is a significant undertaking. Fortunately, the approach described in this book is an evolutionary way to achieve this goal. When finished, the entire corporation becomes one large business process that is managed as a hierarchy. To illustrate this, the business process corresponding to the corporate areas

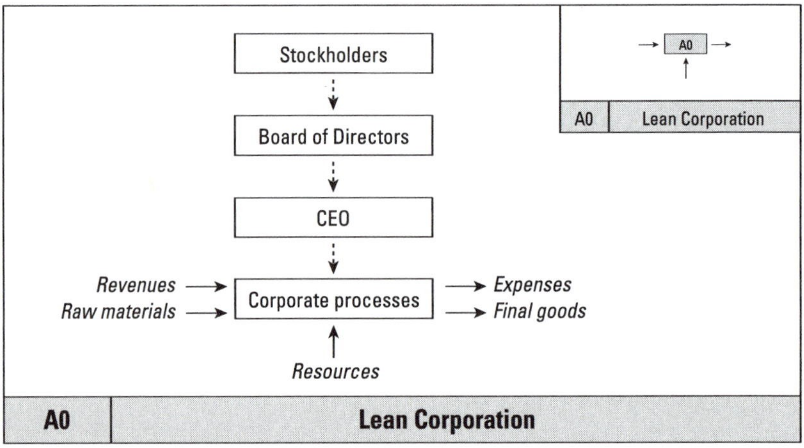

Figure 9-10. Lean corporation

defined in the chapter is displayed using node-descendent views in Figures 9-10 through 9-16.

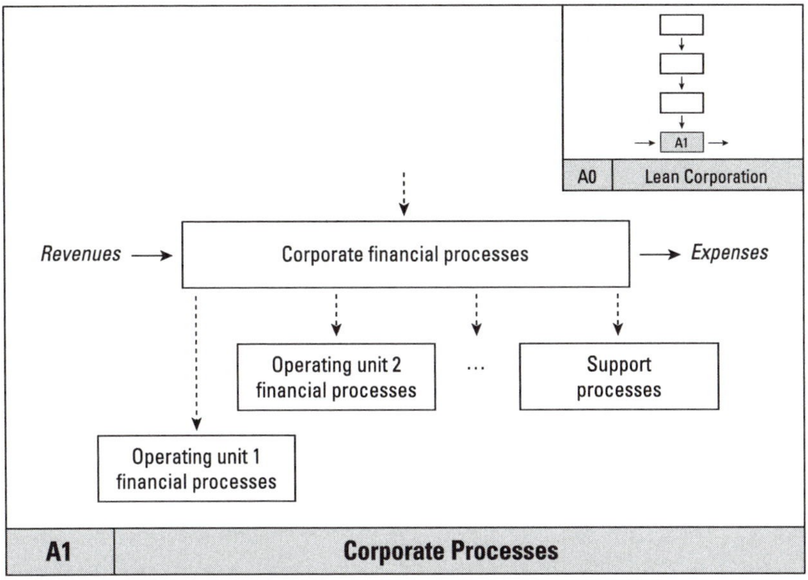

Figure 9-11. Corporate processes

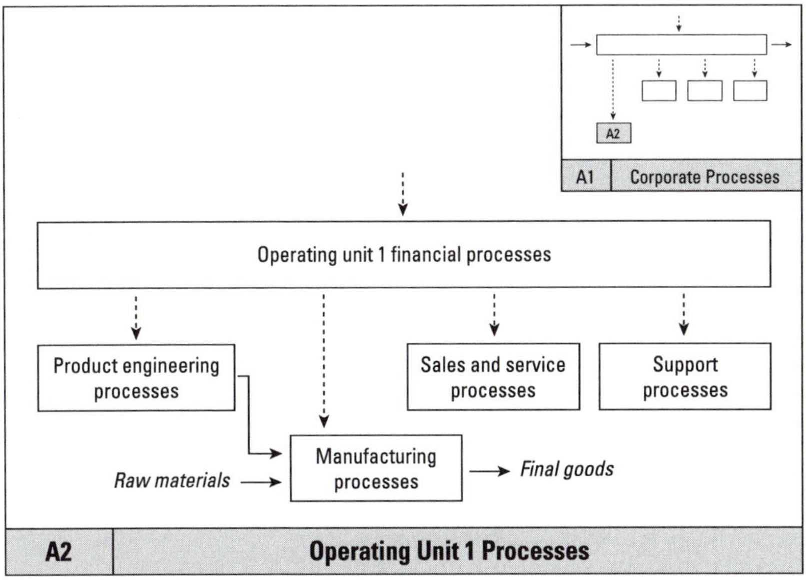

Figure 9-12. Operating unit 1 processes

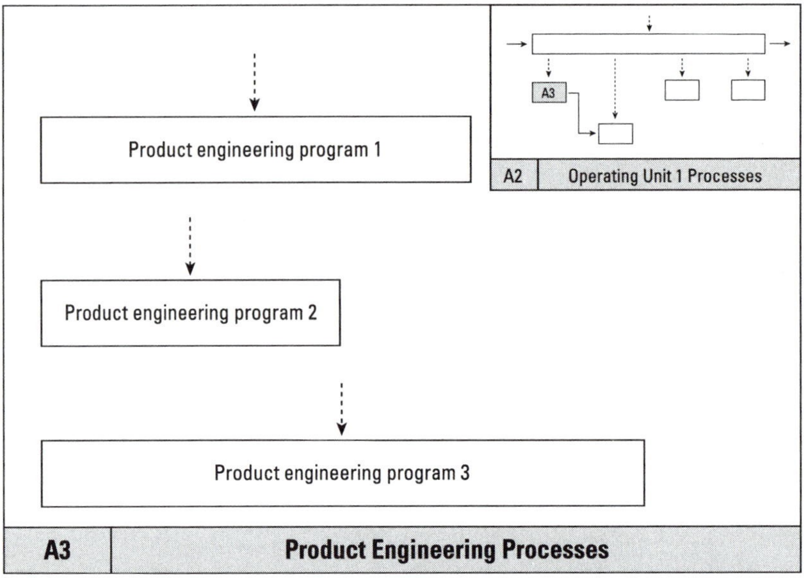

Figure 9-13. Product engineering processes

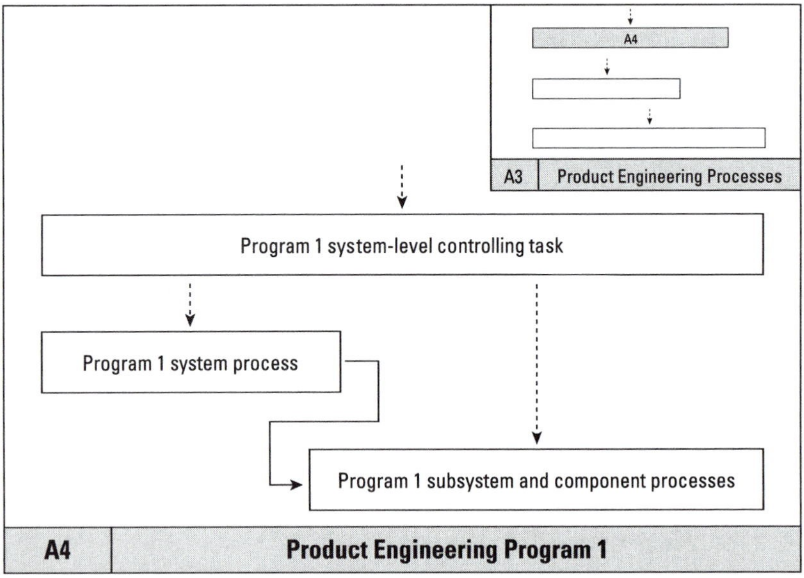

Figure 9-14. Product engineering program 1

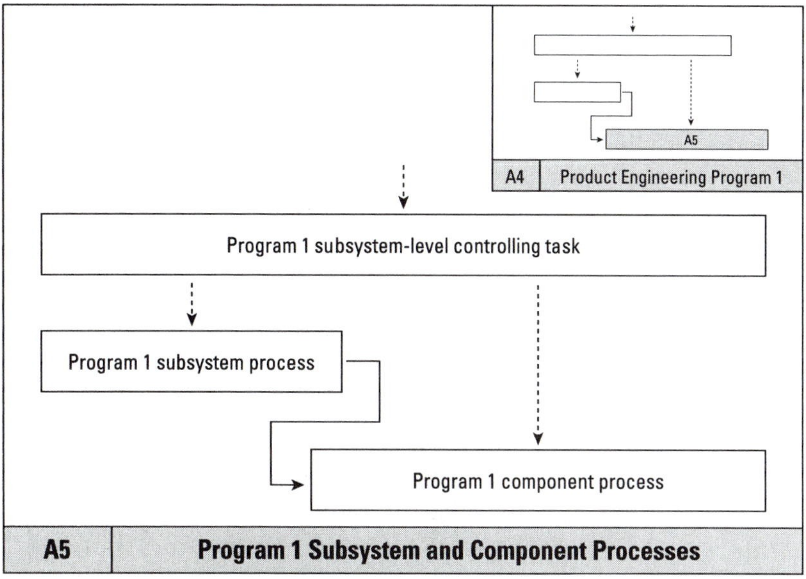

Figure 9-15. Program 1 subsystem and component processes

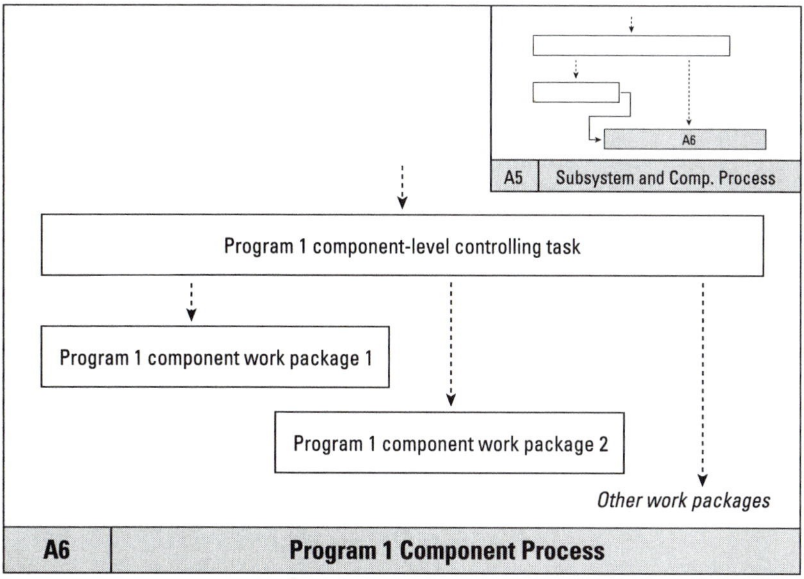

Figure 9-16. Program 1 component process

Representing business processes in the format shown in Figures 9-10 through 9-16 facilitates their management using the lean philosophy. The corporate hierarchies (organizational structure and program structure) implement clearly defined roles and responsibilities. Decoupled processes and systems are established by analyzing the business processes that are created from the IDEF0 process models. Requirement roll-down is achieved according to the program structure. Web-enabled technologies are used to manage all corporate information including the generation of the financial statements.

The application of the concepts in this book to actual corporations is straightforward. A simplified example is presented in Part IV to further demonstrate the approaches. The only difference between the example and actual applications is in the size and complexity of the business processes; otherwise, the approaches used are the same. The transformation process is evolutionary and usually takes several years to perform, but the end result is the creation of a lean corporation.

PART IV

Looking at Examples of Lean Business Processes

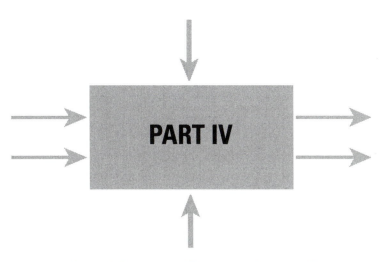

Chapter 10

An Example of Discovering Your Business Processes

Business processes are effectively discovered using the twelve-step procedure presented in Chapter 6. To further demonstrate this procedure, this chapter gives you an example implementation. This implementation is typical of actual implementations, except that it has been reduced in size and complexity so that the main ideas can be presented more easily.

The example uses the acceleration and fuel economy of an automobile as the system-level performance requirements to be optimized, and the process used to assess these requirements is discovered. This example is further developed in Chapters 11 and 12 to illustrate how the discovered business processes are reengineered and implemented.

Step 1: Determine Which Business Processes to Discover

The first step in discovering your business processes is to determine which ones to discover. For this example, the process to discover is the one used to assess vehicle acceleration and fuel economy performance. A hypothetical vehicle engineering organization is created, and three groups are identified to be involved in the project; these are the vehicle performance group, engine performance group, and engine component group.

- The vehicle performance group is a system-level group that is responsible for analyzing the vehicle acceleration and fuel economy.
- The engine performance group is a subsystem-level group that is responsible for analyzing engine power and fuel consumption.

- The engine component group is a component-level group that is responsible for analyzing the mechanical performance of the power-generating components in the engine.

The three groups are specifically selected to be system-, subsystem-, and component-level groups so that the requirement roll-down process can be demonstrated.

The objective of the business process discovery project is to determine which process to use to assess vehicle acceleration and fuel economy performance. The goal is to make the design process visible in terms of time, quality, and cost. Time and cost are made visible by creating a program plan that includes tasks with durations, linkages, and resource requirements. Quality is made visible through the use of performance reviews. The system-level performance review is used to establish an overall rating for the vehicle based on customers' needs and wants. Achieving a high overall rating is a balancing process, where trade-offs are made to create the greatest value to the customer.

Step 2: Formalize the Project

Formalizing the project includes documenting the project objective and scope, selecting a project manager, and establishing a timeline. The project objective is to determine the process used for the assessment of vehicle acceleration and fuel economy performance. The project scope corresponding to this objective is to define the inputs, outputs, requirements, and resources used for the tasks that constitute this process and to create the performance reviews that correspond to the system, subsystem, and component requirements.

Each group included in the project has one section leader identified who is responsible for defining the work tasks in his or her group. The project manager is selected from the system-level vertical group. This is done because the system-level vertical group is responsible for performing the business process, and you want to have the people who perform the process responsible for discovering it.

The timeline shown in Chapter 6 (Figure 6-1) is used. All steps are given one week, except for Steps 3 and 11. Step 3 is a controlling task, thus it runs parallel to the tasks that it controls (controlling tasks are discussed in Chapter 4). Step 11 is the documentation of the procedures, which is done only after the success of the project is determined, as part of the implementation of the process.

After the project is formalized, it must be approved by management. The manager who is one level above the highest level group included in the project approves the project. When this is done, the project officially begins.

Step 3: Establish Formats and Hierarchies

Now that the project is formalized and approved, the formats and hierarchies must be established. The formats describe how the information will be collected. The data needed and numbering schemes are determined and are specified as templates. (You can create your own templates using the ones in this chapter as examples.)

The first hierarchy to create is the organization hierarchy. Only the groups included in the project and their management levels need to be shown. The organization structure for this example is shown in Figure 10-1.

The groups included in the project are shown in boxes. Notice, however, that the Powertrain Performance Group is not included in the project. This was done to demonstrate that business process discovery can be done using any selection of groups. If interactions with the Powertrain Performance Group are part of the business processes, they will show up in the discovery project as external inputs. It is not uncommon for a business process to couple groups at different levels of the organization structure. Two of the selected groups are support groups, while a third is a horizontal group.

Next, the product hierarchy is created. The product hierarchy represents the decomposition of the vehicle system into subsystems and components. The organization structure was designed with this in mind, using the concepts presented in Chapters 4 and 5. The result is that the product hierarchy corresponds to the vertical reporting structure of the organization (program structure) and the breakdown of the components integrated by these groups. This is shown in Figure 10-2.

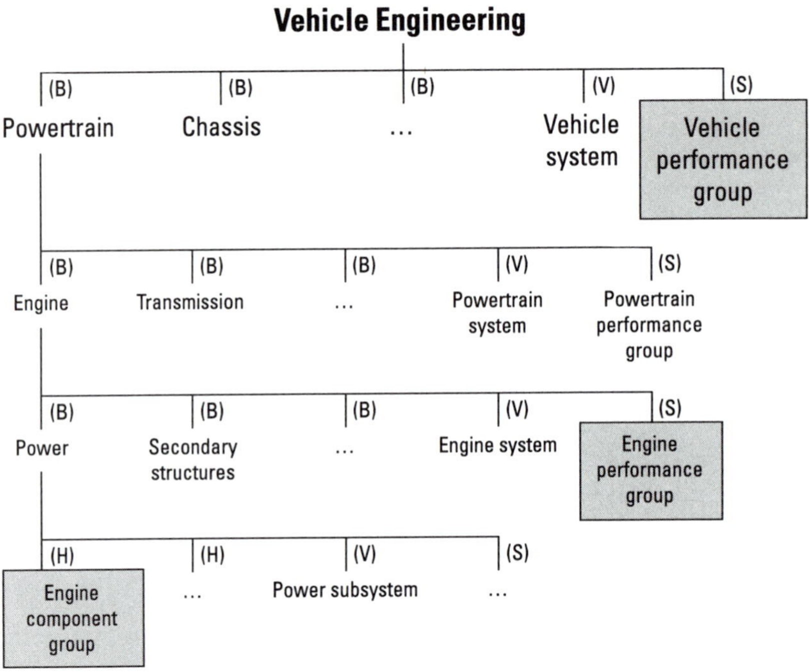

Figure 10-1. Organization structure for the example

Each node in the product hierarchy will have an associated performance review document. The vehicle system group will have the system-level performance review. The Engine System and Power Subsystem groups will have subsystem-level performance reviews. These three performance reviews are created for this example. The component-level performance reviews list component design specifications, as discussed in Chapter 5. Their creation is relatively straightforward, thus they are not presented in this example.

Other hierarchies are developed as the other steps are performed. They are described as they are created.

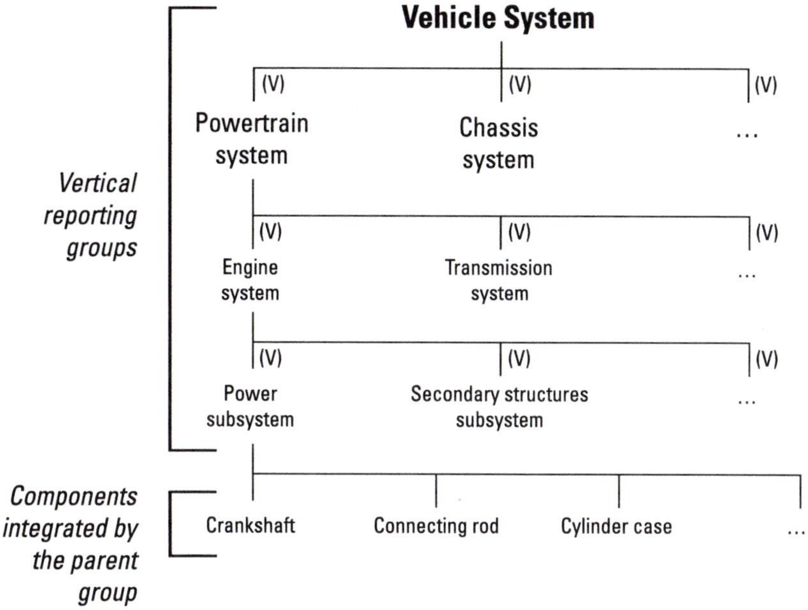

Figure 10-2. Product hierarchy for the example

Step 4: Document the Outputs

For this step, the section leaders document their outputs. Outputs are the items that are created from the execution of tasks. They are documented first to focus on the end results (deliverables) that are produced by the process. For this example, the Vehicle Performance Group conducts simulations to predict the performance of the vehicle. Their outputs are shown in Table 10-1.

The Engine Performance group conducts simulations to predict the performance of the engine. Their outputs are shown in Table 10-2.

The Engine Components Group conducts simulations to predict the performance of the components. Their ouputs are shown in Table 10-3.

The two columns corresponding to the output and requirement numbers are not used in this step. These numbers are assigned in later steps. Modifications and additions to the outputs are done during the input–output negotiation meeting (see

Chapter 6). Some outputs are inputs to other tasks. Others are compared to requirements and are shown on performance reviews.

Table 10-1. Vehicle Performance Group Outputs

Output #	Output Name	Output Type	Output Units	Product Hierarchy Node	Requirement #
	0–30 mph time	Scalar value	s	Vehicle System	
	0–60 mph time	Scalar value	s	Vehicle System	
	1/4 mile time	Scalar value	s	Vehicle System	
	1/4 mile speed	Scalar value	mph	Vehicle System	
	45–65 mph time	Scalar value	s	Vehicle System	
	City fuel economy	Scalar value	mpg	Vehicle System	
	Highway fuel economy	Scalar value	mpg	Vehicle System	
	Driving range	Scalar value	miles	Vehicle System	
	Annual fuel cost	Scalar value	USD	Vehicle System	

Table 10-2. Engine Performance Group Outputs

Output #	Output Name	Output Type	Output Units	Product Hierarchy Node	Requirement #
	Engine brake horsepower	Function	hp vs. rpm	Engine System	
	Engine brake torque	Function	ft-lbs vs. rpm	Engine System	
	Engine peak horsepower	Scalar value	hp	Engine System	
	Engine peak torque	Scalar value	ft-lbs	Engine System	
	Engine cylinder pressures at peak horsepower	Functions	MPa vs. s	Engine System	
	Engine zero-torque line	Function	ft-lbs vs. rpm	Engine System	
	Engine brake specific fuel consumption	Function	lbs/bhp-hr vs. rpm	Engine System	
	Crankshaft loading at peak horsepower	Functions	N vs. s	Engine System	
	Connecting rod loading at peak horsepower	Functions	N vs. s	Engine System	
	Cylinder case loading at peak horsepower	Functions	N vs. s	Engine System	

Table 10-3. Engine Component Group Outputs

Output #	Output Name	Output Type	Output Units	Product Hierarchy Node	Requirement #
	Crankshaft stress at peak horsepower	Scalar value	MPa	Crankshaft	
	Crankshaft fatigue diagram at peak horsepower	Plot	MPa vs. MPa	Crankshaft	
	Crankshaft safety factor at peak horsepower	Scalar value		Crankshaft	
	Connecting rod stress at peak horsepower	Scalar value	MPa	Connecting Rod	
	Connecting rod fatigue diagram at peak horsepower	Plot	MPa vs. MPa	Connecting Rod	
	Connecting rod safety factor at peak horsepower	Scalar value		Connecting Rod	
	Cylinder case stress at peak horsepower	Scalar value	MPa	Cylinder Case	
	Cylinder case fatigue diagram at peak horsepower	Plot	MPa vs. MPa	Cylinder Case	
	Cylinder case safety factor at peak horsepower	Scalar value		Cylinder Case	

Step 5: Document the Controls

The next step is to document the controls. In this example, the controls are the performance requirements used to assess the outputs. Outputs and their associated performance requirements are closely related. Often they are identical, except that the requirement specifies the desired value (target), while the output specifies the value that is achieved. For this example, the outputs for the Vehicle Performance Group will all have corresponding requirements. Thus, all that is needed is to copy the output names to requirement names and fill out the rest of the information. The requirements are shown in Table 10-4.

Table 10-4. Vehicle Performance Group Requirements

Requirement Number	Requirement Name	Requirement Type	Requirement Units	Product Hierarchy Node	Performance Review Node
VEH.PRF.ACC-1	0–30 mph time rating function	0–100 rating	s	Vehicle System	Acceleration
VEH.PRF.ACC-2	0–60 mph time rating function	0–100 rating	s	Vehicle System	Acceleration
VEH.PRF.ACC-3	1/4 mile time rating function	0–100 rating	s	Vehicle System	Acceleration
VEH.PRF.ACC-4	1/4 mile speed rating function	0–100 rating	mph	Vehicle System	Acceleration
VEH.PRF.ACC-5	45–65 mph time rating function	0–100 rating	s	Vehicle System	Acceleration
VEH.FE.OFE-1	City fuel economy rating function	0–100 rating	mpg	Vehicle System	Overall Fuel Economy
VEH.FE.OFE-2	Highway fuel economy rating function	0–100 rating	mpg	Vehicle System	Overall Fuel Economy
VEH.CNV.SR-1	Driving range rating function	0–100 rating	miles	Vehicle System	Service and Range
VEH.VAL.OC-1	Annual fuel cost rating function	0–100 rating	USD	Vehicle System	Operating Cost

The requirement type indicates how the item is assessed. For vehicle level requirements, the assessment is done using 0–100 ratings. These allow the system to be optimized and balanced to achieve the highest value to the customer. Each requirement identifies the product hierarchy node with which it is associated; this determines the performance review in which the requirements appear. The corresponding performance review node is also specified. Requirement numbering for the example uses the performance review hierarchy path, followed by a number. For example, requirement VEH.PRF.ACC-1 is the first requirement in the branch of the performance review from Vehicle System (VEH) to Performance (PRF) to Acceleration (ACC). Requirement information is owned by the group that owns the corresponding outputs.

The assessment of system-level requirements is usually program specific. Typically, a competitive assessment is conducted to determine appropriate target values. As discussed in Chapter 5, there are many useful ways to assess the performance of a requirement. The easiest approach is to consider mean values, as is done in this chapter. In Chapter 11, a more comprehensive approach is presented as an example of reengineering the business process.

Rating functions can be determined from tests, surveys, or from published data. For this example, data from a product-rating publication was analyzed for each vehicle's 0–60 time and overall fuel economy. The average value of the performance parameters were calculated at each grade level. Then, a numerical rating was assigned to these average values using the grading scale shown in Chapter 5 (e.g., in Table 5-1, excellent = 95, very good = 85, and so on). These data points were then linearly interpolated and extrapolated to create the rating functions. The result for the overall fuel economy rating function is shown in Figure 10-3.

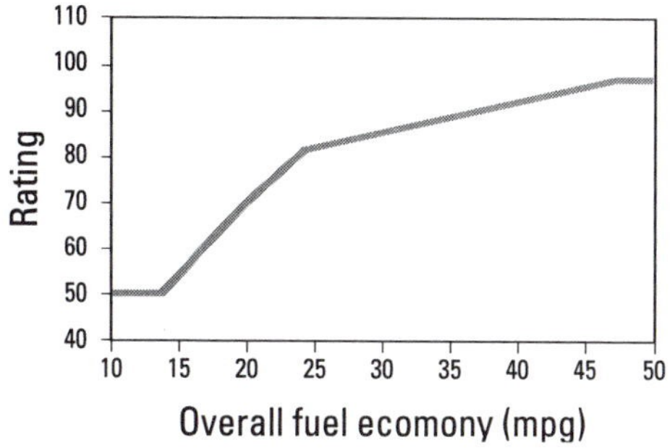

Figure 10-3. Overall fuel economy rating function

Similarly, the 0–60 mph time rating function was determined and is shown in Figure 10-4.

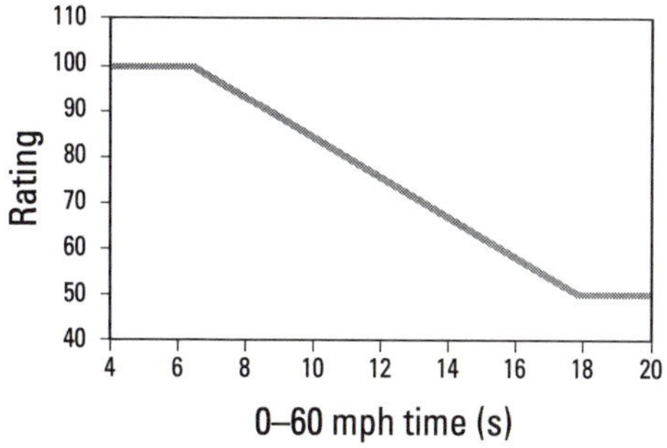

Figure 10-4. Time rating function for 0–60 mph

Each system-level requirement should have a corresponding rating function based on a unified rating scale (0–100). Then, the performance review hierarchy serves as a summary of the ratings at each level. The highest level node is the overall rating. This is shown later in Chapter 12 (Figures 12-2 and 12-10). It is not necessary to develop the assessment rating functions during this step of the business process discovery project, but this was done for this example to demonstrate how these rating functions are developed and used.

The requirements for the Engine Performance Group and Engine Component Group are shown in Tables 10-5 and 10-6, respectively.

The requirement types for subsystem- and component-level requirements are simple target values that are determined by the optimization of the system. This includes minimum and maximum requirement types, as shown. Each group's requirements are associated with their corresponding product hierarchy node and performance review node. Requirements are numbered according to the previously specified numbering scheme.

Step 6: Document the Tasks

After the outputs and requirements are determined, it is time to organize them into tasks. Tasks are the building blocks of programs, so they must be determined with this application in mind. The basic idea is that programs specify content. This content is translated into requirements that are needed to produce the desired product. The requirements then dictate which tasks should be executed based on the relation of requirements to outputs. Generally, several outputs will correspond to the same requirement, as in the case for analysis and test tasks. Furthermore, the program will have constraints as to the time, cost, and quality needs. Thus, a risk assessment is needed to determine an acceptably balanced plan.

Tasks are generally organized based on the performance requirements that they assess. Outputs that are related to the same requirement node are candidates for becoming a task. For the

Table 10-5. Engine Performance Group Requirements

Requirement Number	Requirement Name	Requirement Type	Requirement Units	Product Hierarchy Node	Performance Review Node
ENG.PRF-1	Engine peak horsepower target	Minimum	hp	Engine System	Performance
ENG.PRF-2	Engine RPM at peak horsepower target	Maximum	rpm	Engine System	Performance
ENG.PRF-3	Engine peak torque target	Minimum	ft-lbs	Engine System	Performance
ENG.PRF-4	Engine RPM at peak torque target	Maximum	rpm	Engine System	Performance
ENG.FE-1	Engine brake specific fuel consumption target	Maximum	lbs/bhp-hr	Engine System	Fuel Economy
ENG.CRK-1	Crankshaft loading at peak horsepower target	Maximum	N	Engine System	Crankshaft
ENG.CRD-1	Connecting rod loading at peak horsepower target	Maximum	N	Engine System	Connecting Rod
ENG.CCS-1	Cylinder case loading at peak horsepower target	Maximum	N	Engine System	Cylinder Case

Table 10-6. Engine Component Group Requirements

Requirement Number	Requirement Name	Requirement Type	Requirement Units	Product Hierarchy Node	Performance Review Node
PWR.CRK-1	Crankshaft stress at peak horsepower target	Maximum	MPa	Power Subsystem	Crankshaft
PWR.CRK-2	Crankshaft safety factor at peak horsepower target	Minimum		Power Subsystem	Crankshaft
PWR.CRD-1	Connecting rod stress at peak horsepower target	Maximum	MPa	Power Subsystem	Connecting Rod
PWR.CRD-2	Connecting rod safety factor at peak horsepower target	Minimum		Power Subsystem	Connecting Rod
PWR.CCS-1	Cylinder case stress at peak horsepower target	Maximum	MPa	Power Subsystem	Cylinder Case
PWR.CCS-2	Cylinder case safety factor at peak horsepower target	Minimum		Power Subsystem	Cylinder Case

Vehicle Performance Group, this automatically leads to four tasks. These tasks are shown in Table 10-7, and the numbered outputs are shown in Table 10-8.

Table 10-7. Vehicle Performance Group Tasks

Task Number	Task Name	Task Type	Task Duration (Days)	Organization Structure Node
VE.VPG.1	Vehicle Acceleration	Analysis	5	Vehicle Performance Group
VE.VPG.2	Vehicle Fuel Economy	Analysis	5	Vehicle Performance Group
VE.VPG.3	Vehicle Driving Range	Analysis	0.1	Vehicle Performance Group
VE.VPG.4	Vehicle Annual Fuel Cost	Analysis	0.1	Vehicle Performance Group

Table 10-8. Vehicle Performance Group Numbered Outputs

Output Number	Output Name	Output Type	Output Units	Product Hierarchy Node	Require-ment Number
VE.VPG.1-1	0–30 mph time	Scalar value	s	Vehicle System	VEH.PRF.ACC-1
VE.VPG.1-2	0–60 mph time	Scalar value	s	Vehicle System	VEH.PRF.ACC-2
VE.VPG.1-3	1/4 mile time	Scalar value	s	Vehicle System	VEH.PRF.ACC-3
VE.VPG.1-4	1/4 mile speed	Scalar value	mph	Vehicle System	VEH.PRF.ACC-4
VE.VPG.1-5	45–65 mph time	Scalar value	s	Vehicle System	VEH.PRF.ACC-5
VE.VPG.2-1	City fuel economy	Scalar value	mpg	Vehicle System	VEH.FE.OFE-1
VE.VPG.2-2	Highway fuel economy	Scalar value	mpg	Vehicle System	VEH.FE.OFE-2
VE.VPG.3-1	Driving range	Scalar value	miles	Vehicle System	VEH.CNV.SR-1
VE.VPG.4-1	Annual fuel cost	Scalar value	USD	Vehicle System	VEH.VAL.OC-1

The task type indicates the nature of the task. Common task types for product engineering are design, analysis, test, and so on. For this example, all task types are analysis. Task duration is entered to represent the average amount of time the task takes to complete in worker-days. This information is used to create project timing. The organization hierarchy node for each task is specified. This is the group that owns the task. Tasks are numbered based on the owner's node in the organization hierarchy. The task number is the path to that node, followed by a number. For example, task VE.VPG.1 is the first task corresponding to the path from Vehicle Engineering (VE) to Vehicle Performance Group (VPG).

Outputs are assigned numbers by appending a number to the task number. For example VE.VPG.1-1 is the first output of task VE.VPG.1.

The Engine Performance Group and Engine Component Group tasks are identified using the same approach; each group defines three tasks. The resulting tasks and numbered outputs are shown in Tables 10-9 through 10-12.

With the tasks, outputs, and requirements defined, the master lists can be created. This is done in Step 7.

Table 10-9. Engine Performance Group Tasks

Task Number	Task Name	Task Type	Task Duration (Days)	Organization Structure Node
EE.EPG.1	Engine Performance	Analysis	20	Engine Performance Group
EE.EPG.2	Engine Fuel Economy	Analysis	20	Engine Performance Group
EE.EPG.3	Engine Dynamic Loading	Analysis	5	Engine Performance Group

Table 10-10. Engine Performance Group Numbered Outputs

Output Number	Output Name	Output Type	Output Units	Product Hierarchy Node	Require-ment Number
EE.EPG.1-1	Engine brake horsepower	Function	hp vs. rpm	Engine System	ENG.PRF-1
EE.EPG.1-2	Engine brake torque	Function	ft-lbs vs. rpm	Engine System	ENG.PRF-2
EE.EPG.1-3	Engine peak horsepower	Scalar value	hp	Engine System	ENG.PRF-3
EE.EPG.1-4	Engine peak torque	Scalar value	ft-lbs	Engine System	ENG.PRF-4
EE.EPG.1-5	Engine cylinder pressures at peak horsepower	Functions	MPa vs. s	Engine System	
EE.EPG.1-6	Engine zero-torque line	Function	ft-lbs vs. rpm	Engine System	
EE.EPG.2-1	Engine brake specific fuel consumption	Function	lbs/bhp-hr vs. rpm	Engine System	ENG.FE-1
EE.EPG.3-1	Crankshaft loading at peak horsepower	Functions	N vs. s	Engine System	ENG.CRK-1
EE.EPG.3-2	Connecting rod loading at peak horsepower	Functions	N vs. s	Engine System	ENG.CRD-1
EE.EPG.3-3	Cylinder case loading at peak horsepower	Functions	N vs. s	Engine System	ENG.CCS-2

Table 10-11. Engine Component Group Tasks

Task Number	Task Name	Task Type	Task Duration (Days)	Organization Structure Node
PE.ECG.1	Crankshaft Durability	Analysis	10	Engine Component Group
PE.ECG.2	Connecting Rod Durability	Analysis	5	Engine Component Group
PE.ECG.3	Cylinder Case Durability	Analysis	20	Engine Component Group

Table 10-12. Engine Component Group Numbered Outputs

Output Number	Output Name	Output Type	Output Units	Product Hierarchy Node	Require-ment Number
PE.ECG.1-1	Crankshaft stress at peak horsepower	Scalar value	MPa	Crankshaft	PWR.CRK-1
PE.ECG.1-2	Crankshaft fatigue diagram at peak horsepower	Plot	MPa vs. MPa	Crankshaft	
PE.ECG.1-3	Crankshaft safety factor at peak horsepower	Scalar value		Crankshaft	PWR.CRK-2
PE.ECG.2-1	Connecting rod stress at peak horsepower	Scalar value	MPa	Connecting Rod	PWR.CRD-1
PE.ECG.2-2	Connecting rod fatigue diagram at peak horsepower	Plot	MPa vs. MPa	Connecting Rod	
PE.ECG.2-3	Connecting rod safety factor at peak horsepower	Scalar value		Connecting Rod	PWR.CRD-2
PE.ECG.3-1	Cylinder case stress at peak horsepower	Scalar value	MPa	Cylinder Case	PWR.CCS-1
PE.ECG.3-2	Cylinder case fatigue diagram at peak horsepower	Plot	MPa vs. MPa	Cylinder Case	
PE.ECG.3-3	Cylinder case safety factor at peak horsepower	Scalar value		Cylinder Case	PWR.CCS-2

Step 7: Create the Master Lists

The next step is to create the master lists of tasks, outputs, and requirements. These lists are used to select the inputs for the tasks. A small number of items (<100) can be displayed as lists. A large number of items (>100) can be displayed using hierarchies. Tasks are usually displayed in the organization hierarchy, outputs in the product hierarchy, and requirements in their corresponding performance review hierarchies. Although this example has a small number of items, they are displayed using hierarchies to demonstrate this functionality. This is shown in Figures 10-5 through 10-9.

- Vehicle Engineering
  - Vehicle Performance Group
    - VE.VPG.1 Vehicle Acceleration
    - VE.VPG.2 Vehicle Fuel Economy
    - VE.VPG.3 Vehicle Driving Range
    - VE.VPG.4 Vehicle Annual Fuel Cost
  - Powertrain
    - Engine
      - Engine Performance Group
        - EE.EPG.1 Engine Performance
        - EE.EPG.2 Engine Fuel Economy
        - EE.EPG.3 Engine Dynamic Loading
      - Power
        - Engine Component Group
          - PE.ECG.1 Crankshaft Durability
          - PE.ECG.2 Connecting Rod Durability
          - PE.ECG.3 Cylinder Case Durability
        - Power Subsystem
      - Secondary Structures
      - Engine System
    - Transmission
    - Powertrain System
    - Powertrain Performance Group
  - Chassis
  - Vehicle System

Figure 10-5. Master list of tasks displayed in the organization hierarchy

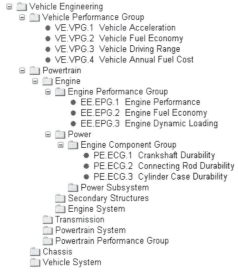

- Vehicle System
  - VE.VPG.1-1 0-30 mph time
  - VE.VPG.1-2 0-60 mph time
  - VE.VPG.1-3 1/4 mile time
  - VE.VPG.1-4 1/4 mile speed
  - VE.VPG.1-5 45-65 mph time
  - VE.VPG.2-1 City fuel economy
  - VE.VPG.2-2 Highway fuel economy
  - VE.VPG.3-1 Driving range
  - VE.VPG.4-1 Annual fuel cost
  - Powertrain System
    - Engine System
      - Power Subsystem
        - EE.EPG.1-1 Engine brake horsepower
        - EE.EPG.1-2 Engine brake torque
        - EE.EPG.1-3 Engine peak horsepower
        - EE.EPG.1-4 Engine peak torque
        - EE.EPG.1-5 Engine cylinder pressures at peak horsepower
        - EE.EPG.1-6 Engine zero-torque line
        - EE.EPG.2-1 Engine brake specific fuel consumption
        - EE.EPG.3-1 Crankshaft loading at peak horsepower
        - EE.EPG.3-2 Connecting rod loading at peak horsepower
        - EE.EPG.3-3 Cylinder case loading at peak horsepower
      - Crankshaft
        - PE.ECG.1-1 Crankshaft stress at peak horsepower
        - PE.ECG.1-2 Crankshaft fatigue diagram at peak horsepower
        - PE.ECG.1-3 Crankshaft safety factor at peak horsepower
      - Connection Rod
        - PE.ECG.2-1 Connecting rod stress at peak horsepower
        - PE.ECG.2-2 Connecting rod fatigue diagram at peak horsepower
        - PE.ECG.2-3 Connecting rod safety factor at peak horsepower
      - Cylinder Case
        - PE.ECG.3-1 Cylinder case stress at peak horsepower
        - PE.ECG.3-2 Cylinder case fatigue diagram at peak horsepower
        - PE.ECG.3-3 Cylinder case safety factor at peak horsepower
      - Secondary Structures System
    - Transmission System
  - Chassis System

Figure 10-6. Master list of outputs displayed in the product hierarchy

- Vehicle System
  - Performance
    - Acceleration
      - VEH.PRF.ACC-1 0-30 mph time
      - VEH.PRF.ACC-2 0-60 mph time
      - VEH.PRF.ACC-3 1/4 mile time
      - VEH.PRF.ACC-4 1/4 mile speed
      - VEH.PRF.ACC-5 45-65 mph time
  - Fuel Economy
    - Overal Fuel Economy
      - VEH.FE.OFE-1 City fuel economy
      - VEH.FE.OFE-2 Highway fuel economy
  - Convenience
    - Service and Range
      - VEH.CNV.SR-1 Driving range
  - Value
    - Operating Cost
      - VEH.VAL.OC-1 Annual fuel cost

Figure 10-7. Vehicle system-level requirements displayed in the vehicle system performance review hierarchy

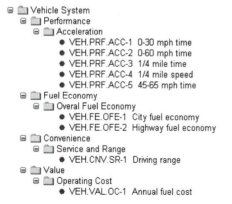

- Engine System
  - Performance
    - ENG.PRF-1 Engine peak horsepower target
    - ENG.PRF-2 Engine RPM at peak horsepower target
    - ENG.PRF-3 Engine peak torque target
    - ENG.PRF-4 Engine RPM at peak torque target
  - Fuel Economy
    - ENG.FE-1 Engine brake specific fuel consumption target
  - Crankshaft
    - ENG.CRK-1 Crankshaft loading at peak horsepower target
  - Connecting Rod
    - ENG.CRD-1 Connecting rod loading at peak horsepower target
  - Cylinder Case
    - ENG.CCS-1 Cylinder case loading at peak horsepower target

Figure 10-8. Engine system-level requirements displayed in the engine system performance review hierarchy

- Power Subsystem
  - Crankshaft
    - PWR.CRK-1 Crankshaft stress at peak horsepower target
    - PWR.CRK-2 Crankshaft safety factor at peak horsepower target
  - Connection Rod
    - PWR.CRD-1 Connecting rod stress at peak horsepower target
    - PWR.CRD-2 Connecting rod safety factor at peak horsepower target
  - Cylinder Case
    - PWR.CCS-1 Cylinder case stress at peak horsepower target
    - PWR.CCS-2 Cylinder case safety factor at peak horsepower target

Figure 10-9. Power subsystem-level requirements displayed in the power subsystem performance review hierarchy

Step 8: Select Inputs

In this step, inputs are selected for each of the tasks. This establishes the input–output linkages between the tasks, which allow the business processes to be identified. Each task owner identifies the items that are needed as inputs to his or her tasks. Inputs are selected from the master list of outputs. If an input is needed that is not on the master list, it must be added by a group that is involved in the project or created as an external input. Ownership of these inputs can effectively be established using an input–output negotiation meeting, as described in Chapter 6.

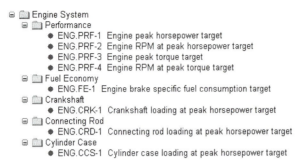

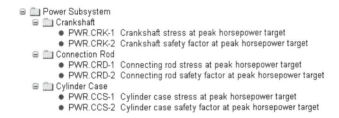

In this example, each group was able to locate its internal inputs from the master list of outputs. The remaining inputs needed are external inputs that are supplied by groups not involved in the project. The project manager acts as the owner of

the external inputs during the input–output negotiation meeting in order to prevent duplicate items from being created.

External inputs are assembled together into groups of items that are needed at the same time during program execution and from the same groups. This produces the bill of materials for the program that indicates what items are needed, by whom, and when. External inputs are documented using the same format as outputs, allowing the external inputs and outputs to be displayed together. The suppliers of the external inputs are identified after the input–output negotiation meeting. This is helpful in two ways:

- **First, the groups that supply the outputs become aware of the items needed by other groups and the timing for these items.** Thus, they can better schedule their work so that these items are supplied on time.
- **Second, in the future, the supplying groups can document their tasks using the external inputs as a starting point for the definition of their outputs and tasks.** This facilitates their becoming part of the defined business process.

The external inputs needed for this example are shown in Table 10-13.

The inputs for the three groups involved in the project are shown in Tables 10-14 through 10-16.

When discovering business processes, only a small number of groups will document their tasks initially. Consequently, many external inputs are created. These external inputs indicate which groups interact directly with the other groups included in the process. They are the next set of groups that should document their work in terms of tasks models. Adding groups progressively in this manner is an extremely effective way to discover large, complex business processes. In this example, the external inputs correspond to the Vehicle System, Engine System, and Transmission System groups. These groups would be next in line for adding their tasks to the process.

Table 10-13. External Inputs for This Example

External Input Number	External Input Name	External Input Type	External Input Units	Product Hierarchy Node	Estimated Cost
VEH.1-1	Driveline mechanical efficiency	Scalar value	%	Vehicle System	$0
VEH.1-2	Vehicle rolling resist-ance	Scalar value	N	Vehicle System	$0
VEH.1-3	Vehicle aerodynamic drag	Scalar value	N	Vehicle System	$0
VEH.1-4	Vehicle mass	Scalar value	Kg	Vehicle System	$0
VEH.1-5	Rear axle ratio	Scalar value		Vehicle System	$0
VEH.1-6	Tire radius in loaded condition	Scalar value	m	Vehicle System	$0
VEH.2-1	City driving cycle	Table		Vehicle System	$0
VEH.2-2	Highway driving cycle	Table		Vehicle System	$0
VEH.3-1	Gas tank capacity	Scalar value	gal	Vehicle System	$0
VEH.4-1	Fuel cost per gallon	Scalar value	USD	Vehicle System	$0
TRN.1-1	Transmission shift schedule	Table		Transmission System	$0
TRN.1-2	Transmission gear ratios	Table		Transmission System	$0
ENG.1-1	Engine performance model	File	SI	Engine System	$400
ENG.2-1	Engine fuel economy model	File	SI	Engine System	$400
ENG.3-1	Engine dynamic model	File	SI	Engine System	$600
ENG.4-1	Crankshaft FEA model	File	SI	Engine System	$800
ENG.5-1	Connecting rod FEA model	File	SI	Engine System	$150
ENG.6-1	Cylinder case FEA model	File	SI	Engine System	$5,000

Table 10-14. Vehicle Performance Group Inputs

Task Number	Task Name	Input Number	Input Name
VE.VPG.1	Vehicle Acceleration	EE.EPG.1-1	Engine brake horsepower
VE.VPG.1	Vehicle Acceleration	VEH.1-1	Driveline mechanical efficiency
VE.VPG.1	Vehicle Acceleration	VEH.1-2	Vehicle rolling resistance
VE.VPG.1	Vehicle Acceleration	VEH.1-3	Vehicle aerodynamic drag
VE.VPG.1	Vehicle Acceleration	VEH.1-4	Vehicle mass
VE.VPG.1	Vehicle Acceleration	TRN.1-1	Transmission shift schedule
VE.VPG.1	Vehicle Acceleration	TRN.1-2	Transmission gear ratios
VE.VPG.1	Vehicle Acceleration	VEH.1-5	Rear axle ratio
VE.VPG.1	Vehicle Acceleration	VEH.1-6	Tire radius in loaded condition
VE.VPG.2	Vehicle Fuel Economy	VEH.2-1	City driving cycle
VE.VPG.2	Vehicle Fuel Economy	VEH.2-2	Highway driving cycle
VE.VPG.2	Vehicle Fuel Economy	VEH.1-1	Driveline mechanical efficiency
VE.VPG.2	Vehicle Fuel Economy	VEH.1-2	Vehicle rolling resistance
VE.VPG.2	Vehicle Fuel Economy	VEH.1-3	Vehicle aerodynamic drag
VE.VPG.2	Vehicle Fuel Economy	VEH.1-4	Vehicle mass
VE.VPG.2	Vehicle Fuel Economy	TRN.1-1	Transmission shift schedule
VE.VPG.2	Vehicle Fuel Economy	TRN.1-2	Transmission gear ratios
VE.VPG.2	Vehicle Fuel Economy	VEH.1-5	Rear axle ratio
VE.VPG.2	Vehicle Fuel Economy	VEH.1-6	Tire radius in loaded condition
VE.VPG.2	Vehicle Fuel Economy	EE.EPG.2-1	Engine brake specific fuel consumption
VE.VPG.3	Vehicle Driving Range	VE.VPG.2-2	Highway fuel economy
VE.VPG.3	Vehicle Driving Range	VEH.3-1	Gas tank capacity
VE.VPG.4	Vehicle Annual Fuel Cost	VE.VPG.2-1	City fuel economy
VE.VPG.4	Vehicle Annual Fuel Cost	VE.VPG.2-2	Highway fuel economy
VE.VPG.4	Vehicle Annual Fuel Cost	VEH.4-1	Fuel cost per gallon

Table 10-15. Engine Performance Group Inputs

Task Number	Task Name	Input Number	Input Name
EE.EPG.1	Engine Performance	ENG.1-1	Engine performance model
EE.EPG.2	Engine Fuel Economy	ENG.2-1	Engine fuel economy model
EE.EPG.3	Engine Dynamic Loading	EE.EPG.1-5	Engine cylinder pressures at peak horsepower
EE.EPG.3	Engine Dynamic Loading	ENG.3-1	Engine dynamic model

Table 10-16. Engine Component Group Inputs

Task Number	Task Name	Input Number	Input Name
PE.ECG.1	Crankshaft Durability	ENG.4-1	Crankshaft FEA model
PE.ECG.1	Crankshaft Durability	EE.EPG.3-1	Crankshaft loading at peak horse-power
PE.ECG.2	Connecting Rod Durability	ENG.5-1	Connecting rod FEA model
PE.ECG.2	Connecting Rod Durability	EE.EPG.3-2	Connecting rod loading at peak horsepower
PE.ECG.3	Cylinder Case Durability	ENG.6-1	Cylinder case FEA model
PE.ECG.3	Cylinder Case Durability	EE.EPG.3-3	Cylinder case loading at peak horse-power

Step 9: Validate the Process

After the tasks are defined in terms of input–output linkages, the business process can be validated. If the project includes many tasks, this may be the first time anyone has actually seen the resulting business process. The selection of outputs as inputs to tasks automatically link the tasks together. This determines the order in which the tasks should be conducted. The process is validated by selecting a set of requirements (or outputs) and then determining the corresponding processes. This is done manually or by creating a simple software application for this purpose. The resulting process corresponding to the selection of all the requirements in this example is shown in Figure 10-10.

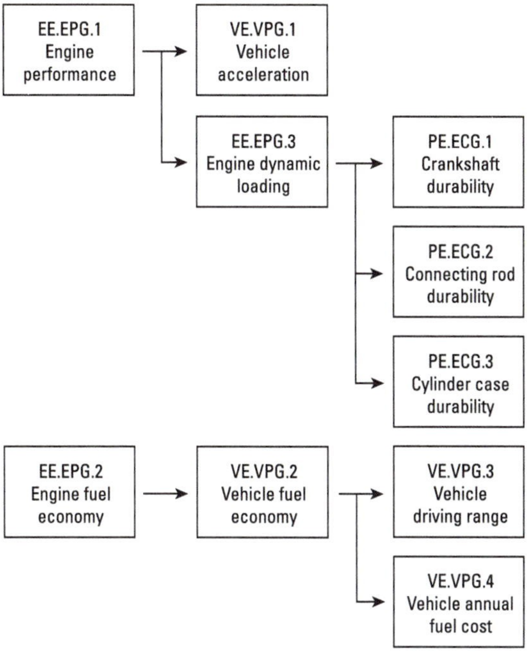

Figure 10-10. Discovered process for the example

Creating different processes using different selections of outputs or requirements allow the input–output linkages and requirement-to-output relationships to be evaluated. The project manager reviews the discovered processes with the task owners and modifies the input-output linkages and/or requirement-to-output relationships, as needed. At this point, the goal is only to define the current process. Efforts to reengineer the processes (see Chapter 11) are done after an accurate baseline process is developed. This allows the reengineered processes to be compared to the existing processes and the improvements to be quantified.

Step 10: Document the Resources

The resources are documented to allow programs to be analyzed based on resource needs, scheduling, and cost. Both the resource hierarchy and the resource items are defined. The resource hierarchy defines and organizes resources into groupings, which are designed to represent the functional capabilities of the resources. Then, the generic and actual resources are placed in the resource hierarchy at a node. Generic resources are mapped to specific resources. For people resources, the mapping is based on the education and training of the individual; individuals with more education and training can perform many different jobs. (This is presented in Chapter 8.) The resource hierarchy with the generic resources needed for this example is shown in Figure 10-11.

- Resources
  - People
    - Engineers
      - PPL.ENG-1 Vehicle Integration Engineer
      - PPL.ENG-2 Engine Performance Engineer
      - PPL.ENG-3 Engine Dynamics Engineer
      - PPL.ENG-4 Engine Component Engineer
  - Equipment
    - Software
      - EQP.SW-1 Vehicle simulation software
      - EQP.SW-2 Engine simulation software
      - EQP.SW-3 Dynamics simulation software
      - EQP.SW-4 Structural analysis software
    - Computers
      - EQP.EN-1 Personal computer
      - EQP.EN-2 Workstation computer
  - Information
    - Work Instructions
      - INF.WI-1 VE.VPG.1 work instructions
      - INF.WI-2 VE.VPG.2 work instructions
      - INF.WI-3 VE.VPG.3 work instructions
      - INF.WI-4 VE.VPG.4 work instructions
      - INF.WI-5 EE.EPG.1 work instructions
      - INF.WI-6 EE.EPG.2 work instructions
      - INF.WI-7 EE.EPG.3 work instructions
      - INF.WI-8 PE.ECG.1 work instructions
      - INF.WI-9 PE.ECG.2 work instructions
      - INF.WI-10 PE.ECG.3 work instructions

Figure 10-11. Resource hierarchy for the example

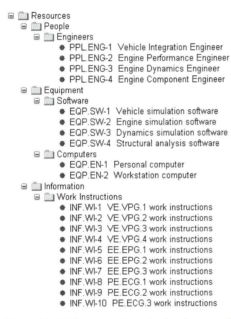

The generic resources needed for the three groups' tasks are shown in Tables 10-17 through 10-19.

Table 10-17. Vehicle Performance Group Resources

Task Number	Task Name	Resource Number	Resource Name
VE.VPG.1	Vehicle Acceleration	PPL.ENG-1	Vehicle Integration Engineer
VE.VPG.1	Vehicle Acceleration	EQP.SW-1	Vehicle simulation software
VE.VPG.1	Vehicle Acceleration	EQP.EN-1	Personal computer
VE.VPG.1	Vehicle Acceleration	INF.WI-1	VE.VPG.1 work instructions
VE.VPG.2	Vehicle Fuel Economy	PPL.ENG-1	Vehicle Integration Engineer
VE.VPG.2	Vehicle Fuel Economy	EQP.SW-1	Vehicle simulation software
VE.VPG.2	Vehicle Fuel Economy	EQP.EN-1	Personal computer
VE.VPG.2	Vehicle Fuel Economy	INF.WI-2	VE.VPG.2 work instructions
VE.VPG.3	Vehicle Driving Range	PPL.ENG-1	Vehicle Integration Engineer
VE.VPG.3	Vehicle Driving Range	EQP.SW-1	Vehicle simulation software
VE.VPG.3	Vehicle Driving Range	EQP.EN-1	Personal computer
VE.VPG.3	Vehicle Driving Range	INF.WI-3	VE.VPG.3 work instructions
VE.VPG.4	Vehicle Annual Fuel Cost	PPL.ENG-1	Vehicle Integration Engineer
VE.VPG.4	Vehicle Annual Fuel Cost	EQP.SW-1	Vehicle simulation software
VE.VPG.4	Vehicle Annual Fuel Cost	EQP.EN-1	Personal computer
VE.VPG.4	Vehicle Annual Fuel Cost	INF.WI-4	VE.VPG.4 work instructions

Table 10-18. Engine Performance Group Resources

Task Number	Task Name	Resource Number	Resource Name
EE.EPG.1	Engine Performance	PPL.ENG-2	Engine Performance Engineer
EE.EPG.1	Engine Performance	EQP.SW-2	Engine simulation software
EE.EPG.1	Engine Performance	EQP.EN-1	Personal computer
EE.EPG.1	Engine Performance	INF.WI-5	EE.EPG.1 work instructions
EE.EPG.2	Engine Fuel Economy	PPL.ENG-2	Engine Performance Engineer
EE.EPG.2	Engine Fuel Economy	EQP.SW-2	Engine simulation software
EE.EPG.2	Engine Fuel Economy	EQP.EN-1	Personal computer
EE.EPG.2	Engine Fuel Economy	INF.WI-6	EE.EPG.2 work instructions
EE.EPG.3	Engine Dynamic Loading	PPL.ENG-3	Engine Dynamics Engineer
EE.EPG.3	Engine Dynamic Loading	EQP.SW-3	Dynamics simulation software
EE.EPG.3	Engine Dynamic Loading	EQP.EN-2	Workstation computer
EE.EPG.3	Engine Dynamic Loading	INF.WI-7	EE.EPG.3 work instructions

Table 10-19. Engine Component Group Resources

Task Number	Task Name	Resource Number	Resource Name
PE.ECG.1	Crankshaft Durability	PPL.ENG-4	Engine Component Engineer
PE.ECG.1	Crankshaft Durability	EQP.SW-4	Structural analysis software
PE.ECG.1	Crankshaft Durability	EQP.EN-2	Workstation computer
PE.ECG.1	Crankshaft Durability	INF.WI-8	PE.ECG.1 work instructions
PE.ECG.2	Connecting Rod Durability	PPL.ENG-4	Engine Component Engineer
PE.ECG.2	Connecting Rod Durability	EQP.SW-4	Structural analysis software
PE.ECG.2	Connecting Rod Durability	EQP.EN-2	Workstation computer
PE.ECG.2	Connecting Rod Durability	INF.WI-9	PE.ECG.2 work instructions
PE.ECG.3	Cylinder Case Durability	PPL.ENG-4	Engine Component Engineer
PE.ECG.3	Cylinder Case Durability	EQP.SW-4	Structural analysis software
PE.ECG.3	Cylinder Case Durability	EQP.EN-2	Workstation computer
PE.ECG.3	Cylinder Case Durability	INF.WI-10	PE.ECG.3 work instructions

Step 11: Document the Procedures

The procedures are documented last, often after the project is formally closed. Sometimes, this step is delayed until after the business processes are reengineered. Regardless, establishing work procedures is one the most important aspects of creating lean corporations.

Procedures are defined by the groups that own the tasks. A job category is defined by a collection of procedures that are assembled into a single document. Procedures also define the training and education needed for the individual who performs the tasks. For this example, the work procedures are not documented. This is done after the project is closed (see the following section). The typical content of a procedure document is shown in Chapter 6.

Step 12: Close the Project

The last step is to close the project, which usually requires that the project be presented to management and documented in a report. (The project results can be presented to management using the display formats in this book.) Several different business processes can be presented that correspond to the selection of different sets of outputs or requirements, along with program assessment reports.

A simple report can be generated by documenting the tasks models, hierarchies, and specific data that was generated during the project. The hierarchies and specific data can be shown using detailed tables. The task models can be documented using the standard summary format (ANSI/PMI 99-001-2000), as shown in Figures 10-12 through 10-14.

VE.VPG.1 Vehicle Acceleration

Inputs	
EE.EPG.1-1	Engine brake horsepower
VEH.1-1	Driveline mechanical efficiency
VEH.1-2	Vehicle rolling resistance
VEH.1-3	Vehicle aerodynamic drag
VEH.1-4	Vehicle mass
TRN.1-1	Transmission shift schedule
TRN.1-2	Transmission gear ratios
VEH.1-5	Rear axle ratio
VEH.1-6	Tire radius in loaded condition
Outputs	
VE.VPG.1-1	0-30 mph time
VE.VPG.1-2	0-60 mph time
VE.VPG.1-3	1/4 mile time
VE.VPG.1-4	1/4 mile speed
VE.VPG.1-5	45-65 mph time
Resources	
PPL.ENG-1	Vehicle Integration Engineer
EQP.SW-1	Vehicle simulation software
EQP.EN-1	Personal computer
INF.WI-1	VE.VPG.1 work instructions
Controls	
VEH.PRF.ACC-1	0-30 mph time rating function
VEH.PRF.ACC-2	0-60 mph time rating function
VEH.PRF.ACC-3	1/4 mile time rating function
VEH.PRF.ACC-4	1/4 mile speed rating function
VEH.PRF.ACC-5	45-65 mph time rating function

VE.VPG.2 Vehicle Fuel Economy

Inputs	
VEH.2-1	City driving cycle
VEH.2-2	Highway driving cycle
VEH.1-1	Driveline mechanical efficiency
VEH.1-2	Vehicle rolling resistance
VEH.1-3	Vehicle aerodynamic drag
VEH.1-4	Vehicle mass
TRN.1-1	Transmission shift schedule
TRN.1-2	Transmission gear ratios
VEH.1-5	Rear axle ratio
VEH.1-6	Tire radius in loaded condition
EE.EPG.2-1	Engine brake specific fuel consumption
Outputs	
VE.VPG.2-1	City fuel economy
VE.VPG.2-2	Highway fuel economy
Resources	
PPL.ENG-1	Vehicle Integration Engineer
EQP.SW-1	Vehicle simulation software
EQP.EN-1	Personal computer
INF.WI-2	VE.VPG.2 work instructions
Controls	
VEH.FE.OFE-1	City fuel economy rating function
VEH.FE.OFE-2	Highway fuel economy rating function

VE.VPG.3 Vehicle Driving Range

Inputs	
VE.VPG.2-2	Highway fuel economy
VEH.3-1	Gas tank capacity
Outputs	
VE.VPG.3-1	Driving range
Resources	
PPL.ENG-1	Vehicle Integration Engineer
EQP.SW-1	Vehicle simulation software
EQP.EN-1	Personal computer
INF.WI-3	VE.VPG.3 work instructions
Controls	
VEH.CNV.SR-1	Driving range rating function

VE.VPG.4 Vehicle Annual Fuel Cost

Inputs	
VE.VPG.2-1	City fuel economy
VE.VPG.2-2	Highway fuel economy
VEH.4-1	Fuel cost per gallon
Outputs	
VE.VPG.4-1	Annual fuel cost
Resources	
PPL.ENG-1	Vehicle Integration Engineer
EQP.SW-1	Vehicle simulation software
EQP.EN-1	Personal computer
INF.WI-4	VE.VPG.4 work instructions
Controls	
VEH.VAL.OC-1	Annual fuel cost rating function

Figure 10-12. Task Model Summaries for VE.VPG.1, VE.VPG.2, VE.VPG.3 and VE.VPG.4

EE.EPG.1 Engine Performance

Inputs	
ENG.1-1	Engine performance model
Outputs	
EE.EPG.1-1	Engine brake horsepower
EE.EPG.1-2	Engine brake torque
EE.EPG.1-3	Engine peak horsepower
EE.EPG.1-4	Engine peak torque
EE.EPG.1-5	Engine cylinder pressures at peak horsepower
EE.EPG.1-6	Engine zero-torque line
Resources	
PPL.ENG-2	Engine Performance Engineer
EQP.SW-2	Engine simulation software
EQP.EN-1	Personal computer
INF.WI-5	EE.EPG.1 work instructions
Controls	
ENG.PRF-1	Engine peak horsepower target
ENG.PRF-2	Engine RPM at peak horse-power target
ENG.PRF-3	Engine peak torque target
ENG.PRF-4	Engine RPM at peak torque target

EE.EPG.2 Engine Fuel Economy

Inputs	
ENG.2-1	Engine fuel economy model
Outputs	
EE.EPG.2-1	Engine brake specific fuel consumption
Resources	
PPL.ENG-2	Engine Performance Engineer
EQP.SW-2	Engine simulation software
EQP.EN-1	Personal computer
INF.WI-6	EE.EPG.2 work instructions
Controls	
ENG.FE-1	Engine brake specific fuel consumption target

EE.EPG.3 Engine Dynamic Loading

Inputs	
EE.EPG.1-5	Engine cylinder pressures at peak horsepower
ENG.3-1	Engine dynamic model
Outputs	
EE.EPG.3-1	Crankshaft loading at peak horsepower
EE.EPG.3-2	Connecting rod loading at peak horsepower
EE.EPG.3-3	Cylinder case loading at peak horsepower
Resources	
PPL.ENG-3	Engine Dynamics Engineer
EQP.SW-3	Dynamics simulation software
EQP.EN-2	Workstation computer
INF.WI-7	EE.EPG.3 work instructions
Controls	
ENG.CRK-1	Crankshaft loading at peak horsepower target
ENG.CRD-1	Connecting rod loading at peak horsepower target
ENG.CCS-1	Cylinder case loading at peak horsepower target

PE.ECG.1 Crankshaft Durability

Inputs	
ENG.6-1	Crankshaft FEA model
EE.EPG.3-3	Crankshaft loading at peak horsepower
Outputs	
PE.ECG.1-1	Crankshaft stress at peak horsepower
PE.ECG.1-2	Crankshaft fatigue diagram at peak horsepower
PE.ECG.1-3	Crankshaft safety factor at peak horsepower
Resources	
PPL.ENG-4	Engine Component Engineer
EQP.SW-4	Structural analysis software
EQP.EN-2	Workstation computer
INF.WI-8	PE.ECG.1 work instructions
Controls	
PWR.CRK-1	Crankshaft stress at peak horsepower target
PWR.CRK-2	Crankshaft safety factor at peak horsepower target

Figure 10-13. Task Model Summaries for EE.EPG.1, EE.EPG.2, EE.EPG.3 and PE.ECG.1

PE.ECG.2 Connecting Rod Durability	
Inputs	
ENG.5-1	Connecting rod FEA model
EE.EPG.3-2	Connecting rod loading at peak horsepower
Outputs	
PE.ECG.2-1	Connecting rod stress at peak horsepower
PE.ECG.2-2	Connecting rod fatigue diagram at peak horsepower
PE.ECG.2-3	Connecting rod safety factor at peak horsepower
Resources	
PPL.ENG-4	Engine Component Engineer
EQP.SW-4	Structural analysis software
EQP.EN-2	Workstation computer
INF.WI-9	PE.ECG.2 work instructions
Controls	
PWR.CRD-1	Connecting rod stress at peak horsepower target
PWR.CRD-2	Connecting rod safety factor at peak horsepower target

PE.ECG.3 Cylinder Case Durability	
Inputs	
ENG.6-1	Cylinder case FEA model
EE.EPG.3-3	Cylinder case loading at peak horsepower
Outputs	
PE.ECG.3-1	Cylinder case stress at peak horsepower
PE.ECG.3-2	Cylinder case fatigue diagram at peak horsepower
PE.ECG.3-3	Cylinder case safety factor at peak horsepower
Resources	
PPL.ENG-4	Engine Component Engineer
EQP.SW-4	Structural analysis software
EQP.EN-2	Workstation computer
INF.WI-10	PE.ECG.3 work instructions
Controls	
PWR.CCS-1	Cylinder case stress at peak horsepower target
PWR.CCS-2	Cylinder case safety factor at peak horsepower target

Figure 10-14. Task Model Summaries for PE.ECG.2 and PE.ECG.3

For this example, the business process was relatively simple, so the main concepts could be presented easily. However, the use of the twelve-step procedure is no more difficult to apply to large, complex processes than it is for small, simple processes.

In Chapter 11, the discovered business process is reengineered using several different approaches to further demonstrate the concepts in this book.

Chapter 11

An Example of Reengineering Your Business Processes

In this chapter, the example business process that was discovered in Chapter 10 is reengineered. Depending on the business objectives and the criteria used for the optimization of the process, many different reengineered processes can be developed. Several different criteria are used in this chapter, and the results are discussed.

The baseline process to be reengineered is shown in Chapter 10 (Figure 10-10). This process is typical of processes that are discovered using the lean-corporation approach, except that only a small number of tasks are included to simplify the discussion. Actual business processes have significantly more tasks, but they are reengineered in the same manner.

Process Redesign to Facilitate Requirement Roll-Down

When reviewing the baseline process, you see that it starts with subsystem-level tasks, followed by system-level tasks, and then component-level tasks. This does not facilitate the roll-down of requirements. Therefore, the first redesign revises the tasks so that requirement roll-down can be used.

Requirement roll-down starts with the system-level tasks, in this case, the vehicle acceleration and vehicle fuel economy tasks. The inputs from the engine-performance and engine-economy tasks must be substituted. These consist of engine brake horsepower and engine brake specific fuel consumption curves. Instead of calculating these using the engine tasks, these are parameterized with respect to the characteristics common to all engines. The general characteristics of these engine performance curves are determined from empirical data. Then, specific parameter values are selected to represent a modern 200 brake horsepower engine.

Next engine brake horsepower is parameterized using six independent variables. These are throttle position, rpm, maximum brake horsepower, rpm at maximum brake horsepower, maximum brake torque, and rpm at maximum brake torque. The maximum horsepower and torque curves corresponding to wide open throttle are created by modeling engine torque as a variable radius arc. The radius value and slope of the arc are determined from the maximum brake horsepower, rpm at maximum brake horsepower, maximum brake torque, and rpm at maximum brake torque. Using the parameterized model, the maximum engine brake horsepower and torque are represented by the curves shown in Figures 11-1 and 11-2.

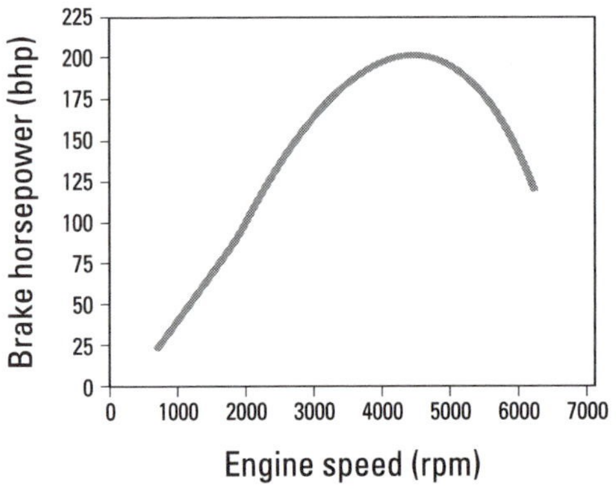

Figure 11-1. Parameterized brake horsepower

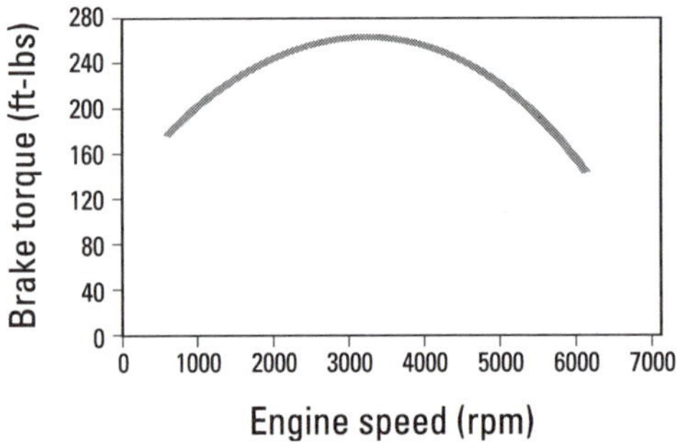

Figure 11-2. Parameterized brake torque

Throttle position dictates how much of the maximum horsepower and torque is used. A value of 100 percent corresponds to a wide-open throttle condition, which represents the maximum level. The throttle position corresponding to the minimum value is referred to as the zero-torque line. This is the value that is needed just to keep the engine running under zero external loading. The zero-torque line is a function of rpm and is modeled as a straight line, as shown in Figure 11-3.

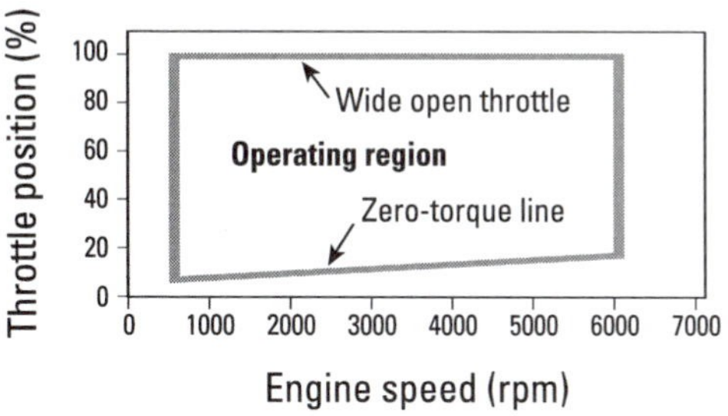

Figure 11-3. Engine operating region

Results for any engine load can be calculated by interpolating between the curves corresponding to wide open throttle and the zero-torque line. Therefore, vehicle performance can be determined from these models.

Brake specific fuel consumption is parameterized using five independent variables. These are throttle position, rpm, minimum brake specific fuel consumption for wide open throttle, rpm at minimum brake specific fuel consumption for wide open throttle, and a coefficient that controls the flatness of the curve. A quadratic function is used to model brake specific fuel consumption. The coefficient that controls the flatness of the curve is selected based on the type of engine that is used (L4, V6, V8, and so on). Using the parameterized model, the engine brake specific fuel consumption is modeled in Figure 11-4.

Results for any engine load are calculated in the same way as for engine brake horsepower and torque: by interpolating between the curves corresponding to wide open throttle and the zero-torque line. Therefore, vehicle fuel economy can be determined from this model.

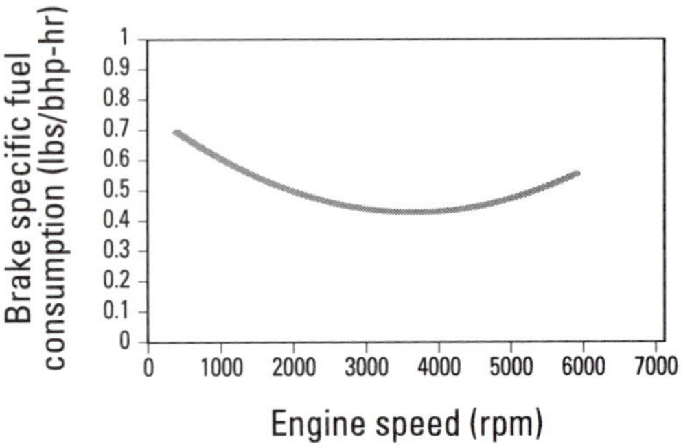

Figure 11-4. Parameterized brake specific fuel consumption

VE.VPG.1 Vehicle Acceleration	
Inputs	
VEH.1-1	Driveline mechanical efficiency
VEH.1-2	Vehicle rolling resistance
VEH.1-3	Vehicle aerodynamic drag
VEH.1-4	Vehicle mass
TRN.1-1	Transmission shift schedule
TRN.1-2	Transmission gear ratios
VEH.1-5	Rear axle ratio
VEH.1-6	Tire radius in loaded condition
Outputs	
VE.VPG.1-1	0-30 mph time
VE.VPG.1-2	0-60 mph time
VE.VPG.1-3	1/4 mile time
VE.VPG.1-4	1/4 mile speed
VE.VPG.1-5	45-65 mph time
VE.VPG.1-6	Engine brake horsepower
VE.VPG.1-7	Engine brake torque
VE.VPG.1-8	Engine zero-torque line
Resources	
PPL.ENG-1	Vehicle Integration Engineer
EQP.SW-1	Vehicle simulation software
EQP.EN-1	Personal computer
INF.WI-1	VE.VPG.1 work instructions
Controls	
VEH.PRF.ACC-1	0-30 mph time rating function
VEH.PRF.ACC-2	0-60 mph time rating function
VEH.PRF.ACC-3	1/4 mile time rating function
VEH.PRF.ACC-4	1/4 mile speed rating function
VEH.PRF.ACC-5	45-65 mph time rating function

VE.VPG.2 Vehicle Fuel Economy	
Inputs	
VEH.2-1	City driving cycle
VEH.2-2	Highway driving cycle
VEH.1-1	Driveline mechanical efficiency
VEH.1-2	Vehicle rolling resistance
VEH.1-3	Vehicle aerodynamic drag
VEH.1-4	Vehicle mass
TRN.1-1	Transmission shift schedule
TRN.1-2	Transmission gear ratios
VEH.1-5	Rear axle ratio
VEH.1-6	Tire radius in loaded condition
Outputs	
VE.VPG.2-1	City fuel economy
VE.VPG.2-2	Highway fuel economy
VE.VPG.2-3	Engine brake specific fuel consumption
Resources	
PPL.ENG-1	Vehicle Integration Engineer
EQP.SW-1	Vehicle simulation software
EQP.EN-1	Personal computer
INF.WI-2	VE.VPG.2 work instructions
Controls	
VEH.FE.OFE-1	City fuel economy rating function
VEH.FE.OFE-2	Highway fuel economy rating function

Figure 11-5. Revised vehicle acceleration and fuel economy task models for requirement roll-down

The vehicle acceleration and fuel economy tasks are revised to use the parameterized models. This effectively converts these tasks from analysis to synthesis. The required brake horsepower, torque, zero-torque line, and specific fuel consumption needed to achieve the vehicle acceleration and fuel economy targets are estimated by the tasks, and the results are used as inputs to the engine performance and fuel economy tasks and as preliminary target values for the associated engine-level requirements. The revised task models are shown in Figures 11-5 and 11-6.

EE.EPG.1 Engine Performance	
Inputs	
VE.VPG.1-6	Engine brake horsepower
VE.VPG.1-7	Engine brake torque
VE.VPG.1-8	Engine zero-torque line
ENG.1-1	Engine performance model
Outputs	
EE.EPG.1-1	Engine brake horsepower
EE.EPG.1-2	Engine brake torque
EE.EPG.1-3	Engine peak horsepower
EE.EPG.1-4	Engine peak torque
EE.EPG.1-5	Engine cylinder pressures at peak horsepower
EE.EPG.1-6	Engine zero-torque line
Resources	
PPL.ENG-2	Engine Performance Engineer
EQP.SW-2	Engine simulation software
EQP.EN-1	Personal computer
INF.WI-5	EE.EPG.1 work instructions
Controls	
ENG.PRF-1	Engine peak horsepower target
ENG.PRF-2	Engine RPM at peak horsepower target
ENG.PRF-3	Engine peak torque target
ENG.PRF-4	Engine RPM at peak torque target

EE.EPG.2 Engine Fuel Economy	
Inputs	
VE.VPG.2-3	Engine brake specific fuel consumption
ENG.2-1	Engine fuel economy model
Outputs	
EE.EPG.2-1	Engine brake specific fuel consumption
Resources	
PPL.ENG-2	Engine Performance Engineer
EQP.SW-2	Engine simulation software
EQP.EN-1	Personal computer
INF.WI-6	EE.EPG.2 work instructions
Controls	
ENG.FE-1	Engine brake specific fuel consumption target

Figure 11-6. Revised engine performance and fuel economy task models for requirement roll-down

Now the entire process is recreated using the revised task models. The result is shown in Figure 11-7.

This revised process is better suited for requirement roll-down. Note that the system and subsystem subprocesses overlap. This is typical of actual processes and allows the overall duration of the process to be minimized. The overall process duration has been increased from 45 to 50 days.

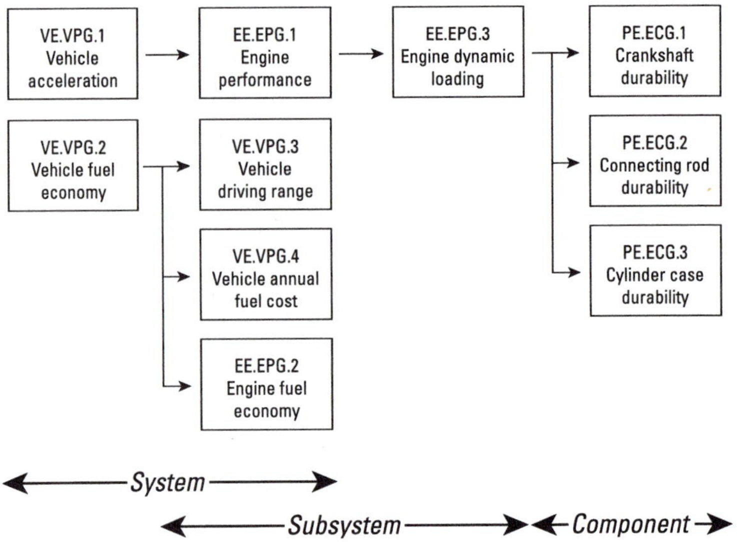

Figure 11-7. Revised process optimized for requirement roll-down

Process Redesign for Optimized Threads

The revised process is then reevaluated. It is apparent that the process is too functionally oriented instead of process oriented. What the process needs are optimized threads, where each thread can be assigned to a single worker. Threads are developed that correspond to system-, subsystem-, and component-level tasks. Each of these threads runs in parallel and relates its outputs to vehicle-level requirements. This is different than the traditional way of doing requirement roll-down, in which the system-, subsystem-, and component-level tasks are run in series—and their outputs are related only to their parent subsystem or system requirements. The traditional way of doing requirement roll-down not only takes too much time but also generally does not produce optimized systems. (This is shown in Chapter 12.) So, the requirement roll-down procedure presented in Chapter 5 is used.

For this example, the program structure is designed to mirror the product structure. Thus, the three levels of vertical groups are used to develop process threads. The critical path is through the vehicle acceleration task, so this task should go first. The vehicle fuel economy task can go next. This is done by making the vehicle acceleration task a predecessor to the vehicle fuel economy task. Note that this is not required by the input and output relationships, so it is handled differently by including the linkages as discretionary constraints, as described in Chapter 6. Discretionary constraints are enforced only when these tasks occur in the same program.

First, the vehicle-level tasks are made into a single thread. This requires that the vehicle fuel economy and annual fuel cost tasks be assigned discretionary constraints that correspond to the vehicle acceleration and vehicle driving range tasks, respectively. The resulting task models are shown in Figure 11-8.

VE.VPG.2 Vehicle Fuel Economy	
Inputs	
VEH.2-1	City driving cycle
VEH.2-2	Highway driving cycle
VEH.1-1	Driveline mechanical efficiency
VEH.1-2	Vehicle rolling resistance
VEH.1-3	Vehicle aerodynamic drag
VEH.1-4	Vehicle mass
TRN.1-1	Transmission shift schedule
TRN.1-2	Transmission gear ratios
VEH.1-5	Rear axle ratio
VEH.1-6	Tire radius in loaded condition
Outputs	
VE.VPG.2-1	City fuel economy
VE.VPG.2-2	Highway fuel economy
VE.VPG.2-3	Engine brake specific fuel consumption
Resources	
PPL.ENG-1	Vehicle Integration Engineer
EQP.SW-1	Vehicle simulation software
EQP.EN-1	Personal computer
INF.WI-2	VE.VPG.2 work instructions
Controls	
VEH.FE.OFE-1	City fuel economy rating function
VEH.FE.OFE-2	Highway fuel economy rating function
Discretionary Constraints	
VE.VPG.1	Vehicle acceleration

VE.VPG.4 Vehicle Annual Fuel Cost	
Inputs	
VE.VPG.2-1	City fuel economy
VE.VPG.2-2	Highway fuel economy
VEH.4-1	Fuel cost per gallon
Outputs	
VE.VPG.4-1	Annual fuel cost
Resources	
PPL.ENG-1	Vehicle Integration Engineer
EQP.SW-1	Vehicle simulation software
EQP.EN-1	Personal computer
INF.WI-4	VE.VPG.4 work instructions
Controls	
VEH.VAL.OC-1	Annual fuel cost rating function
Discretionary Constraints	
VE.VPG.3	Vehicle driving range

Figure 11-8. Revised vehicle fuel economy and vehicle annual fuel cost task models for optimized vehicle-level thread

The revised process with the optimized vehicle-level thread is shown in Figure 11-9.

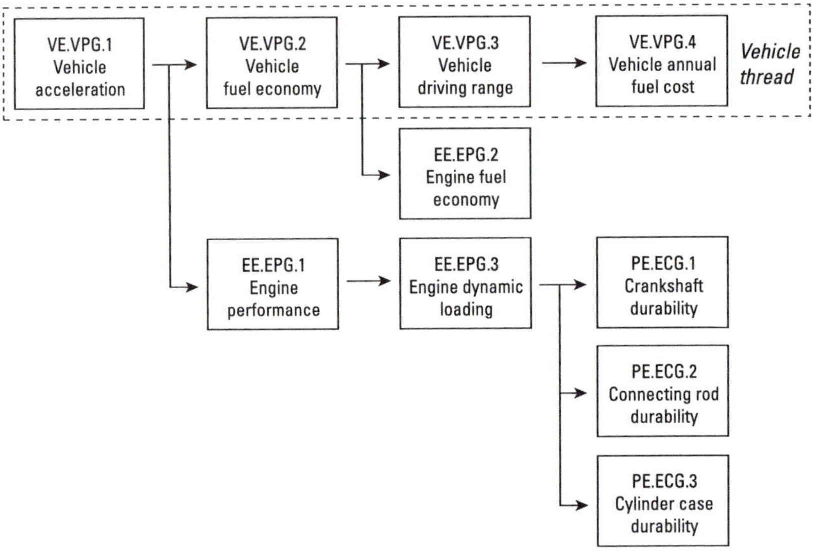

Figure 11-9. Revised process with optimized vehicle-level thread

Next, the engine performance and engine fuel economy tasks are made into a thread by adding the engine performance task as a discretionary constraint to the engine fuel economy task. The engine dynamic loading task is then put into the component thread by substituting the cylinder pressure input (EE.EPG.1-5) with the engine brake horsepower (VE.VPG.1-6) and brake torque (VE.VPG.1-7) inputs. (Cylinder pressures can be estimated from brake horsepower and torque). This has the advantages of moving the engine dynamic loading task into the component-level thread and allowing the thread to start earlier in the process. The resulting task models are shown in Figure 11-10.

The final revised process with all of the optimized process threads is shown in Figure 11-11.

The redesigned process has the same duration as the baseline process (45 days), but it is more efficient in terms of resource utilization. The reason is that the revised process has a reduced number of handoffs. It is also better suited to handle iterations, as described in the following section.

EE.EPG.3 Engine Dynamic Loading	
Inputs	
VE.VPG.1-6	Engine brake horsepower
VE.VPG.1-7	Engine brake torque
ENG.3-1	Engine dynamic model
Outputs	
EE.EPG.3-1	Crankshaft loading at peak horsepower
EE.EPG.3-2	Connecting rod loading at peak horsepower
EE.EPG.3-3	Cylinder case loading at peak horsepower
Resources	
PPL.ENG-3	Engine Dynamics Engineer
EQP.SW-3	Dynamics simulation software
EQP.EN-2	Workstation computer
INF.WI-7	EE.EPG.3 work instructions
Controls	
ENG.CRK-1	Crankshaft loading at peak horsepower target
ENG.CRD-1	Connecting rod loading at peak horsepower target
ENG.CCS-1	Cylinder case loading at peak horsepower target

PE.ECG.2 Connecting Rod Durability	
Inputs	
ENG.5-1	Connecting rod FEA model
EE.EPG.3-2	Connecting rod loading at peak horsepower
Outputs	
PE.ECG.2-1	Connecting rod stress at peak horsepower
PE.ECG.2-2	Connecting rod fatigue diagram at peak horsepower
PE.ECG.2-3	Connecting rod safety factor at peak horsepower
Resources	
PPL.ENG-4	Engine Component Engineer
EQP.SW-4	Structural analysis software
EQP.EN-2	Workstation computer
INF.WI-9	PE.ECG.2 work instructions
Controls	
PWR.CRD-1	Connecting rod stress at peak horsepower target
PWR.CRD-2	Connecting rod safety factor at peak horsepower target
Discretionary Constraints	
PE.ECG.1	Crankshaft durability

PE.ECG.3 Cylinder Case Durability	
Inputs	
ENG.6-1	Cylinder case FEA model
EE.EPG.3-3	Cylinder case loading at peak horsepower
Outputs	
PE.ECG.3-1	Cylinder case stress at peak horsepower
PE.ECG.3-2	Cylinder case fatigue diagram at peak horsepower
PE.ECG.3-3	Cylinder case safety factor at peak horsepower-
Resources	
PPL.ENG-4	Engine Component Engineer
EQP.SW-4	Structural analysis software
EQP.EN-2	Workstation computer
INF.WI-10	PE.ECG.3 work instructions
Controls	
PWR.CCS-1	Cylinder case stress at peak horsepower target
PWR.CCS-2	Cylinder case safety factor at peak horsepower target
Discretionary Constraints	
PE.ECG.2	Connecting rod durability

Figure 11-10. Revised engine dynamic loading, connecting rod durability, and cylinder case durability task models for optimized subsystem- and component-level threads

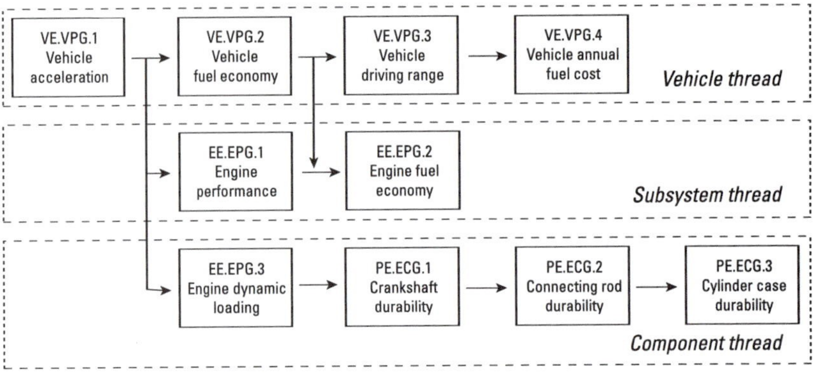

Figure 11-11. Final revised process with optimized process threads

Process Redesign to Handle Iterations

All product design processes require a balancing of the system performance requirements to produce the best value to the customer. In this example, there are trade-offs between vehicle performance and fuel economy. This causes the corresponding tasks to be part of a feedback loop. The best way to handle these feedback loops is to isolate them in subprocesses, as shown in Figure 11-12.

Isolating feedback loops in subprocesses allows iterations to be conducted efficiently. All downstream tasks are decoupled from the subprocess iterations, preventing wasted effort from occurring by eliminating the need to have the downstream tasks reexecuted due to changes in the outputs from tasks in the feedback loop. Only the final outputs are passed to the downstream tasks after the iterations are complete.

Process Redesign to Include Controlling Tasks

Controlling tasks are run in parallel to the tasks they control and are implemented according to the program structure, with one controlling task for each vertical manager assigned to the program. This establishes a clear chain of command, with one person responsible for the management of a given set of tasks.

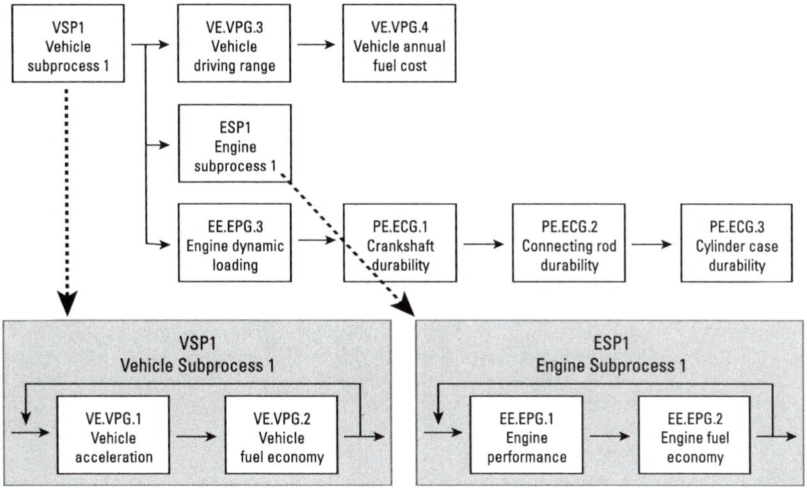

Figure 11-12. Revised process showing potential iteration loops

Controlling tasks are easily added to the redesigned process in Figure 11-12. The resulting controlling task models are shown in Figure 11-13.

The resulting process with controlling tasks is shown in Figure 11-14.

The control arrows in Figure 11-14 are shown using dotted lines to illustrate the hierarchical relationship between the controlling tasks. To reduce clutter, control arrows are not usually shown when displaying processes. Controlling tasks also allow the resources associated with them to be managed. They are assigned workers just like any other task. Management of controlling tasks uses the hierarchy between controlling tasks, thus effectively dividing large, complex processes into manageable subprocesses. The subprocesses are defined based on the structure of the controlling tasks. This is best illustrated using node-descendent views. The process in Figure 11-14 is redisplayed in this format in Figures 11-15 through 11-19.

VE.VLC.1 Vehicle-Level Controlling Task

Inputs	
All controlled tasks' outputs	
Outputs	
VE.VLC.1-1	Vehicle-level performance review
VE.VLC.1-2	Vehicle-level bill of materials
VE.VLC.1-3	Vehicle-level program plan
VE.VLC.1-4	Vehicle-level program statistics
Resources	
PPL.ENG-5	Vehicle Integration Engineer
EQP.SW-5	Project management software
EQP.EN-1	Personal computer
INF.WI-11	VE.VLC.1 work instructions
Controls	
Parent controlling task	

EE.ELC.1 Engine-Level Controlling Task

Inputs	
All controlled tasks' outputs	
Outputs	
EE.ELC.1-1	Engine-level performance review
EE.ELC.1-2	Engine-level bill of materials
EE.ELC.1-3	Engine-level program plan
EE.ELC.1-4	Engine-level program statistics
Resources	
PPL.ENG-6	Engine Integration Engineer
EQP.SW-5	Project management software
EQP.EN-1	Personal computer
INF.WI-12	EE.ELC.1 work instructions
Controls	
Parent controlling task	

PE.CLC.1 Component-Level Controlling Task

Inputs	
All controlled tasks' outputs	
Outputs	
PE.CLC.1-1	Component-level performance review
PE.CLC.1-2	Component-level bill of materials
PE.CLC.1-3	Component-level program plan
PE.CLC.1-4	Component-level program statistics
Resources	
PPL.ENG-7	Engine Component Integration Engineer
EQP.SW-5	Project management software
EQP.EN-1	Personal computer
INF.WI-13	PE.CLC.1 work instructions
Controls	
Parent controlling task	

Figure 11-13. Controlling task models

While it is a bit excessive to display the original process in the node-descendent view format shown in Figures 11-15 through 11-19, this was done to demonstrate the approach. For actual processes that include hundreds of tasks, each figure would correspond to its own subprocess, which is managed by the person responsible for the controlling task.

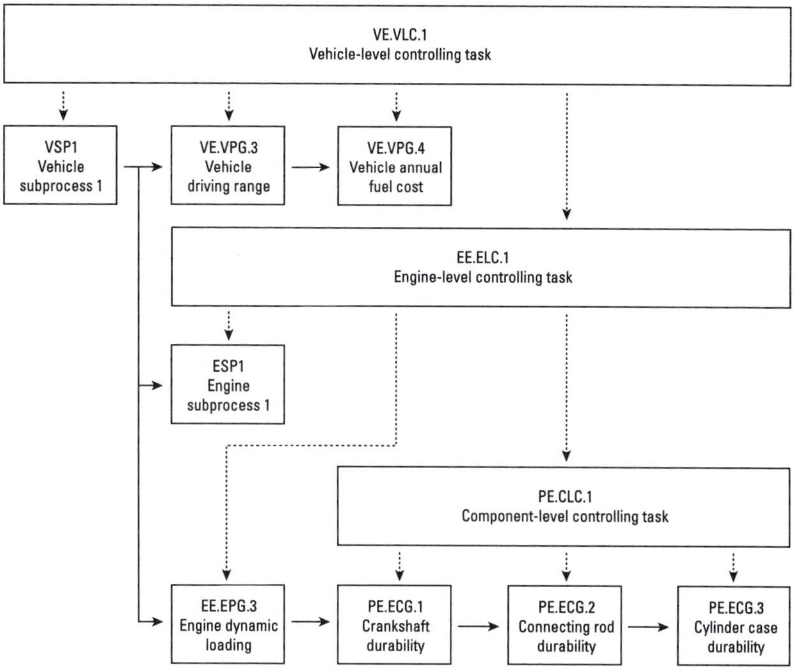

Figure 11-14. Resulting process with controlling tasks

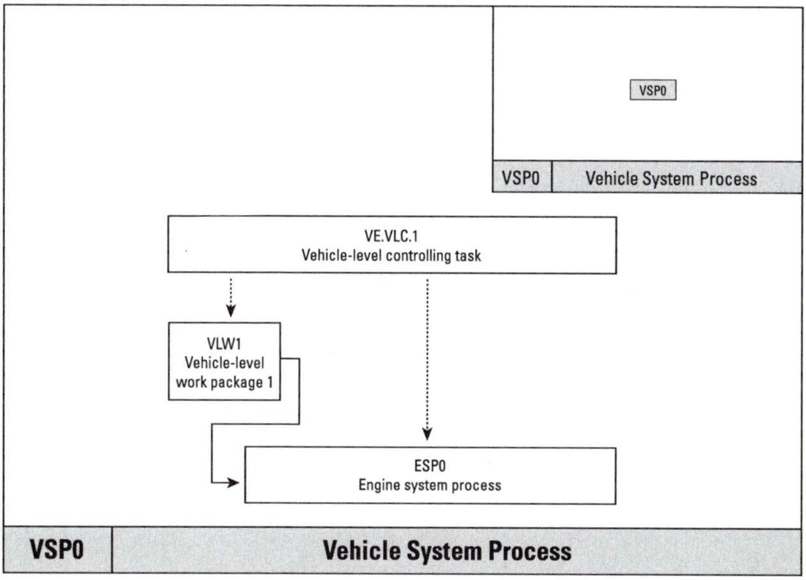

Figure 11-15. Vehicle system process

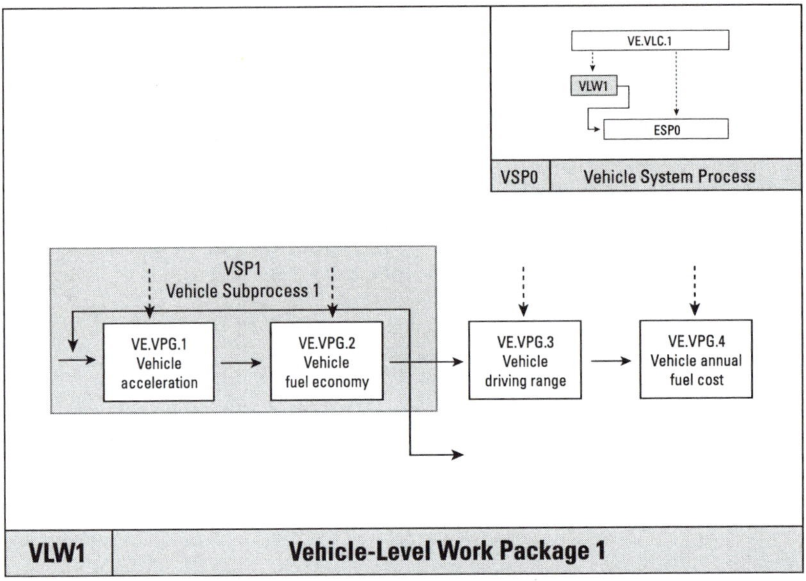

Figure 11-16. Vehicle-level work package 1

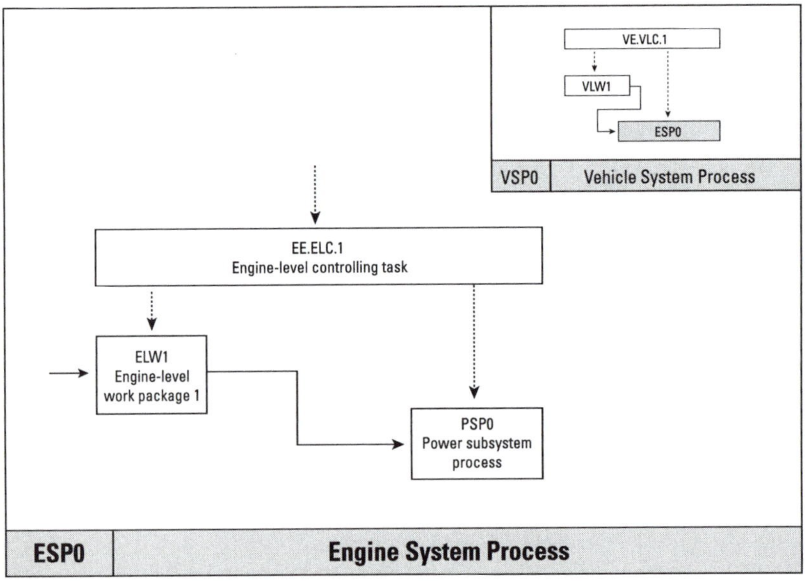

Figure 11-17. Engine system process

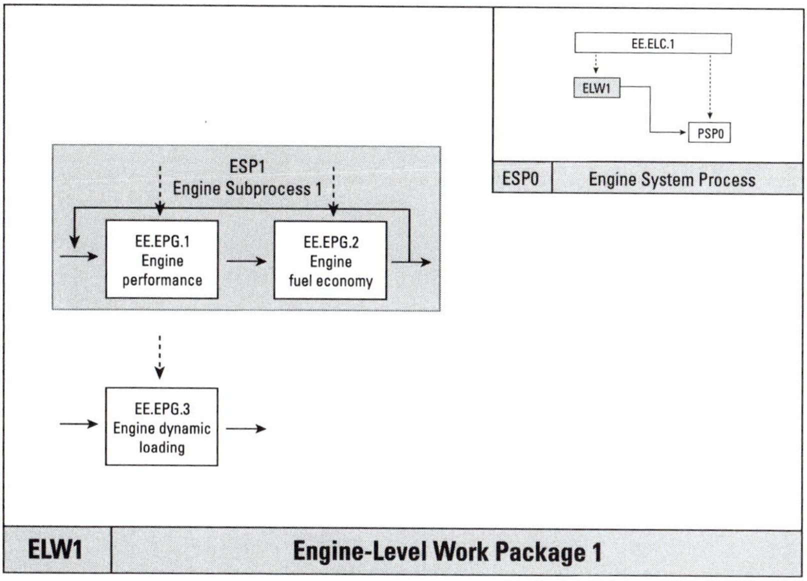

Figure 11-18. Engine-level work package 1

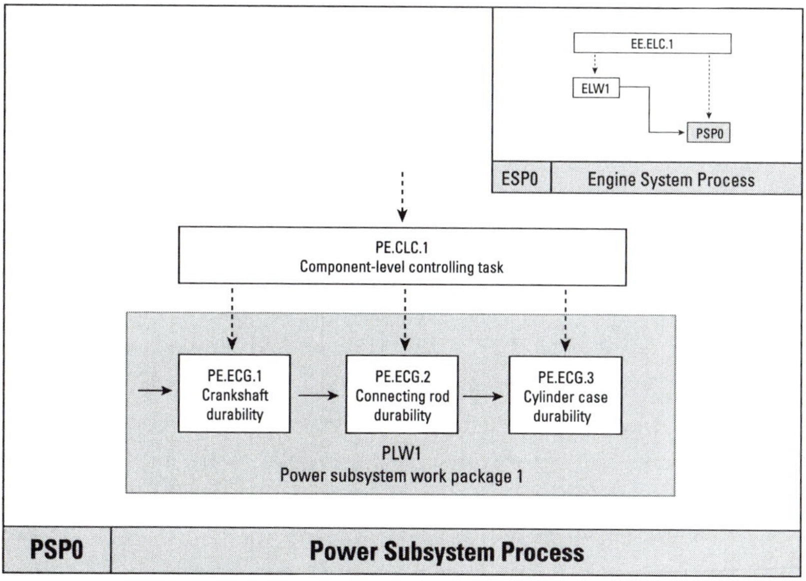

Figure 11-19. Power subsystem process

Reengineered Process Assessment

Refer to Figure 11-14 for the reengineered process. The new process is assessed for quality, cost, and time. Quality is assessed using performance reviews. These are the same as for the baseline process and have the format shown in Chapter 10 (Figures 10-7 through 10-9). Time is assessed as the total duration needed to execute the process. This assessment is shown in Figure 11-20.

Program Timing	Duration
VSP0 Vehicle System Process	50
VE.VLC.1 Vehicle-Level Controlling Task	50
VLW1 Vehicle-Level Work Package 1	10.2
VSP1 Vehicle Subprocess 1	10
VE.VPG.1 Vehicle Acceleration	5
VE.VPG.2 Vehicle Fuel Economy	5
VE.VPG.3 Vehicle Driving Range	0.1
VE.VPG.4 Vehicle Annual Fuel Cost	0.1
ESP0 Engine System Process	40
EE.ELC.1 Engine-Level Controlling Task	40
ELW1 Engine-Level Work Package 1	40
ESP1 Engine Subprocess 1	40
EE.EPG.1 Engine Performance	20
EE.EPG.2 Engine Fuel Economy	20
EE.EPG.3 Engine Dynamic Loading	5
PSP0 Power Subsystem Process	35
PE.CLC.1 Component-Level Controling Task	35
PLW1 Power Subsystem-Level Work Package 1	35
PE.ECG.1 Crankshaft Durability	10
PE.ECG.2 Connecting Rod Durability	5
PE.ECG.3 Cylinder Case Durability	20

Figure 11-20. Reengineered process time assessment

Cost is assessed by calculating the cost of materials and resources needed to perform the process. Material costs are determined from the bill of materials (external inputs). These costs are shown in Chapter 10 (see Table 10-13). For this assessment, the engineering personnel, software, computer, and work instruction resources are cost at \$50, \$10, \$5 and \$0 per hour, respectively with a 100 percent utilization rate for the regular work tasks and a 10 percent utilization rate for the controlling-type tasks. This assessment is shown in Figure 11-21.

Displaying the quality, time, and cost assessments in hierarchy form makes it easy to view the results. This allows these three assessment areas to be balanced based on risk. Chapter 12 presents an example execution of this reengineered process.

Program Cost	Estimated Cost
☐ VSP0 Vehicle System Process	$60,754
◆ VE.VLC.1 Vehicle-Level Controlling Task	$2,600
⊟ ☐ VLW1 Vehicle-Level Work Package 1	$5,304
⊟ ☐ VSP1 Vehicle Subprocess 1	$5,200
◆ VE.VPG.1 Vehicle Acceleration	$2,600
◆ VE.VPG.2 Vehicle Fuel Economy	$2,600
◆ VE.VPG.3 Vehicle Driving Range	$52
◆ VE.VPG.4 Vehicle Annual Fuel Cost	$52
⊞ ☐ VLW1.BOM Bill of Materials	$0
⊟ ☐ ESP0 Engine System Process	$52,850
◆ EE.ELC.1 Engine-Level Controlling Task	$2,080
⊟ ☐ ELW1 Engine-Level Work Package 1	$24,800
⊟ ☐ ESP1 Engine Subprocess 1	$20,800
◆ EE.EPG.1 Engine Performance	$10,400
◆ EE.EPG.2 Engine Fuel Economy	$10,400
◆ EE.EPG.3 Engine Dynamic Loading	$2,600
⊟ ☐ ELW1.BOM Bill of Materials	$1,400
◆ ENG.1-1 Engine performance model	$400
◆ ENG.2-1 Engine fuel economy model	$400
◆ ENG.3-1 Engine dynamic model	$600
⊟ ☐ PSP0 Power Subsystem Process	$25,970
◆ PE.CLC.1 Component-Level Controling Task	$1,820
⊟ ☐ PLW1 Power Subsystem-Level Work Package 1	$24,150
◆ PE.ECG.1 Crankshaft Durability	$5,200
◆ PE.ECG.2 Connecting Rod Durability	$2,600
◆ PE.ECG.3 Cylinder Case Durability	$10,400
⊟ ☐ PLW1.BOM Bill of Materials	$5,950
◆ ENG.4-1 Crankshaft FEA model	$800
◆ ENG.5-1 Connecting rod FEA model	$150
◆ ENG.6-1 Cylinder case FEA model	$5,000

Figure 11-21. Reengineered process cost assessment

Chapter 12

An Example of Implementing New Business Processes

This chapter demonstrates how to implement new business processes. A simulated implementation is conducted using the reengineered business process shown in Chapter 11 (Figure 11-14). The traditional five sub-processes of program management are used: program initiation, program planning, program execution, program control, and program close-out.

First, the program objectives are established. Then, these objectives are rolled-down to create the business process. The work breakdown structure and organizational breakdown structure are automatically determined from the program structure, organization structure, and the included work tasks. These are used to create the program timing and cost assessment reports. Then, the process is executed and the results are presented, including the performance reviews used to ensure the quality of the product produced from the program's business process.

Program Initiation

The first step in implementing new business processes is program initiation. In this step, program objectives are identified at the system level and are translated into measurable attributes so that the success of the program can be determined.

Program Objectives

For this example, a production vehicle (called the current design vehicle) is redesigned to achieve the best-in-class rating according to a product rating publication. The current overall vehicle ratings are shown in Figure 12-1.

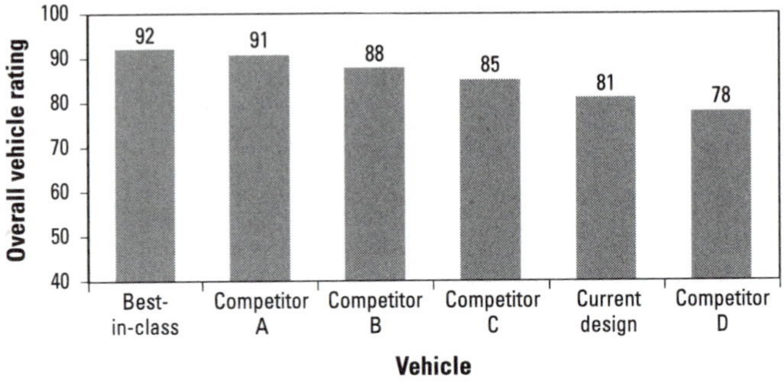

Figure 12-1. Current overall vehicle ratings

A single program objective is used for this example: to determine the optimal design modifications to the current design vehicle so that it can achieve the best-in-class rating. The program objective is translated into measurable attributes using a system-level performance review. This performance review corresponds to that used in a product-rating publication. The overall vehicle rating is calculated as the weighted average of the ratings achieved in each of the performance areas included in the performance review. The best-in-class overall vehicle rating of 92 is selected as the target value for the modified vehicle design (called the modified design vehicle).

Vehicle-Level Performance Review

An analysis of the evaluation criteria is done, and the relative weightings for each performance area are determined along with their corresponding rating functions. This allows measurable performance levels to be rated and combined into an overall vehicle rating. Using this information, a vehicle-level performance review is created. The overall vehicle rating can now be determined as a function of the individual performance levels. The vehicle-level performance review for the current design vehicle is shown in Figure 12-2.

Numerical values for each individual performance area and the resulting overall vehicle rating allow the current design vehicle to be assessed objectively and compared to other vehicles in its class. This is used to determine which areas of performance require improvement and what target values are needed to achieve the program objectives. The success of the program will be judged based on the vehicle-level performance review.

Performance Review	Target Value	Actual Value	Rating
Overall Vehicle			81
Performance			94
Acceleration			94
VEH.PRF.ACC-1 0-30 mph time	2.9	3	98
VEH.PRF.ACC-2 0-60 mph time	8	8.3	95
VEH.PRF.ACC-3 1/4 mile time	16	16.4	92
VEH.PRF.ACC-4 1/4 mile speed	90	85	92
VEH.PRF.ACC-5 45-65 mph time	5	5.7	93
Fuel Economy			65
Overall Fuel Economy			65
VEH.FE.OFE-1 City fuel economy	20	15	65
VEH.FE.OFE-2 Highway fuel economy	30	21	65
Convenience			90
Service and Range			90
VEH.CNV.SR-1 Driving range	350	325	90
Value			75
Operating Cost			75
VEH.VAL.OC-1 Annual fuel cost	1,000	1,300	75

Figure 12-2. Current design vehicle performance review

Program Planning

The next step in implementing new business processes is program planning. In this step, program objectives are rolled down to each level of the organization structure. Then, the detailed business processes that support the program objective are determined.

Business Objective Roll-Down

The process shown in Chapter 8 (Figure 8-3) is used to roll-down the business objective to each level in the corporation. A CEO-level business objective is created that corresponds to the program objective of best-in-class overall vehicle rating. This is then rolled down to the next level of management, which in this example is the Director of Vehicle Engineering. This Director reviews the business objective with each of his or her subordinate managers to determine how each will support it. The assigned vertical manager for the program begins the business process planning. The other managers begin planning how to support the vertical manager.

The program manager is responsible for the vehicle-level performance review. A review of the data shows that overall fuel economy and operating cost are the two main areas that need improvement. Improving these areas to the best-in-class levels will result in a best-in-class rating for the current design vehicle. Therefore, the overall fuel economy and operating cost areas are selected for improvements. The other system-level managers review this information and determine whether they should be involved in the process to achieve the program goals. If they should be involved, they meet with their subordinate managers to determine which managers at this level should be involved in the process. This roll-down process proceeds down to the department level, where the organizational structure changes from upper-management to the horizontal groups that execute the majority of the tasks in the process.

At the department level, a vertical manager is assigned responsibility for managing the work packages that will be conducted to support the program. Horizontal group managers determine what work they recommend be conducted and the risk associated with each item. This allows upper-management to balance timing, cost, and risk for each program. Risk is assessed using the DFMEA approach, as discussed in Chapter 5. The result is given to the responsible vertical manager. The vertical manager can then develop several proposed plans with varying levels of timing, cost, and risk.

The subsystem and system vertical managers do the same and give their proposed plans to their respective vertical managers. This proceeds to the highest level vertical manager, who presents the results in summary to his or her direct manager (the Director of Vehicle Engineering, in this example). The Director of Vehicle Engineering then meets with the CEO to balance the timing, cost, and risk associated with the program. The result is an optimized program plan and corresponding budget that is approved by the CEO. For this example, only the optimized business process is shown. The intermediate processes that are developed during program objective roll-down have the same format as the optimized plan.

If the business objectives cannot be addressed using capabilities within the corporation, outside resources would be used and managed as external inputs. Long-term planning would then be conducted to develop these needs. This could include the establishment of a program to develop technologies and skills needed to improve vehicle overall fuel economy and operating cost. For this example, however, the needed capabilities do exist, so long-term planning is not necessary.

Optimized Business Process

During the business objective roll-down process, it was determined that all of the areas listed in the vehicle performance review need to be assessed, because these areas are highly coupled. The twenty-three requirements that were created during the business process discovery example in Chapter 10 are used as the selected requirements to be included in the program. The tasks that need to be performed in the process are determined from the relation of the requirements to task outputs and the input–output linkages to predecessor tasks. The resulting process corresponds to that shown in Chapter 11 (Figure 11-14). Obviously, an actual implementation would have many more tasks than are shown in this example. The small number of tasks included in the example is only to make the discussion simpler.

Quality, cost, and time assessments are easily created from the optimized process, as described in Chapter 8. These assessments are displayed in the work breakdown structure and organizational breakdown structure, which are described in the following sections.

Work Breakdown Structure

The work breakdown structure (WBS) is automatically determined from the program structure and the work tasks that are included in the program. Work packages are defined that consist of all the work tasks being conducted by a single group relative to a specific program. These work packages are placed in the program structure at their vertical management nodes to create the WBS. The resulting WBS for this example is shown in Figure 12-3.

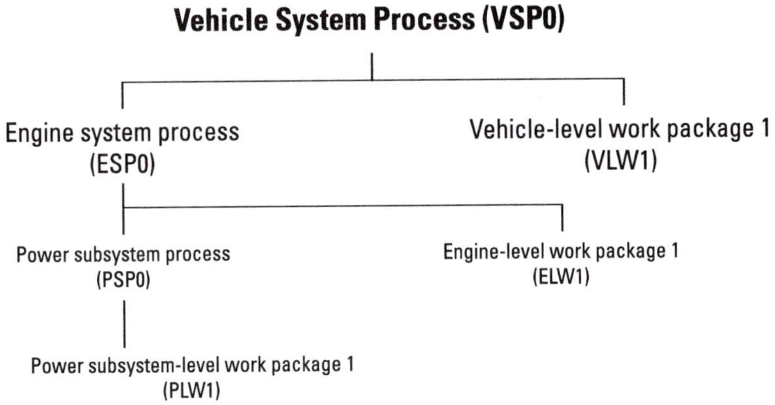

Figure 12-3. Work breakdown structure for the example

Organizational Breakdown Structure

The organizational breakdown structure (OBS) is automatically determined from the organization structure and the defined work packages. The work packages are placed in the organizational structure corresponding to the groups that perform the work packages. The resulting OBS for this example is shown in Figure 12-4.

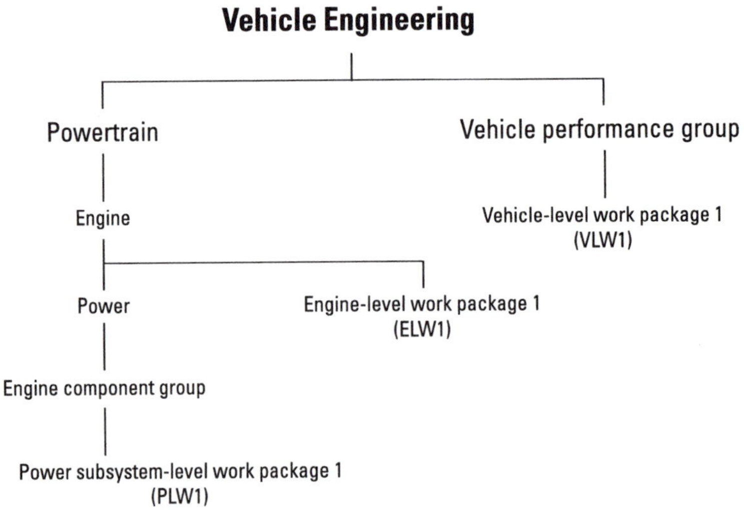

Figure 12-4. Organizational breakdown structure for the example

Process Assessment Reports

Four process assessment reports are presented for this example. These are the program timing, bill of materials, program cost, and product performance reviews. Other reports would be generated, as needed, during program execution and program closeout. The process assessment reports are created using hierarchies that facilitate the management of the business processes.

The program timing report is a tree-table view with timing information (attributes) corresponding to work tasks (items) displayed in the WBS (hierarchy). The program timing report for this example is shown in Figure 12-5.

Program Timing	Duration	Target Start	Target Finish	Float
VSP0 Vehicle System Process	50	0	50	0
• VE.VLC.1 Vehicle-Level Controlling Task	50	0	50	0
VLW1 Vehicle-Level Work Package 1	10.2	0	10.2	39.8
VSP1 Vehicle Subprocess 1	10	0	10	0
• VE.VPG.1 Vehicle Acceleration	5	0	5	0
• VE.VPG.2 Vehicle Fuel Economy	5	5	10	0
• VE.VPG.3 Vehicle Driving Range	0.1	10	10.1	39.8
• VE.VPG.4 Vehicle Annual Fuel Cost	0.1	10.1	10.2	39.8
ESP0 Engine System Process	40	10	50	0
• EE.ELC.1 Engine-Level Controlling Task	40	10	50	0
ELW1 Engine-Level Work Package 1	40	10	50	0
ESP1 Engine Subprocess 1	40	20	40	0
• EE.EPG.1 Engine Performance	20	10	30	0
• EE.EPG.2 Engine Fuel Economy	20	30	50	0
• EE.EPG.3 Engine Dynamic Loading	5	10	15	0
PSP0 Power Subsystem Process	35	15	50	0
• PE.CLC.1 Component-Level Controling Task	35	15	50	0
PLW1 Power Subsystem-Level Work Package 1	35	15	50	0
• PE.ECG.1 Crankshaft Durability	10	15	25	0
• PE.ECG.2 Connecting Rod Durability	5	25	30	0
• PE.ECG.3 Cylinder Case Durability	20	30	50	0

Figure 12-5. Program timing report for the example

The program timing report is used primarily by the vertical managers. Each vertical manager manages one or more nodes in the program timing report. Each node contains one or more work packages. The timing information and the values of float (see Chapter 7) are displayed.

The program bill of materials (BOM) report shows what materials are needed and when. These materials are the external inputs needed to perform the process. The BOM report is a tree-table view with timing information (attributes) corresponding to external inputs (items) displayed in the WBS (hierarchy). The program BOM report for this example is shown in Figure 12-6.

Bill of Materials	Day Needed	Day Received	Float
VSP0 Vehicle System Process			
VLW1 Vehicle-Level Work Package 1			
• VEH.1-1 Driveline mechanical efficiency	0		0
• VEH.1-2 Vehicle rolling resistance	0		0
• VEH.1-3 Vehicle aerodynamic drag	0		0
• VEH.1-4 Vehicle mass	0		0
• VEH.1-5 Rear axle ratio	0		0
• VEH.1-6 Tire radius in loaded condition	0		0
• VEH.2-1 City driving cycle	5		0
• VEH.2-2 Highway driving cycle	5		0
• VEH.3-1 Gas tank capacity	10		39.8
• VEH.4-1 Fuel cost per gallon	10.1		39.8
• TRN.1-1 Transmission shift schedule	0		0
• TRN.1-2 Transmission gear ratios	0		0
ESP0 Engine System Process			
ELW1 Engine-Level Work Package 1			
• ENG.1-1 Engine performance model	10		0
• ENG.2-1 Engine fuel economy model	30		0
• ENG.3-1 Engine dynamic model	10		0
PSP0 Power Subsystem Process			
PLW1 Power Subsystem-Level Work Package 1			
• ENG.4-1 Crankshaft FEA model	15		0
• ENG.5-1 Connecting rod FEA model	25		0
• ENG.6-1 Cylinder case FEA model	30		0

Figure 12-6. Program BOM report for the example

The program BOM report is used primarily by the vertical managers, because they are responsible for scheduling the external inputs. Each work package contains its own BOM that it needs to perform its task. When the same external input is used by more than one work package, it is assigned to the one that uses it first. Having a separate BOM for each work package facilitates the transfer of management responsibility for the work packages between the vertical managers. This is done to balance the vertical manager's workload. The timing information and the values of float are displayed.

The program cost report shows the total resource and material costs of the program. The program cost report is a tree-table view with cost information (attributes) corresponding to resources and materials (items) displayed in the WBS (hierarchy). The program cost report for this example is shown in Figure 12-7.

The program cost report is used primarily by the vertical managers. Estimated and actual costs are tracked throughout the program. This allows the financial performance of the program to be actively managed.

Program Cost	Estimated Cost	Actual Cost	Variance
VSP0 Vehicle System Process	$60,754		$0
• VE.VLC.1 Vehicle-Level Controlling Task	$2,600		$0
VLW1 Vehicle-Level Work Package 1	$5,304		$0
VSP1 Vehicle Subprocess 1	$5,200		$0
• VE.VPG.1 Vehicle Acceleration	$2,600		$0
• VE.VPG.2 Vehicle Fuel Economy	$2,600		$0
• VE.VPG.3 Vehicle Driving Range	$52		$0
• VE.VPG.4 Vehicle Annual Fuel Cost	$52		$0
VLW1.BOM Bill of Materials	$0		$0
ESP0 Engine System Process	$52,850		$0
• EE.ELC.1 Engine-Level Controlling Task	$2,080		$0
ELW1 Engine-Level Work Package 1	$24,800		$0
ESP1 Engine Subprocess 1	$20,800		$0
• EE.EPG.1 Engine Performance	$10,400		$0
• EE.EPG.2 Engine Fuel Economy	$10,400		$0
• EE.EPG.3 Engine Dynamic Loading	$2,600		$0
ELW1.BOM Bill of Materials	$1,400		$0
• ENG.1-1 Engine performance model	$400		$0
• ENG.2-1 Engine fuel economy model	$400		$0
• ENG.3-1 Engine dynamic model	$600		$0
PSP0 Power Subsystem Process	$25,970		$0
• PE.CLC.1 Component-Level Controling Task	$1,820		$0
PLW1 Power Subsystem-Level Work Package 1	$24,150		$0
• PE.ECG.1 Crankshaft Durability	$5,200		$0
• PE.ECG.2 Connecting Rod Durability	$2,600		$0
• PE.ECG.3 Cylinder Case Durability	$10,400		$0
PLW1.BOM Bill of Materials	$5,950		$0
• ENG.4-1 Crankshaft FEA model	$800		$0
• ENG.5-1 Connecting rod FEA model	$150		$0
• ENG.6-1 Cylinder case FEA model	$5,000		$0

Figure 12-7. Program cost report for the example.

Program Approval

The last step in program planning is program approval. Commitments from the resource managers and the material suppliers are obtained. Then the program is officially approved. Budgets are allocated for the costs associated with the program. These are used to acquire the resources and materials needed to execute the program.

Program Execution and Control

The business process is then executed and controlled. The vertical managers coordinate their portions of the program according to their responsibilities established in the program structure. Materials are acquired by the vertical managers according to the schedule in the BOM. The scheduling of the resources is done by the managers of the horizontal and support groups. The OBS is used to show all work that is needed from the groups for all programs.

Resources are then scheduled using the generic-to-specific

resource mapping table. This shows which resources are capable of performing the specific roles and usages. The format of the resource mapping is shown in Chapter 8. The resources are rated based on their capability to perform the work task. For critical tasks, the highest rating resources can be used. For noncritical tasks, lower rating resources can be used. When the specific resources are selected, they are reserved.

Vehicle-Level Work Package

The vehicle-level work package starts first. Materials are obtained according to the schedule in the vehicle-level work package BOM. Subprocess VSP1 is executed first. It is a feedback loop. The first execution is called the baseline (refer to Figure 12-2). To determine the optimal design modifications to the system, a sensitivity study is performed. This identifies the vehicle-level factors that are most sensitive to improving the performance and fuel economy. This is done, and the resulting design sensitivity charts are shown in Figures 12-8 and 12-9.

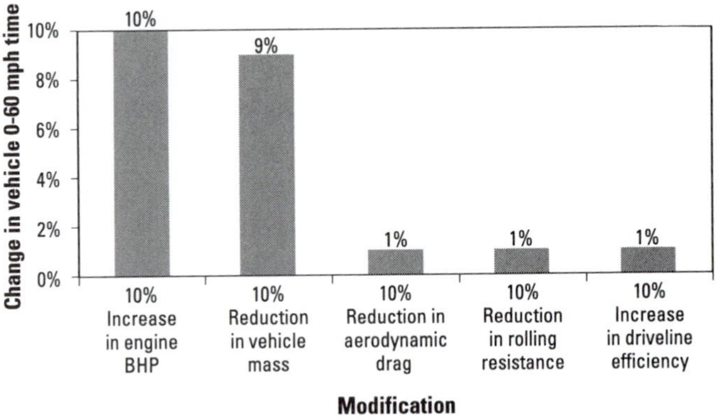

Figure 12-8. Vehicle-level sensitivity study for vehicle acceleration

The most sensitive factor for vehicle acceleration is engine brake horsepower (BHP). The most sensitive factor for vehicle fuel economy is engine brake specific fuel consumption (BSFC). Vehicle mass is the second most sensitive factor in both cases. So, the potential is evaluated to see how much improvement can be expected from the most sensitive items, looking at competitors for this information. Seeing that many competitive products have significantly better performance in these areas indicates that these items can be improved. Modified engine BHP and BSFC functions are developed that would achieve the desired overall vehicle rating. These functions become the outputs of the subprocess, which are used as design targets for the engine system-level performance and fuel economy tasks.

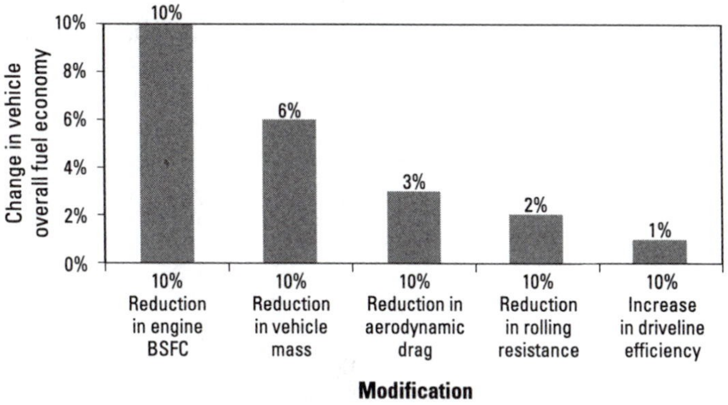

Figure 12-9. Vehicle-level sensitivity study for vehicle fuel economy

The other two vehicle-level tasks are executed. The resulting performance variable results are listed on the modified design vehicle performance review in Figure 12-10.

Performance Review	Target Value	Actual Value	Rating
Overall Vehicle			92
Performance			94
Acceleration			94
VEH.PRF.ACC-1 0-30 mph time	2.9	3	98
VEH.PRF.ACC-2 0-60 mph time	8	8.3	95
VEH.PRF.ACC-3 1/4 mile time	16	16.4	92
VEH.PRF.ACC-4 1/4 mile speed	90	85	92
VEH.PRF.ACC-5 45-65 mph time	5	5.7	93
Fuel Economy			87
Overall Fuel Economy			87
VEH.FE.OFE-1 City fuel economy	20	17	88
VEH.FE.OFE-2 Highway fuel economy	30	26	86
Convenience			100
Service and Range			100
VEH.CNV.SR-1 Driving range	350	360	100
Value			87
Operating Cost			87
VEH.VAL.OC-1 Annual fuel cost	1,000	1,200	87

Figure 12-10. Modified design vehicle performance review

Engine System-Level Work Package

The engine system-level work package begins next. Materials are obtained according to the schedule in the engine system-level work package BOM. Subprocess ESP1 and task EE.EPG.3 are executed in parallel. ESP1 is a feedback loop. The two tasks are performed to establish the baseline results. To determine the optimal design modifications to the system, a sensitivity study is performed. This identifies the engine-level factors that are most sensitive to improving the vehicle acceleration and fuel economy. This is done, and the resulting design sensitivity charts are shown in Figures 12-11 and 12-12.

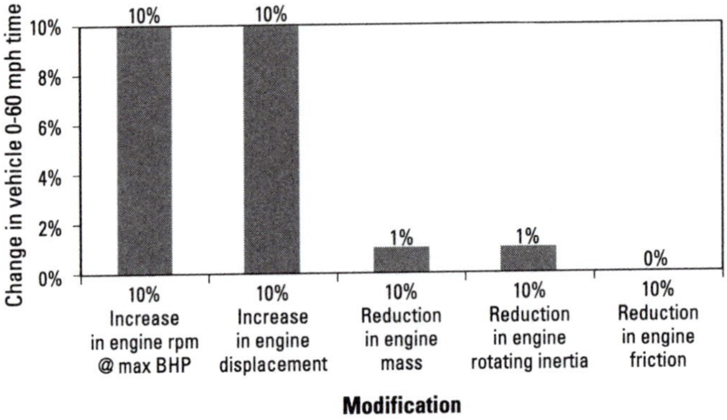

Figure 12-11. Engine-level sensitivity study for vehicle acceleration

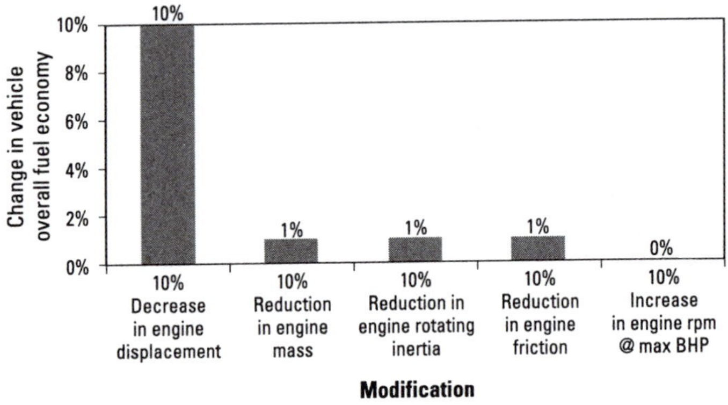

Figure 12-12. Engine-level sensitivity study for vehicle fuel economy

The design sensitivity charts show that increased engine rpm at maximum horsepower and decreased engine displacement are needed to increase fuel economy and performance. This allows a smaller displacement engine to produce more power. Optimal engine factors are determined. These factors are used to determine the design changes to the engine. The modified engine performance requirements are then listed on the engine system performance review. This is shown in Figure 12-13.

Performance Review	Target Value	Actual Value	Assessment
Overall Engine System			R=0, Y=0, G=8
Performance			R=0, Y=0, G=4
• ENG.PRF-1 Engine peak horsepower target	200	201	green
• ENG.PRF-2 Engine RPM at peak horsepower target	5200	5230	green
• ENG.PRF-3 Engine peak torque target	260	262	green
• ENG.PRF-4 Engine RPM at peak torque target	3300	3320	green
Fuel Economy			R=0, Y=0, G=1
• ENG.FE-1 Engine brake specific fuel consumption target	0.5	0.49	green
Crankshaft			R=0, Y=0, G=1
• ENG.CRK-1 Crankshaft loading at peak horsepower target	2000	2000	green
Connecting Rod			R=0, Y=0, G=1
• ENG.CRD-1 Connecting rod loading at peak horsepower target	2000	1800	green
Cylinder Case			R=0, Y=0, G=1
• ENG.CCS-1 Cylinder case loading at peak horsepower target	2000	1900	green

Figure 12-13. Engine system performance review

Power Subsystem-Level Work Package

The power subsystem-level work package is started last. This work package includes three tasks that are executed in series. No feedback loops exist, so the tasks are executed once; no design sensitivity analysis is needed. Materials are obtained according to the schedule in the power subsystem-level work package BOM. The component loading is supplied by the engine dynamic-loading task (EE.EPG.3). The component tasks are executed, and the resulting performance requirements are listed on the power subsystem performance review. This is shown in Figure 12-14.

Performance Review	Target Value	Actual Value	Assessment
Overall Power Subsystem			R=0, Y=0, G=6
Crankshaft			R=0, Y=0, G=2
• PWR.CRK-1 Crankshaft stress at peak horsepower target	100.0	95.0	green
• PWR.CRK-2 Crankshaft safety factor at peak horsepower target	2.0	2.1	green
Connecting Rod			R=0, Y=0, G=2
• PWR.CRD-1 Connecting rod stress at peak horsepower target	160.0	155.0	green
• PWR.CRD-2 Connecting rod safety factor at peak horsepower target	2.0	2.1	green
Cylinder Case			R=0, Y=0, G=2
• PWR.CCS-1 Cylinder case stress at peak horsepower target	75.0	75.0	green
• PWR.CCS-2 Cylinder case safety factor at peak horsepower target	2.0	2.0	green

Figure 12-14. Power subsystem performance review

Program Close Out

The last step in implementing new business processes is program close out. A final accounting of the program cost is made, accounting budgets are closed, and program outputs are delivered to their customers. Any remaining resources and materials are released to be used on other programs. An assessment of the success of the program and all final documentation are completed.

The results for the program are reviewed, and new programs are initiated. For this example, all of the performance requirements are met. A new program will be initiated to obtain prototype parts and validate them from the bottom up using tests. Components will be validated first, followed by subsystems, and then the total vehicle system. The resulting designs will proceed into preparation for production and sale to the public.

The example presented in this chapter shows a simplified implementation of reengineered business processes.

Doing Requirement Roll-Down the Wrong Way

As a side note, this section shows you how the traditional requirement roll-down process can generate the wrong outcome. Recall that, in Chapter 5, requirement roll-down in the lean philosophy is fundamentally different than the traditional method of requirement roll-down. In the traditional method, the design sensitivities shown in Figures 12-11 and 12-12 would have been related to engine BHP and engine BSFC, not to vehicle acceleration and vehicle fuel economy. These were determined and are shown in Figure 12-15 and 12-16.

Using traditional requirement roll-down, the optimal changes to the engine would have been identified as increased engine rpm at maximum horsepower and decreased engine friction, not increased engine rpm at maximum horsepower and decreased engine displacement, as was determined using the lean philosophy's system engineering approach. This shows how the same analysis models can be used to generate different estimates for the optimal design changes in a subsystem or component.

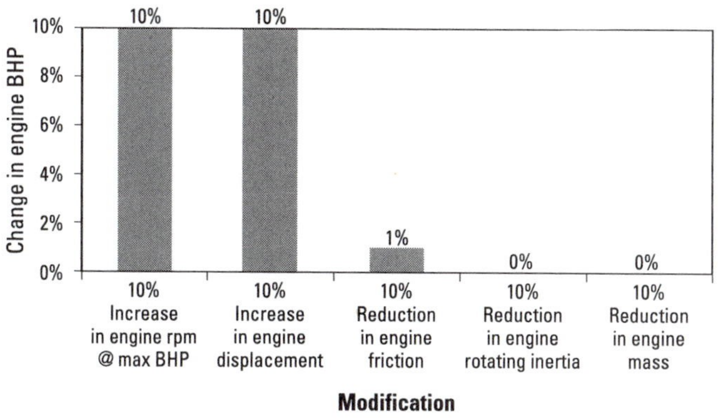

Figure 12-15. Engine-level sensitivity study for engine BHP

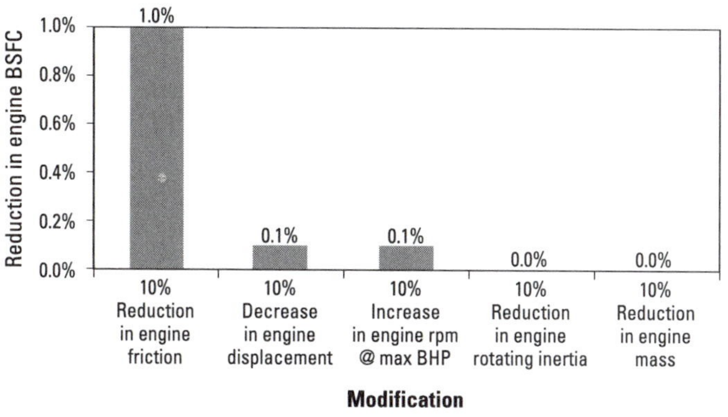

Figure 12-16. Engine-level sensitivity study for engine BSFC

The traditional requirement roll-down process falls into the trap of optimizing subsystems and components, not the overall system. This is not a defect in the theory, but a limitation in its application. Theoretically, traditional requirement roll-down will work if the complex relationships between system, subsystems, and components can be determined. However, in application, making this determination is difficult to do. In many cases, traditional requirement roll-down fails to produce the desired system-level results. In contrast, the lean philosophy's system engineering approach to requirement roll-down nearly always produces the desired system-level results. This is illustrated by the high success level of Design for Six Sigma (DFSS) projects, which use the same system engineering approach as the lean philosophy.

Also, the traditional approach to requirement roll-down causes the system-, subsystem-, and component-level tasks to be conducted in series. This causes the overall duration of the process to be longer that when these tasks can be run in parallel using optimized process threads.

Finally, allowing all of the subsystem and component suppliers to determine the effects of their design changes on system-level performance allows them to design their parts better. All they need to know is how the interfaces of their subsystems and components interact with the rest of the system. These can be represented using simplified models, as shown in Chapter 4. Many subsystem and component suppliers already do this, allowing them to optimize their subsystems and components with respect to system-level performance, thereby creating the maximum value for their customers.

Conclusion

Applying the concepts in this book should be straightforward. Depending on the goals of a corporation, different levels of implementation can be conducted. The minimum implementation involves only standardized work and process redesign. From this starting point, virtually all aspects of corporate processes can be managed, including property management, quality control, and financial accounting.

The procedures that are presented throughout this book allow any organization to begin the transition to the lean state. The hardest part is getting started and, as with most things, management support is critical. Make sure you have strong management support at the correct levels. As you discover your business processes, you will gain the knowledge needed to reengineer them, even complex processes. After all, the more complex the business process, the more effective the procedure is. The minimum you will get is a better understanding of your current processes. The maximum you will get is the creation of a lean corporation.

Bibliography

Chapter 1

Ohno, Taiichi. *Toyota Production System: Beyond Large-Scale Production*. Portland, Oregon: Productivity Press, 1988.

Shingo, Shigeo. *A Study of the Toyota Production System: From an Industrial Engineering Viewpoint*. Cambridge, Massachusetts: Productivity Press, 1989.

Shingo, Shigeo. *Non-stock Production: The Shingo System for Continuous Improvement*. Cambridge, Massachusetts: Productivity Press, 1988.

Shingo, Shigeo. *Zero Quality Control: Source Inspection and the Poka-Yoke System*. Cambridge, Massachusetts: Productivity Press, 1986.

Levinson, William A. *Henry Ford's Lean Vision: Enduring Principles from the First Ford Motor Plant*. New York: Productivity Press, 2002.

Taylor, Frederick W. *The Principles of Scientific Management*. Mineola, New York: Dover Publications, 1988.

Chapter 2

Federal Information Processing Standards Publication 183: *Integration Definition for Function Modeling (IDEF0)*. Washington DC: National Institute of Standards and Technology, 1993.

Goldratt, Eliyahu M. *The Goal: A Process of Ongoing Improvement*. Great Barrington, Massachusetts: North River Press, 1984.

Chapter 3

Federal Information Processing Standards Publication 183. *Integration Definition for Function Modeling (IDEF0)*. Washington DC: National Institute of Standards and Technology, 1993.

Lombardi, Vince. *Coaching for Teamwork: Winning Concepts for Business in the Twenty-First Century*. Bellevue, Washington: Reinforcement Press, 1996.

Hammer, Michael. *Beyond Reengineering: How the Process-Centered Organization is Changing Our Work and Our Lives.* New York: HarperBusiness, 1996.

Schwarzkopf, H. Norman. *It Doesn't Take a Hero: General H. Norman Schwarzkopf, the Autobiography*. New York: Bantam Books, 1992.

Chapter 4

Mulready, Dick (Richard C.). *Advanced Engine Development at Pratt & Whitney: The Inside Story of Eight Special Projects.* Warrendale, Pennsylvania: Society of Automotive Engineers, 2001.

Hurty, W. C. "Dynamic Analysis of Structural Systems using Component Modes." *AIAA Journal,* Vol. 3, No. 4, 1965, pp. 678–685.

Craig, R. R. Jr., and Bampton, M. C. C. "Coupling of Substructures for Dynamic Analysis." *AIAA Journal,* Vol. 6, No. 7, 1968, pp. 1313–1319.

Guyan, R. J. "Reduction of Stiffness and Mass Matrices." *AIAA Journal,* Vol. 3, No. 2, 1965, p. 380.

Morgan, J. A., Pierre, C., and Hulbert, G. M. "Calculation of Component Mode Synthesis Matrices from Measured Frequency Response Functions, Part 1: Theory." *ASME Journal of Vibration and Acoustics,* Vol. 120, No. 2, 1998, pp. 503–508.

Morgan, J. A., Pierre, C., and Hulbert, G. M. "Calculation of Component Mode Synthesis Matrices from Measured Frequency Response Functions, Part 2: Application." *ASME Journal of Vibration and Acoustics,* Vol. 120, No. 2, 1998, pp. 509–516.

Morgan, J. A., Pierre, C., and Hulbert, G. M. "Forced Response of Coupled Substructures Using Experimentally Based Component Mode Synthesis." *AIAA Journal,* Vol. 35, No. 2, 1997, pp. 334–339.

Du, H.Y. Isaac, Morgan, Jeff, Wong, Jason M., and Salmon, Richard "Modeling and Correlation of Driveshaft Whirl Dynamics for RWD Sport Utility Vehicles." *SAE paper 2001-01-1503,* 2001, pp. 1–8.

Chapter 5

Powers, Charles H. *Vilfredo Pareto.* Newbury Park, California: Sage Publications, 1986.

SAE Publication J1739. *Potential Failure Mode and Effects Analysis in Design (Design FMEA), Potential Failure Mode and Effects in Manufacturing and Assembly Processes (Process FMEA), and Potential Failure Mode and Effects Analysis for Machinery (Machinery FMEA).* Warrendale, Pennsylvania: Society of Automotive Engineers, 1994.

Breyfogle, Forrest W. *Implementing Six Sigma: Smarter Solutions Using Statistical Methods.* New York: John Wiley, 1999.

George, Michael L. *Lean Six Sigma: Combining Six Sigma Quality with Lean Speed.* New York: McGraw-Hill, 2002.

Yang, Kai, and El-Haik, Basem. *Design for Six Sigma: A Roadmap for Product Development.* New York: McGraw-Hill, 2003.

Chapter 6

Technical Specification IS0/TS 16949:2002: *Quality management systems—Particular requirements for the application of ISO 9001:2000 for automotive production and relevant part organizations,* Second Edition (2002-03-01). Switzerland: International Organization for Standardization, 2002.

Project Management Institute. *A Guide to the Project Management Body of Knowledge (PMBOK® Guide),* 2000 Edition. Newton Square, Pennsylvania: Project Management Institute, 2000.

Chapter 7

Hammer, Michael, and Champy, James. *Reengineering the Corporation: A Manifesto for Business Revolution.* New York: HarperBusiness, 1993.

Chapter 8

Project Management Institute. *A Guide to the Project Management Body of Knowledge (PMBOK® Guide),* 2000 Edition. Newton Square, Pennsylvania: Project Management Institute, 2000.

Heldman. Kim. *PMP: Project Management Professional Study Guide.* San Francisco, California: Sybex, 2002.

Stover, Teresa S. *Microsoft Project Version 2002 Inside Out.* Redmond, Washington: Microsoft Press, 2002.

Chapter 9

None.

Chapter 10

Project Management Institute. *A Guide to the Project Management Body of Knowledge (PMBOK® Guide),* 2000 Edition. Newton Square, Pennsylvania: Project Management Institute, 2000.

Chapter 11

Obert, Edward F. *Internal Combustion Engines Analysis and Practice,* Second Edition. Scranton, Pennsylvania: Haddon Craftsmen, 1950.

Chapter 12

Robert Bosch GmbH. *Automotive Handbook,* Fifth Edition. Stuttgart, Germany: Robert Bosch GmbH, 2000.

Index

Page numbers in *italics* indicate illustrations. Page numbers in **bold** indicate tables.

About the Author

In 1985, Dr. Jeffrey Morgan began his career with General Motors under the University of Cincinnati's student co-op program. In 1988, he received a BSME degree from the University of Cincinnati and became an associate engineer with the former Chevrolet-Pontiac-GM of Canada (C-P-C) Powertrain Division. Dr. Morgan received a MSE degree in mechanical engineering from the University of Michigan in 1991. In 1992, he entered the GM Technical Education Ph.D. program, and in 1996 he received a Ph.D. degree in mechanical engineering from the University of Michigan.

In 2001, Dr. Morgan received a prestigious Charles F. "Boss" Kettering Award for his work in creating and implementing a lean business process reengineering methodology at General Motors. This methodology was then independently researched and developed during a one-year leave of absence starting in February, 2002. The result of this effort was published in the book Creating Lean Corporations. Dr. Morgan continues to work at General Motors as a senior project engineer where he is responsible for technology development in the areas of powertrain structural dynamics and acoustics and for the application of lean management principles to the product engineering process.